SPHERES OF INFLUENCE

SPHERES
OF
INFLUENCE

The Great Powers Partition Europe,
from Munich to Yalta

LLOYD C. GARDNER

ELEPHANT PAPERBACKS
Ivan R. Dee, Publisher, Chicago

SPHERES OF INFLUENCE. Copyright ©1993 by Lloyd C. Gardner. This book was originally published in 1993 by Ivan R. Dee.

First ELEPHANT PAPERBACK edition published 1994 by Ivan R. Dee, Inc., 1332 North Halsted Street, Chicago 60622. Manufactured in the United States of America and printed on acid-free paper.

Library of Congress Cataloging-in-Publication Data:
Gardner, Lloyd C., 1934–
    Spheres of influence : the great powers partition Europe,
  from Munich to Yalta / Lloyd C. Gardner
      p.   cm.
    Includes bibliographical references and index.
    ISBN 1-56663-058-4
    1. World War, 1939–1945—Diplomatic history. 2. Spheres of
influence. 3. Reconstruction (1939–1951). 4. Europe—History—
1945–. I. Title.
D749.G37 1993
940.53'142—dc20   92-40147

To Warren F. Kimball

who took us on a journey of understanding,
from Lend-Lease to Yalta

Contents

Preface

The trouble is that Mr. Churchill has the same
attitude toward royalty that many New York
business men had toward Tammany Hall during its
worst period of corruption—namely, that it is
simpler to deal with a corrupt, continuing, going
concern that knows the language than it is to
trade with neophytes in politics who believe in
principles.

Raymond Daniell, New York Times,
December 10, 1944

Has anyone who is wringing his hands and
beating his breast about these developments any
better plan for winning the peace than one which
enlists the principal nations of Europe as the
primary guardians?

Walter Lippmann, December 21, 1944

THE SUDDEN COLLAPSE of the Soviet Empire in Eastern
Europe has reopened debate once again on the origins of the
cold war. Russian scholars, in particular, have set to work filling
in the "white spaces" in Stalinist accounts, from the 1939
Nazi-Soviet pact through the 1945 Yalta Conference. For the
first time a copy of the 1939 agreement dividing Eastern
Europe into spheres of influence has been uncovered in Russian
archives; for the first time also, historians can see the original
order Stalin signed in 1940 for the execution of thousands of
Polish officers in the Katyn Forest when Poland was partitioned
between Germany and Russia.

As the quotations from Raymond Daniell and Walter Lippmann make clear, contemporary observers were well aware of the basic issues confronting the Big Three as World War II came to an end. Even without access to secret archives, enough was already known about Stalin's determination to dominate Eastern Europe. Churchill's efforts to meet that challenge were regarded by Washington as reactionary—not unlike Neville Chamberlain's morally repugnant and ultimately short-sighted appeasement schemes. This dynamic eventually forced Roosevelt to confront the most difficult choice of the war: he could abandon the Grand Alliance and declare separate war aims for the United States, or he could try to minimize differences for the sake of preserving the wartime "partnership" as a transitional stage to what he hoped would evolve into a reasonably secure peace. For FDR the choice seemed obvious. The "beautiful ideas" of the Atlantic Charter would have to be postponed until postwar stability permitted their return. Roosevelt never really let on—at least in public—what the terms of his choices were, or how his own thought had evolved during the war. In press conferences he hinted at the difficulties of peacemaking, but the trail of those clues (as was often the case with FDR) led to no certain destination.

"This war is not as in the past," Stalin once instructed Yugoslav communists. "Whoever occupies a territory also imposes on it his own social system" as far "as his army can reach." British policymakers were never sure what Stalin intended, and like their American counterparts they fluctuated about how to respond to the challenge. Churchill wanted assurance from Stalin that Russia would not interfere, either through the Red Army or the Communist party, in Britain's traditional sphere of influence. If such arrangements lasted until Churchill could persuade the Americans to take a more active role in Central European affairs, all the better. He would do all he could after Yalta, in part for domestic political purposes, to "roll back" Soviet gains; but always first in his mind was the reconstruction of empire battlements where they touched on the borders of the Russian glacis.

American policymakers thought Churchill's wartime strategy terribly dangerous. Any such arrangement with the Soviet

Union was inherently unstable, in their view, and likely to produce exactly the sort of situation that had led to war in the past. Churchill had been Neville Chamberlain's most determined opponent, but his approach to the postwar settlement seemed destined, Washington believed, to repeat Chamberlain's error in trusting Hitler to honor a spheres-of-influence arrangement.

Roosevelt had stood aside in 1938 when Chamberlain sought to give Hitler a free hand in Eastern Europe and as the prime minister proposed repartitioning Africa to encourage Germany to rejoin the bearers of the "white man's burden." But when it appeared that Chamberlain's successor, Churchill, was prepared in 1942 to yield the Baltic states and divide the Balkans in order to appease Stalin, the president protested strongly.

Despite Churchill's bulldog reputation and his antiappeasement rhetoric, his "peripheral" political and military strategies protected imperial interests in the Mediterranean and delayed the second front in Europe. Still worse, Americans worried that the prime minister would drag them along into Southeastern Europe to insure the success of a spheres-of-influence bargain. Churchill could hope all he wanted that Anglo-American military force would rectify the situation at war's end—but then it would be too late.

Churchill defended himself early on against American accusations by appealing to Roosevelt to understand that he had little to offer Stalin to keep him in the war except assurances that Russian territorial demands would be satisfied. He had resisted that path, he insisted, but saw no other way. As it became apparent that the question was not how to keep Russia in the war but where the boundaries would fall between "systems," the prime minister fretted that Roosevelt's aloofness weakened the allies' ability to bargain with Stalin.

At the outset of American involvement in wartime diplomacy, when Franklin Roosevelt met Churchill off the coast of

Newfoundland to write the Atlantic Charter in August 1941, and then a few weeks later when he made the decision to extend Lend-Lease aid to the Soviet Union, the president had high hopes for Big Three cooperation. He looked toward agreements among the victors that could form the basis for a reasonable peace settlement, one that could be defended as fair to the smaller nations and colonial peoples struggling for independence, yet not challenge the security needs of the great powers.

Having begun the war with the "beautiful ideas" of the Atlantic Charter as his guide, Roosevelt later refused to jeopardize the Grand Alliance to preserve the principle of self-determination. From his rigid opposition to Churchill's acquiescence in Russian demands for the Baltic states to his concessions on Polish issues at Yalta, Roosevelt followed a difficult path. He continued to turn over possible alternatives—for example, economic inducements—but nothing the State Department offered him, still less Churchill's post-Yalta maneuvers, satisfied his first requirement: holding the Grand Alliance together through the peacemaking process.

Perhaps the most complex and fascinating aspects of Roosevelt's wartime diplomacy involved his conviction that what he negotiated stood on a different level from Churchill's similar arrangements with Stalin. If the British prime minister parceled out the peoples and lands of Europe, that was part of the bad Old World diplomacy. But if FDR talked with Stalin about the Big Three or Big Four running things after the war, that was a prelude to a just peace. Even if the president went beyond Churchill in making concessions, these were somehow different both in terms of permanence and implication—because America was destined to play a different role in world history. Woodrow Wilson's vision of these matters was not wrong, he had just gone about it in the wrong way. FDR would not make that mistake.

Roosevelt thus sought a way out in a two-phase approach to the postwar world. The president was determined, as he assured his wartime partners at Yalta, that the peace would be written by the three of them sitting around that table. He opposed efforts by his advisers at Yalta to create machinery to implement the "beautiful ideas" of the Atlantic Charter for fear of destroying the fragile unity of the Grand Alliance. If that alliance was to become the way to move beyond spheres of influence, it had to survive the transition to peace. The latest partition of Europe was for FDR not the last word to be said on the results of the war, only a preliminary stage. He hoped he could convince the others—and his critics at home—that peace-making was a process, not a solution in itself.

Unfortunately, Roosevelt could do little to prepare the American public or his successor (even had he confided in Harry Truman) for the harsh realities of the peacemaking process. Russian postwar behavior in Eastern Europe appeared inexplicable, except in terms of confrontation. Even so, FDR succeeded both in holding the alliance together until war's end and in laying a basis for a future peace. Had the Grand Alliance fallen apart at Yalta or immediately after because Roosevelt refused to recognize Russia's security demands, however twisted Stalin's visions, however brutal his methods, however terrible the immediate consequences for those peoples who fell under his control, the uneasy equilibrium of the cold war might have deteriorated into something much worse—a series of civil wars or possibly an even darker Orwellian condition of localized wars along an uncertain border.

On one of his visits to Ronald Reagan's America, Soviet leader Mikhail Gorbachev paid a special tribute to Franklin Roosevelt. Half a century ago, he said, President Roosevelt had spoken of four essential freedoms: freedom of speech, freedom of worship, freedom from want, and freedom from fear. "And this ideal has not yet been attained in the world and it could not be attained in the world of animosity and confrontation." Bad things happened within the postwar Soviet empire, Gorbachev admitted on another occasion. No one liked all aspects of the peace, but there were objective reasons for what took place.

Walter Lippmann had forecast that spheres of influence were the only solution to the postwar world until the guardians of the peace were themselves reassured that the peace would last. The only alternative to a realistic acceptance of that situation was war. While Stalin and Churchill tried to sort things out between them, seeking to control populations and establish outposts, Roosevelt followed a circuitous path, trying at first to prove Lippmann wrong. In the event, the Big Three collaborated—not always consciously—in avoiding a worse plan. "Civilization is hooped together," wrote William Butler Yeats, "brought under a rule, under the semblance of peace, by manifold illusion. . . ."

Acknowledgments

THIS BOOK IS the result of several strains coming together. In some ways it is a sequel to my study *Safe for Democracy: The Anglo-American Response to Revolution, 1913–1924* (1984). Here the focus is somewhat different, but I view both books as a reinterpretation of the response to war and revolution. The present book gained from a privileged opportunity to put my ideas before others during a series of Russian-American conferences on World War II that began in 1986 in Moscow. I am especially grateful for the comments and insights of my Russian colleagues in those ventures, notably Grigory Sevostianov, Oleg Rzheshevsky, Boris Gilenson, Victor Malkov, and Vladimir Poznyakov, as well as those of members of the American delegation, particularly Mark Stoler, Steve Miner, Ted Wilson, and Ed Bennett.

Warren Kimball, to whom this book is dedicated, has always generously shared his insights on Roosevelt's diplomacy and listened (not always patiently) to my own reconstructions. As the leader of the American delegations to the Russian-American symposia, he has contributed in so many other ways to the still unfinished process of understanding World War II. We are all in his debt. Mark White has given me much time and help in completing the manuscript, and many great conversations. Christopher Thorne did not live to read a word of this manuscript, but his influence is present everywhere in it.

This book continues my happy relationship with Gerard McCauley, a friend and literary agent introduced to me by Bill Williams many years ago, and resumes a publishing relationship to go with a longtime friendship with Ivan Dee, who has helped to bring out what is best in my account of these issues. Thanks, finally, to Erin Gardner Myers, who designed a beautiful jacket to show people what her father's book is about.

L. C. G.

Dutch Neck, New Jersey
November 1992

SPHERES OF INFLUENCE

1

ROOSEVELT'S PROPOSAL

What a fool Roosevelt would have looked if he had launched his precious proposal. What would he have thought of us if we had encouraged him to publish it, as Anthony was so eager to do? And how we, too, would have made ourselves the laughing stock of the world.

Neville Chamberlain, March 1938[1]

AFTER THE WAR it was argued that British Prime Minister Neville Chamberlain had brushed aside an American alternative to appeasement. Had he been willing to consider President Roosevelt's proposal for an international conference, the argument went, the whole sequence of events from 1938 might have been different. There might not even have been a war. Forsaking this "last frail chance to save the world from tyranny otherwise than by war," Winston Churchill later wrote, Chamberlain instead embraced a humiliating policy that would soon send him scurrying off to Munich with a vain offer to meet Hitler's price for peace in Europe: annexation of the Sudetenland to the Third Reich.[2] Left behind in London was British honor. Sullied by the betrayal of Czechoslovakia, Chamberlain's appeasement policy quickly came to symbolize all that was wrong about attempts to settle affairs with dictators via spheres of influence. So it was that the "Lesson of Munich," as presented so forcefully in Churchill's memoirs and repeated by others, became a primary text for wartime and postwar statesmen.

"No event," Churchill lamented in his famous account of the war, "could have been more likely to stave off, or even prevent, war than the arrival of the United States in the circle of European hates and fears. To Britain it was a matter almost of life and death."[3] This was quite a lot to assume about what was, at least at the outset, a vague gesture from the American president.

Churchill insisted on the importance of the Roosevelt "proposal" because it fit well with his determination to educate postwar readers about the folly of appeasement. But speculations about "missed opportunities" often as not misdirect historical inquiries. The January 1938 Roosevelt initiative is especially problematic. Elevated by Churchill to the status of an alternative to appeasement, it gives American policy in the pre-Munich years a clearer definition than is warranted by the evidence.

As Hitler grew bolder, Roosevelt's sympathies—like those of most Americans—lay with England and France. But his 1938 initiative did not go beyond what he had set forth as guiding principles for European policy enunciated four years earlier in his 1934 State of the Union Message to Congress:

> I have made it clear that the United States cannot take part in political arrangements in Europe, but that we stand ready to cooperate at any time in practicable measures on a world basis looking to immediate reduction of armaments and the lowering of the barriers against commerce.

The Roosevelt "proposal" which Churchill refashioned into a major turning point on the road to war originated in a private discussion between the president and his old friend, Under Secretary of State Sumner Welles, about finding a way to aid Anglo-French efforts to reach agreement with Germany without further undermining the position of the smaller nations of

Europe. Welles suggested an international conference to "lend support and impetus" to Anglo-French attempts to reach "a practical understanding with Germany both on colonies and upon security, as well as upon European adjustments."[4]

Roosevelt liked the idea and told Welles to convey it to the British ambassador, Sir Ronald Lindsay. Secretary of State Cordell Hull knew nothing about it until after Welles had talked with Lindsay, and Hull was furious about what he considered a slapdash manner of conducting foreign policy. The secretary had always resented Welles's relationship with FDR, so his pique was not unexpected. But it did not further the plan's chances for success.

When Welles explained the idea to Sir Ronald, he noted that the president was alarmed by the movement of smaller states toward the orbit of the dictators. Something must be done, Welles said, to restore the influence of the democracies "at the earliest possible moment." Toward that end, Roosevelt proposed a conference to lend an economic as well as a political basis to efforts for a settlement with Germany. If His Majesty's Government agreed, Welles told Lindsay on January 12, 1938, the president planned to call an international conference to discuss world economic issues and the arms race.[5]

Lindsay came away from this conversation excited about the apparent shift in American policy toward a deeper involvement in European affairs. In his report to London, the American proposal became identified, then and later, not as a parallel to political appeasement but as an alternative to direct dealings with the dictators. The ambassador's impression was strengthened, moreover, by Welles's sense of urgency. Roosevelt wanted an answer within five days, he said, otherwise he would drop the project.[6]

The British Foreign Office reacted with considerable enthusiasm. True, in this first go-around Roosevelt's ideas seemed more than a little blurry—even confused in places—and, true, the proposal bore all the marks of a hastily assembled package, put together from fragments of old Wilsonian ideas about international cooperation. Nor did it deal directly with critical issues in Central and Eastern Europe. But wasn't this the long-awaited indication that America was emerging from its national solipsism? At least, shouldn't one find out?

Sir Alec Cadogan, Welles's counterpart in the Foreign Office, wrote Prime Minister Chamberlain a note embodying all those reactions. "FDR's readiness to enter the arena," said the diplomat, "is obviously a fact of the first importance, and I should say that we must not discourage him, although the prospects of the success of his system are problematical and the risks, maybe, great."[7]

Chamberlain's response was quite different. The president's intervention was an unexploded "bombshell" that had suddenly landed in his lap, he wrote privately, and would blow everything to smithereens at the very moment his policy was about to bring lasting peace to Europe.[8] Taking advantage of Roosevelt's insistence upon a quick reply, Chamberlain drafted a chilly response suggesting that the president hold back, lest his well-intentioned proposal cut across his own plans. Cadogan managed to recast the message in somewhat friendlier language, but it nonetheless reflected Chamberlain's caution—and his deep suspicion of American motives in general. Might not Germany and Italy use Roosevelt's invitation to "delay consideration of specific points," he wondered, "and to put forward demands over and above what they would put forward to us if we were in direct negotiations with them?"[9]

Chamberlain had long feared that American goals were nothing less than the economic annexation of empire markets. If Roosevelt's conference reopened questions of trade equity among the industrial nations, there was no telling where things might lead.

But when the prime minister spoke to the cabinet, he placed his negative reaction to the president's proposal in somewhat different terms. The whole thing was "rather preposterous," Chamberlain said, beginning with Roosevelt's insistence on a quick reply, and all the rest. Only too typical of his experience with the Americans. What was new here? Nothing, merely a restatement of tired old notions bypassed long ago by the pace of political events. The dictator states would sneer at the proposal. Certainly they would find nothing to entice them into serious negotiations.[10]

Chamberlain knew that his foreign secretary, Anthony Eden, who had been out of the country, would seize on Lindsay's reports to rally opposition to appeasement. Eden was foolishly enamored of the notion, thought Chamberlain, that the Americans could somehow be coaxed into playing a constructive role in Europe. Eden did indeed hope for an American alternative to appeasement. "It may be that you think I exaggerate," the foreign secretary wrote privately before a crucial cabinet debate, "but I truly believe that with the world as it is now, it is almost impossible to overestimate the effect which an indication of United States interest in European affairs may be calculated to produce."[11]

Eden found little support from the men who sat around the cabinet table. Where Chamberlain was convinced of the rightness of his position, his colleagues were in thrall to their fear that any other course meant war. Looking at those faces, Eden knew he must resign. "He seemed to me at this moment," Churchill later wrote, recalling his anxiety the night of Eden's departure, "to embody the life-hope of the British nation.... Now he was gone. I watched the daylight slowly creep in through the windows, and saw before me in mental gaze the vision of Death."[12]

And so the time passed for a positive reply to Roosevelt. Would anything solid have emerged if Chamberlain had encouraged FDR to move ahead? Would the prewar partition of Europe have been avoided? These questions remain unanswered and probably unanswerable except for the speculations of memoir writers like Churchill, whose postwar judgments about men and events have shaped historical interpretations about World War II to the present day. A new look at the events leading to Munich suggests that, contrary to what Churchill and others wrote after the war, appeasement in 1938 was not simply a matter of cowardice or folly, and that the attempted division of Europe was a response to more than Hitler's driving ambition.

As Hitler drove Europe to the precipice of World War II, leaders in the three nations that were eventually forced into alliance to oppose his ambitions had certain fears in common: none of them knew whether they could risk opposing him with arms, or, conversely, whether they could risk *not* opposing him. In the United States, Britain, and the Soviet Union, political and economic systems had had to withstand a series of shocks that left them uncertain, if not precarious. Their governments probably were in less danger than their leaders feared at the time, but internal preoccupations dictated a common desire to preserve (or at least extend) the peace.

Beginning with the Great Depression, the world had become a molten tangle of national hatreds. The 1936 Anti-Comintern pact united Berlin, Rome, and Tokyo in an alliance that gave notice to the rest of the world that preserving the peace was not accorded the same priority in the fascist worldview. Any remaining doubts on that point were quickly erased by the Japanese thrust into China, and the Spanish Civil War.

The Great Depression did not strike Great Britain as fiercely as it hit other industrial nations, but the damage was nevertheless widespread. Still more worrisome was the growing belief that British industry had fallen into an irreversible decline, characterized by a fatalistic ennui. The Conservative government continued to amass huge majorities in Parliament, but its tired leadership inspired few, if any, bold initiatives.

Neville Chamberlain imagined he would change all that. Succeeding Stanley Baldwin as prime minister in the summer of 1937, Chamberlain wrote to his sister Ida, "Now I have only to raise a finger and the whole face of Europe is changed!"[13] Although certainly more active than its predecessor, Chamberlain's cabinet feared fully as much the impact of rearmament spending on the economy and political stability. "We are . . . in danger of undermining ourselves," Sir Warren Fisher, permanent under secretary at the Treasury, had noted in June 1937, "before the Boche feels it desirable to move." Armament spending meant inflation, Chamberlain had declared while still chancellor of the exchequer, "leading to the loss of our export trade, a feverish and artificial boom followed by a disastrous slump, and finally the defeat of the Government."[14]

Appeasement, Chamberlain wrote privately at the end of October 1937, could provide "the ultimate check to the mad armaments race, which if allowed to continue must involve us all in ruin."[15] On the other hand, as he would often explain to the cabinet, if war should come Britain's economic stability would be a key to the nation's defenses. If the enemy knew he could not strike a knockout blow to the British economy, he might not risk war.[16] Another reason, then, to rein in arms expenditures—another reason, first, to avoid war by settling with Germany and Italy.

The heart of the matter in dealing with Germany was, everyone agreed, Eastern Europe. And here Chamberlain had first to maneuver around French commitments. After World War I French leaders had sought to hem in the Germans with a series of security treaties creating the so-called Little Entente. Paris had given its solemn commitment to defend Czechoslovakia with its large, restless German minority, the obvious place for Hitler to expand his power eastward. Still more unfortunate, from Chamberlain's point of view, the French had tied themselves up with Russia in the Czech business. The new prime minister had hoped to undo the French knot by encouraging the Russians and Germans to sign nonaggression pacts with all the states between them.[17]

If Hitler was not interested in that idea—and of course he was not—perhaps he could be induced to think about the repartitioning of Africa?[18] This seemingly fantastic scheme to set the clock back to the pre–World War I era, and correct old mistakes of British statesmen, was nevertheless deemed worthy of serious consideration as perhaps the means to de-Nazify Germany. Various British officials thus encouraged their German contacts to think about such a solution; and they listened carefully to Radio Berlin for hints that Hitler wished to do more than just rave about the injustice of the Versailles Treaty and Germany's lost African colonies. A former finance minister of Rumania told Sir Frederick Leith-Ross, another Treasury expert, to forget about Hitler and Africa: "The sort of country he wanted for his colonies was to be found in Russia."[19]

Yet there appeared some reason to believe that, if not Hitler, those around him were indeed interested in regaining a share of Africa. German needs for raw materials might thus exert a moderating force on Nazi "extremists." Even David Lloyd George, prime minister in the Great War and constant goad to Chamberlain in these later years, joined the call for redistributing colonial "mandates." In the House of Commons he declared his belief that the only way to break the circle of death rapidly forming around Europe was a reshuffling to return Germany to her proper prewar alignment alongside the other metropolitan powers. "Let them put their cards on the table and say what it was they were after."[20]

Chamberlain did not choose to wait for Hitler to put his cards on the table. He preferred to play his first. The prime minister's design followed the lines originally set down by his father Joseph Chamberlain, who, as colonial secretary in Lord Salisbury's cabinet at the turn of the century, had argued unsuccessfully for a global settlement with Germany. Such a pact, the elder Chamberlain had maintained, would ease colonial rivalries, allow Britain breathing space to deal with internal problems, and form a united front of conservative powers in the face of radical movements at home and challenges from abroad.[21]

The Chamberlain "tradition" in foreign policy had then passed from Joseph to Neville through his half-brother Austen, the Conservative foreign secretary who formulated the Locarno Pact with Italy in the mid-1920s, and whose considered recommendation for Eastern Europe was to condemn bolshevism as loudly as possible and otherwise leave Russia to its fate.[22]

Shortly before Neville Chamberlain succeeded Baldwin in 1937, Lord Lothian, a Liberal party stalwart, made his own journey to Berlin to see for himself what this man Hitler was all about. He came away convinced that the situation was "both more dangerous and more soluble than I had thought." "We are . . . to-day once more very much where we were . . . at the beginning of this century," he wrote in a memorandum for the Foreign Office, "when Joseph Chamberlain tried to cut through the toils [coils?] which were beginning to entrap us, except that events move far more rapidly than they did then."[23]

Lothian's recommendation was simple: "In the first place Eastern Europe." There were only two ultimate possibilities in that region—either Germany would take what it wanted by force, or "agreements will be made between Germany and the smaller Eastern European nations on the model of the modern British Commonwealth."[24] Lothian's memorandum was dismissed by nearly everyone in the Foreign Office as an example of what happened when amateurs meddled in diplomacy. "He knows practically nothing of the *inside* of the questions that he is treating," gibed Permanent Under Secretary Sir Robert Vansittart, "but remains happily on the surface."[25]

Chamberlain obviously did not agree. Within a short time Vansittart was shunted to a meaningless position in the Foreign Office. The prime minister had concluded that Sir Robert was a major obstacle to his plans, whatever final form they might take; he was far too anti-German ever to acknowledge any proposal for settling affairs on reasonable terms. "Van had the effect of multiplying . . . [Eden's] natural vibrations," Chamberlain would explain, and now "he will be much steadier."[26] Lothian's belief that Hitler would respect national rights in Eastern Europe might have been naive, but that did not, Chamberlain would argue, negate his point: if Germany moved to restore its "natural" position in Central and Eastern Europe by force, the immediate consequences would be far more serious to those countries, and, consequently, to British interests, than if some way were found to meet Hitler's demands by demonstrating that the West had no desire to encircle Germany or to mount an ideological crusade to overturn the Nazi regime. In return, Germany should respect British imperial concerns, particularly in easing its support for Italian adventures in the Mediterranean or Japanese threats in the Far East.

"The primary issue," Lothian repeated in a letter to the British ambassador in Germany, Nevile Henderson, who agreed, "is whether Germany or France and Russia is going to be predominant in East Central Europe." It had to be made clear that the British would not allow themselves to be dragged into a war that could only benefit the "Communists of Europe." "Once that is clear the sheer strength of Germany will give her local predominance without risk of war."[27]

The hard part was to find a proper opening for initiating conversations. Over Anthony Eden's objections, Chamberlain chose Lord Halifax, a former viceroy for India, for the assignment. In the foreign policy committee's discussions on the colonial question, Halifax had indicated he was far more open to appeasement initiatives than the phalanx of Foreign Office officials. As the discussion turned to possible quid pro quos, Halifax pointed out that the safest way to engage Germany would be to make colonial concessions contingent upon a general settlement. Unless some offer were made, on the other hand, he did not see how Germany could be kept out of Africa without going to war—and probably not even then.[28]

Halifax traveled to Germany in mid-November 1937, ostensibly in response to an invitation to a stag hunt at one of Herman Goering's estates in Bavaria. His conversations with Hitler closely followed the suggestions he had taken with him, to such an extent that when Halifax reported to the cabinet, it was difficult to separate out what the German leader had actually asked of his guest. Thus when Hitler raised the colonial question, he had been given a strong lead in by Halifax and an indication of readiness to negotiate.[29]

Even so, Halifax was uncertain of the direction he wished Hitler to go. One way was to try to persuade the German dictator to give up colonial claims in exchange for a free hand in Europe. The more difficult—"but possibly sounder bargain" —was to try for a colonial settlement at the price of being a good European. It was an altogether tricky proposition, for the idea must be planted with Hitler that London would not oppose a "rather liberally interpreted" "peaceful evolution" of the situation in Eastern Europe—and yet not leave the impression His Majesty's Government cared nothing for the process. "It is going to be very bad, if we get to talks and they break down," Halifax cautioned Chamberlain privately about Foreign Office attitudes. "And therefore I think we must see pretty clearly how far we are really prepared to go."[30]

However carefully Halifax probed Hitler's intentions, the special emissary did not withhold praise for Germany's role in halting the spread of communism. As Halifax recorded his words to Hitler:

> I was not blind to what he had done for Germany and to the achievement from his point of view of keeping Communism out of his country and, as he would feel, of blocking its passage West. And taking England as a whole, there was a much greater degree of understanding of all his work on that side than there had been some time ago.[31]

Halifax received gratifying assurances from both Goering and Hitler, in return, that they did not wish to spend "one drop of blood" because of Eastern Europe—unless war was forced upon them. He therefore expected, Halifax reported to the cabinet, that Germany would work with beaverlike persistence to achieve its aims in that region, "but not in a form to give others cause—or probably occasion—to interfere."

After listening to Halifax's carefully worded report of Hitler's views, Anthony Eden tried to alert his colleagues to what he saw as the basic flaw in the Chamberlain/Halifax premise. The colonial question loomed larger than he had thought, the foreign secretary began, but "Germany clearly did not now wish to connect Central Europe with the colonial question." It was important to realize, therefore, that if the cabinet wished to make colonial concessions part of a general settlement, "that was clearly not Germany's view."[32]

In their discussions with the British a few days later, the French put the same point that Eden had made. Halifax's conversations, they said, actually revealed that Hitler saw *no* connection between Central Europe and the colonial question. The French were also disappointed by Chamberlain's use of the Halifax talks to pressure them to agree that "appropriate concessions might be made" by the Czechs for the sake of a general agreement with Germany.[33]

The prime minister had prepared an answer beforehand to such objections: Italy. What his opponents failed to understand was that despite the Anti-Comintern pact, Italy and Germany had different aims in Europe. While Halifax laid the groundwork with Hitler, Chamberlain would come at the problem through Rome, offering diplomatic recognition of the puppet state Italy had created with the conquest of Abyssinia. Mussolini needed British approval more than he needed the alliance with Germany, Chamberlain told French diplomats, hence it would be possible to bring pressure on Berlin in such a fashion.[34] Divide and conquer—even by using appeasement as your weapon. Like his critics, Chamberlain felt contempt for the Italian dictator, but that was not the point. "If only we could get on terms with the Germans," he wrote to his sister Ida, "I would not care a rap for Musso."[35]

"Why shouldn't we say to Germany," Chamberlain mused, "'give us satisfactory assurances that you won't use force to deal with the Austrians and Czechoslovakians, and we will give you similar assurances that we won't use force to prevent the changes you want, if you can get them by peaceful means.'"[36] But it was never simply a case of not seeking to "prevent the changes" Germany sought, nor even, as Lord Lothian had postulated, of making it clear that Britain would be neutral in a Russo-German contest for supremacy in Eastern Europe. Instead Chamberlain had set himself the task of completing his father's work—a global settlement with Germany. From the time of German unification, or certainly soon thereafter, it had become clear that British economic supremacy was severely challenged. The French had disturbing ambitions in areas of concern to British statesmen, but Germany was the only power that posed a total challenge. Sooner or later matters would have to be settled between them. The Great War (World War I), it turned out, had only delayed the day of reckoning. Chamberlain's father had been right all along.

His father had also been right not to trust the Americans. In the name of all that was holy in international affairs, they would only succeed in causing irreparable damage to British interests. It could almost have been predicted, then, that just as he was ready to go forward with his plans for a German settlement, the Americans would launch some half-baked proposal. For the life of him, Chamberlain could not understand why his critics believed there really was something as serious as an American "alternative" to appeasement.

One need only read, as Chamberlain did, what Roosevelt had to say. In the prime minister's copy of Ambassador Lindsay's report of the conversation with Sumner Welles, someone had underlined these words: *"Traditional policy of freedom from political involvement which U.S. Government has maintained and will maintain is well known. In the determination of political* [frontiers?], *U.S. Government can play no part."* Plain for all to see, Roosevelt had offered no help, only Wilsonian dreams. Lindsay had explained that this meant the president believed there must be agreement on general principles before any territorial adjustments were made, but the blue-pencil underliner at No. 10 Downing Street obviously thought otherwise.[37]

Roosevelt also set great store on the surprise impact of his proposal, Lindsay explained. Hence there would be no time for His Majesty's Government to formulate "constructive suggestions." "Destructive criticisms, reservations or attempts to define issues more clearly can only accomplish very little..., while they will create a disproportionate bad impression" in Washington.[38]

What was one to make of all this? What could be put together here? A solid proposal for an American presence in European affairs? Not likely, thought Chamberlain. More likely a got-up piece of hasty pudding in the Foreign Office to distract him from his destined mission to save the empire from ideologues and crusaders, like Vansittart and his clan. No such collusion existed, except perhaps in Chamberlain's suspicious mind; but because there was no document that could be studied—only Lindsay's report of Welles's conversation—it is scarcely surprising that the prime minister saw the Foreign Office's unusual, indeed totally uncharacteristic, willingness to suspend disbelief in this instance as suspicious in itself.

Lindsay raved on in his descriptions of Roosevelt's apparent willingness to put the American government behind the democracies, but all that one found under the crust were those soft, mushy principles Wilson had brought with him to Paris, and which the Americans had been trying to feed the world ever since. It was all there, every bit of it: equal access for all nations to raw materials headed the list. Germany might go for that—but what would it give in return?[39]

To Chamberlain and those who thought as he did, Roosevelt's proposal aimed to set the clock back to a time when British free-trade principles ruled the marketplace as the British navy ruled the seas. But World War I had destroyed that world. Moreover, even before the New Deal the Americans themselves practiced protectionism. In rejecting Roosevelt's initiative, Chamberlain was also acting out the implications of "imperial preference."

Almost six years earlier in Ottawa, Canada, in the summer of 1932, Chamberlain had led the British delegation to an empire conference that created the imperial preference system. The stakes were high. If the empire was to be saved, it must have an economic basis. The depression had disrupted trade around the world for almost three years, with no end in sight. If London had not acted at Ottawa to give special preferences in its market to empire produce, the future would have looked bleak for the achievements of Victoria's glorious reign.

Watching the events in Ottawa from Albany, New York, Governor Franklin D. Roosevelt, the Democratic candidate for the presidency, had some sharp comments for an English journalist. "I don't think it is practicable, and I don't think it is wise," Roosevelt told Arthur Cummings, "to attempt the creation of an Empire economic unit as that would almost inevitably create antagonistic economic units elsewhere. We on our part, for example, would undoubtedly be tempted to seek exclusive arrangements with Germany." He looked forward to a better time, Roosevelt rambled on, when the United States, Great Britain, and the Empire could act together to promote their political and economic interests around the world, acquiring between them "the moral leadership of the entire world."[40]

Now, in early 1938, Roosevelt's better time was the least favorable moment for a positive response from Neville Chamberlain. It is more than a little ironic that the American initiative had behind it, if one looked closely enough, concern about a possible Anglo-German trade "arrangement" to divide European markets.[41] But right out in front the Roosevelt proposal seemed to be a new approach to outflanking the imperial preference system. Anglo-American trade negotiations had been going on for some months before the president's proposal. British negotiators were especially wary of undertaking the trade assignment precisely because of its political implications. The cabinet saw little or no gain at stake for British trade, and had approved the negotiations, despite fears about the integrity of the Ottawa agreements, because of supposed political benefits.[42]

Ottawa had been Chamberlain's "New Deal," as he told critics at the time, and while he did not exactly rejoice at American anger about supposed trade discrimination, he had few regrets that it widened the distance between London and Washington. He was certainly not unhappy, for example, that Ottawa posed a continuing obstacle to "quixotic" quests in search of Anglo-American cooperation, spawned by then Prime Minister Ramsay MacDonald's infatuation with his supposed powers over American public opinion.

"I know the P.M. has had hankerings after a visit to America in the autumn," Chamberlain wrote to his sister after returning from Canada, "but I have reason to believe that the Americans don't want him and I hope therefore that we shall hear no more about the proposal."[43] He did not change his mind in later years. In contrast to his desire to expand personal connections with Mussolini and Hitler, Chamberlain turned down every invitation to visit Roosevelt. A message from FDR was conveyed to Chamberlain in early June 1937, for example, saying he would welcome a visit because the peace of the world depended upon "an enlightened policy of Anglo-American cooperation." Roosevelt had in mind the "logical occasion" of agreement on trade negotiations for such a visit, as it would provide the opportunity for conversations "on other subjects."[44]

The Americans had "a long way to go yet before they become helpful partners in world affairs," Chamberlain wrote his other sister Hilda, citing efforts to win Washington's support of an appeal to Japan and China to end their hostilities.[45] The prime minister used the Far Eastern situation as a reason for not coming to Washington, as he saw "little prospect" of action by the Western powers to ease tensions there. The conclusion of an Anglo-American commercial agreement "when we have found ways of overcoming its obvious difficulties will undoubtedly be an important step in the right direction."[46]

Chamberlain did not intend to be chivied into a trade agreement that would undermine all that had been accomplished at Ottawa, unless there was an urgent need for American political support. Roosevelt's January 1938 initiative thus appeared to him to be just one more tactic in the American campaign to break through the stalled Anglo-American negotiations and gain a worldwide agreement with economic remedies for political ills. When Lindsay in fact asked Welles how the Japanese question fit into Roosevelt's plan, he was told that once Germany and Italy were engaged in serious negotiations they would withdraw support from Tokyo, leaving Japan no alternative but to make peace within the terms of various treaties guaranteeing China's security.[47]

However well intended, and indeed *because* they were, these were highly pernicious notions for the British. Appeasement, on the other hand, might rescue Britain from unwanted entanglements across the Atlantic as well as from perils closer to home across the English Channel. While the dominant view in the prime minister's office held that the American initiative would also be rejected by the fascist powers as a clumsy effort to maneuver them—thus destroying all chances for negotiating a European settlement—British interests might be still more endangered if Germany and Italy took the proposal seriously.

The president had called for discussion of the "inequities" in the Versailles Treaty. That might actually lead the dictators to demand greater economic concessions than Chamberlain planned to offer. He expressed such a fear in a private message to Ambassador Lindsay. Roosevelt's proposal, he said, had obviously been drawn up without a full knowledge of all that was happening. In fact, no one but the prime minister knew all that was going on, because his distrust of the Foreign Office had led him to use various outside intermediaries, including even his sister-in-law, to establish contacts with potential negotiating partners in Germany and Italy. But never mind that, his point to Lindsay was that any mention of inequities in the Versailles settlement could prompt Germany to put its "colonial claims very high indeed."[48]

Lindsay reported that Chamberlain's attitude was a keen disappointment to the president. In addition, the prime minister's proposal to accord Mussolini de jure recognition of the conquest of Abyssinia as a starting point for serious negotiations added to Roosevelt's irritation. It would be seen in Washington as a corrupt bargain, the ambassador warned, at the expense of American interest in blocking Japan's efforts to legitimize its military conquest of Manchuria.[49]

The wrangle over Anglo-Italian negotiations finally brought matters to a head between Chamberlain and Eden. The foreign secretary's repeated concern not to do anything about Italy "without Roosevelt's approval" created an impasse that could only be resolved by Eden leaving the cabinet.[50] At the climactic cabinet meetings of February 19 and 20, 1938, Chamberlain recited at length his experience with the growing burden of armaments since his term as chancellor of the exchequer. If things continued as they were, within two years the country would face "the gravest financial dislocation."

From the time he became prime minister, therefore, he had

been concerned to find a diplomatic solution to Britain's impending financial crisis. He repeated once again his belief that the route to such a solution lay through Italy. In his mind, he now said, it had always been a matter of concessions to Germany or easing tensions with Italy. Italy was like a "hysterical woman." Faced with the British attitude toward Abyssinia, and German power in Central Europe, Rome was facing a desperate choice.

He could not imagine that Mussolini found Hitler's new threats to Austria palatable, but British diplomacy left him no alternative to acquiescence. He had been informed, Chamberlain went on, that Rome had sought to moderate the German approach to Austria. The purpose of opening negotiations with Italy had always been to stiffen Mussolini's resistance to German pretensions. Here was one of those opportunities, he concluded, "that come at rare intervals and did not recur." If the Italian gambit succeeded, it would "give courage" not only to Rome but to Austria and other small countries threatened by German power.

Eden tried to counter the prime minister's effective (and facile) performance by insisting that there was no evidence that Mussolini faced a desperate choice, or that he had any intention of switching sides. Eden had never believed that Mussolini exerted, or wished to exert, a moderating role in the Austrian question. Recognition of the conquest of Abyssinia would cause a "panic" among Britain's friends in Europe. "There would be an impression of scuttle in England, and alienation of popular opinion in the U.S."[51]

Eden's resignation after two days of cabinet battles—lopsided affairs which the foreign secretary had no chance of winning—sent a signal to European capitals and to Washington that British policy had been determined: a surrender of Southeastern Europe to Berlin. Chamberlain had telephoned him immediately after Eden's resignation, French Premier Camille Chautemps told the American ambassador in Paris, to inform him that there would be no change in British policy. "This was polite but not important."[52]

Chautemps believed that Chamberlain contemplated with relative equanimity German control of Austria, Czechoslovakia, Hungary, and Rumania. The premier doubted his country would be prepared to make the sacrifices necessary under these circumstances to try to maintain the French position in Central and Eastern Europe. Foreign Minister Yvon Delbos said he had also received a reassuring note from Chamberlain. But there was no doubt that Britain had embarked on a policy of turning over Eastern Europe. France would withdraw behind the Maginot Line. German domination, Chautemps believed, would likely last until years of conflict "between Germany and the Russian colossus supported by the other states of Europe" brought it finally to an end.[53]

In Washington, Assistant Secretary of State George Messersmith wrote a long memorandum to Cordell Hull, the secretary of state, analyzing the European situation as it stood near the end of February 1938. Hull passed it on to Roosevelt. Messersmith, who had served in Berlin when Hitler came to power, marveled that it seemed so difficult for some to realize that Germany was proceeding on a fixed course which had not altered since the regime came to power:

> I cannot understand the English attitude. There seems to be . . . a group which believes that they can purchase security through giving Germany a free hand in Southeastern Europe. . . . It now looks as though it has the upper hand. It would be well if they realized that Germany with a free hand in Europe has a good deal freer hand in the rest of the world.[54]

That argument had been used successfully in earlier times against Joe Chamberlain's proposal for an understanding with Berlin to protect the empire. Messersmith believed that British unwillingness to speak "above a whisper" about German aims would not only forfeit a chance to stop Berlin's drive east, it also meant "the gradual disintegration of the British Empire." Finally, German hegemony would also menace the future of the American trade agreements program around the world and create a stronger base for German economic expansion into

South America. "With England and France in a purely second-ary position and with the Empire disintegrated, we in this country would stand practically alone, and that our troubles would come a little later does not give me any comfort."[55]

Roosevelt once observed to an American ambassador in Europe that the "group" which Messersmith had described as in control of British policy had its counterpart in America. These were the "economic royalists" who opposed the New Deal: "They would really like me to be like Neville Chamberlain."[56] Roosevelt's image of himself as a champion of an active, Wilsonian-like foreign policy was not quite a matter of a liberal president opposing conservative isolationists. Certainly FDR saw himself in that picture, struggling against an isolationist Congress, trying to educate public opinion; but the liberal Wilsonian tradition (dating back to Jefferson) was not pro-intervention in European affairs, it was supra-intervention. Rather than partici-pating in Old World politics, it sought to remake Europe (and the world) from the top down.[57]

Roosevelt's 1938 "initiative" for an international conference, with its emphasis on economic issues and disarmament—and its firm statement against U.S. political involvement in Europe—was perfectly in line with the general pattern of the 1930s. France's tragedy, claimed Camille Chautemps, "was that the nation which kept its word—the United States—could not act in Europe and the nation which could act—Great Britain—could not keep its word."[58] More than a little self-serving, and too simplified, Chautemps's appraisal nonetheless captured the dilemma of mobilizing a united front against Hitler's challenge.

The Roosevelt administration had briefly flirted with eco-nomic isolationism at the depths of the depression crisis, but then it proposed to Congress the Reciprocal Trade Agreements Program. Its principal sponsor in the administration was Secre-tary of State Cordell Hull, whose faith in the power of economic liberalism to right all—or most all—political wrongs was widely derided by the inner circle of New Deal "planners" in and around the White House. FDR did not confide in Hull, but the secretary would outlast the planners and his other rivals for control of day-to-day policy.

The first trade treaties under the aegis of the RTA program were made with countries whose products did not really compete with American domestic interests. Hull realized that if his program was to reverse the momentum toward economic and political "blocs," and the resultant march toward war, he would have to maintain support at home while negotiating treaties with powerful industrial rivals. The opening of negotiations with London would, Hull believed, provide the make-or-break test of whether the democracies could bring themselves together in common purpose to meet the fascist challenge abroad and the perils of state socialism at home.[59]

The delay in completing this agreement from early 1937 to near the end of 1938, which Hull blamed on the "oyster shell" attitude spawned by the Ottawa imperial preference system, was maddening to State Department negotiators. "When war was threatening and Germany was pounding at our gates," an assistant secretary lectured the British late in 1938, "it seemed to me tragic that we had not been able to reach and sign an agreement."[60]

Hull had hoped to use the British agreement as a launching pad for the definitive task of creating an American-led "bloc" of thirty or so nations that would ultimately prove too great for Germany to resist. If Nazi trade methods were defeated, Nazism would then recede as a force menacing Europe and the world. But now he was worried about the possibility of a new depression at home, Hull told former Secretary of State Henry L. Stimson at the end of March 1938, and the collapse of the American economy.[61]

The president was also alive to the danger that all his progress in restoring the economy and putting in place New Deal reforms could be washed away in a renewed economic crisis. That possibility loomed large in the fall of 1937 with the onset of an economic recession that left the president and his cabinet groping for answers. Ruminating over lunch about the sudden reversal, Roosevelt talked about the speed of fascist gains around the world. There were people in the United States who might get together, he told Treasury Secretary Henry Morgenthau, to decide they wanted their own man in the White House. Business did not believe him, he said, when he declared that he wanted it to make profits and that he believed in property rights.[62]

Just before the recession began, Roosevelt had traveled to Chicago. In a speech dedicating a bridge, he had called upon the world to quarantine the "epidemic of world lawlessness." Let no one imagine, he said, that if the epidemic spread, America could continue to live in peace and tranquility. The reaction to the speech was overwhelmingly negative, and it continued to provide ammunition for the president's critics for some months after.[63]

Roosevelt was soon juxtaposing his domestic opponents with the "appeasers" in Chamberlain's cabinet. But the reactions to his quarantine speech led him to return to what one historian has called "multilateral appeasement." "Whereas London followed a strategy of bilateral appeasement aimed at keeping the German and Central European Market open even in direct cooperation with the Brownshirts, Washington's Open Door policy followed a concept of multilateral appeasement."[64]

The president did not have the same fear of arms spending that helped to drive Chamberlain toward Munich, but the lingering effects of the 1937 recession drove wedges in the New Deal coalition and brought renewed attacks from Republicans that the administration was destroying the capitalist system. Any serious gesture toward political involvement in Europe was, consequently, out of the question. Former President Herbert Hoover, for example, denounced any move toward an alliance with England and France against Germany. It would have to include Russia, he said, and would thus set the stage for an ideological struggle with all the "hideous elements of the old religious wars." "We can never lead the world onto the paths of righteousness with the dogs of war."[65]

Hoover ended with a telling jab against the notion of a quarantine against lawless nations. "If our so-called planned economy," he said, referring to the New Deal, "is not an infection from the original stream of fascism, it is at least a remarkable coincidence." Speaking to a British correspondent, the banker Thomas Lamont made a different kind of comparison, but it contained the same warning that Roosevelt's New Deal was more dangerous than the external threat of fascist military action. Lamont's comment was all the more remarkable because of his reputation as Wall Street's most ardent internationalist and successful "diplomatist":

> Hitler is menacing the peace of Europe. Franklin Roosevelt has menaced and is continuing to menace the progress of all enterprise and industry in this country. And the war that he is waging on business is far more devastating as far as this country is concerned than the threats that Hitler is throwing at you people.[66]

Interestingly, Neville Chamberlain had a measure of sympathy for Roosevelt's plight. Much would depend on the president's ability to solve the recession, he wrote to his sister Ida. "He has got to restore confidence in the U.S.A. if the rot is to be stopped." Whether he could put things back together, and how long it would take, remained to be seen.[67]

Where Hoover and Lamont deprecated a strong European policy as a way out for a New Deal–weakened America, believing it would only produce socialism, Chamberlain and his advisers similarly feared both the results of arms spending and opening the door to bolshevism in Western Europe by going to war with Germany. Roosevelt's advisers in America and Chamberlain's critics in England believed, on the other hand, that the successes of the autarkic powers would eventually force trade into ever narrower channels and produce a different sort of state planning—fascism. With its huge domestic market, the United States was perhaps best able to cope with self-containment as a theoretical possibility. Yet what price would have to be paid in terms of individual freedoms? "Whatever may be the role of the home market," wrote Ambassador William C. Bullitt from Paris, "the fostering of international trade must remain an element of capital importance for economic prosperity within the national frontiers."[68]

Roosevelt's dilemma was all the more complicated because many, like Bullitt, wanted him to avoid doing anything that might involve the United States in a war over Southeastern Europe. The president had watched Hull's trade treaty efforts with considerable sympathy. Hull's philosophy, the president told Treasury Secretary Morgenthau, was that by increasing world trade he would take up the slack in unemployment and remove the stimulus to the arms race. The president's proposal for an international conference was one way to speed up the process. By the time of the Munich crisis some months later, however, Roosevelt had cast aside the notion that war could be prevented by trade treaties. "Henry, these trade treaties are just too goddamned slow. The world is marching too fast. They're just too slow."[69]

The history of the road to war is often told as a Thomas Hardy tale of missed opportunities, of notes left under doors, of messages that somehow slipped out of sight. Roosevelt's 1938 "note" was in plain view. But it meant different things to each of those who picked it up. After failing to enlist British support for his "multilateral appeasement" proposal, Roosevelt stood aside while Chamberlain pursued "bilateral appeasement" to its unhappy conclusion. He wished the prime minister well at the time of Munich while doubting the outcome. But the Roosevelt proposal never really disappeared, for it became the basis of various statements of American war aims throughout World War II, all of them designed to avoid American participation in a spheres-of-influence "deal" that the other great powers might arrange among them. Yet the pressure to solve political problems was not diminished by the war. And the road to Munich continued on to Yalta.

2 | MUNICH AND THE NAZI-SOVIET PACT

> My poor friend, what have you done? As for us, I
> do not see any other outcome than a fourth
> partition of Poland.
>
> *Vice Commissar Vladimir Potemkin to*
> *the French Ambassador in Moscow,*
> *November 1938*[1]

AT DAWN on March 12, 1938, German troops crossed
the Austrian border. "In Austria we were not met with rifle
shots and bombs," Herman Goering told his judges at the
Nuremberg war crimes trial, "only one thing was thrown at
us, flowers."[2] Hitler's "peaceful" annexation of Austria, the
Anschluss, was followed immediately by a Nazi reign of terror.
Thousands were imprisoned. "The S.S., the S.A. and the
Gestapo are active day and night. Houses are being searched;
money, private property, even the knives, forks and spoons are
being confiscated in Jewish homes." The situation, concluded
the American representative in Vienna, "is worse than it ever
was in Berlin."[3]

In the midst of this turmoil, Chancellor Hitler was asked by
a British interviewer if the Austrian developments would have
any impact on Anglo-German conversations. "On our side,
none at all," replied the Nazi leader, "and I hope none on the

British side. What harm have we done to any foreign country?" The overwhelming majority of the Austrian people desired to become Germans—and now they were.[4]

Not even Chamberlain could now believe that the so-called moderates around Hitler were capable of—or perhaps even interested in—a repartition of Africa, the prime minister's "bait" for a general settlement in Europe. Just a few days before, Chamberlain had outlined for the cabinet his colonial plan. His idea was that the League of Nations mandate system would be abolished, all territory south of the Sahara and north of South Africa would be demilitarized, and equal trade rights would be accorded to each of the administering powers, including Germany. The scheme had the great advantage, he said, that it could be presented to the world not as a diplomatic deal but as a "plan based on high ideals and allotting territory subject to certain principles." It avoided, on the other hand, the accusation that nations were being handed from one power to another "as though they were chattels without regard for their interests."[5] It is hard to see what high ideals and principles Chamberlain meant, except that Germany would somehow be held accountable for its trusteeship of African colonies while drawing from them the fats and oils needed for the "success" of Nazi economic policies at home.

When Ambassador Nevile Henderson described this plot outline to Hitler, the head of the Third Reich let it be known that he had another stage in mind—Central Europe, where he did not wish to be directed by someone from London. Chamberlain was chagrined. Why had Herr Hitler made so much fuss about Germany's lost colonies, the prime minister asked his colleagues, if he now insisted the question could be put back six to ten years, "during which interval they proposed to get their own way in Central Europe?"[6]

What, then, should be British policy? Halifax, now foreign secretary, replied that his general line in the Foreign Office was not to give the Germans the impression we were running after them while showing that "we were not shutting the door."[7] This marvelously ambiguous phrase presumably covered almost every contingency, from reopening the African question to meeting expected German demands on Czechoslovakia.

Halifax presented more specific options at a special meeting of the cabinet foreign policy committee called a few days after the *Anschluss*. He noted three possibilities: a "Grand Alliance" to halt Germany by collective action; a somewhat narrower commitment to Czechoslovakia that would, however, surely entangle Britain in Franco-Soviet assurances to Prague; and, finally, private efforts to persuade both France and Czechoslovakia that they should make the best possible terms with Germany.

The arguments against the first two options were essentially the same: Czechoslovakia was not worth a war that might last years and would very likely destroy the empire. Halifax summed up the consensus. The case for a deterrent commitment rested on the assumption, he said, that once Germany had achieved "hegemony" in Central Europe, Berlin would pick a quarrel with the Western powers. He did not believe that would happen. Second, either of the first two alternatives meant closer association with both France and Russia, and, consequently, an impression in Germany that Britain was plotting encirclement, making any "real settlement" impossible. Finally, Halifax said, he believed he could distinguish between Germany's "racial" efforts, "which no one could question, and a lust for conquest on a Napoleonic scale which he himself did not credit."[8]

It was such a difference, Chamberlain wrote to his sister Ida after this meeting, dealing with Halifax at the Foreign Office instead of Anthony Eden. There was no use crying over spilt milk. Austria was gone. He would like to say to the Germans that what had to be done was to restore confidence. Tell us exactly what you want from the Sudetenland, and if it is reasonable, and if you give us your word you will let them alone, "we will urge the Czechs to accept it."[9]

Chamberlain believed he had freed himself from the incubus of Anthony Eden and the bothersome troublemakers in the Foreign Office, and the change in policymaking was also noted in exactly those places where the prime minister hoped it would be—America, which could not be trusted, and Soviet Russia, an even more unreliable factor. At the moment, Chamberlain was concerned that an old foe, Winston Churchill, was conniving with Russian Ambassador Ivan Maisky, on behalf of their separate agendas, to bring into being the frightful notion of a "Grand Alliance." Whatever the prime minister suspected in this regard was true, as was his assessment that British public opinion was not ready to follow Churchill's lead. For the foreseeable future, Chamberlain had complete freedom of action in foreign policy.[10]

Soviet Foreign Minister Maksim Litvinov's various overtures to Western leaders had made very little headway. It is easy to understand why. From the time of the Bolshevik Revolution the avowed aim of Soviet leaders was the overthrow of the capitalist system worldwide. Moscow's relations with Western capitals were always tenuous, never more so than in the 1930s during the "Depression Decade."

A brief review of Soviet-American relations in those years indicates the atmosphere of mistrust that characterized the general situation. One of Franklin Roosevelt's first foreign policy actions had been to open negotiations with Litvinov leading to the establishment of diplomatic relations in late 1933, but nothing significant resulted from the exchange of ambassadors. Indeed, in some ways things grew worse, when, for example, Ambassador Bullitt tried to pin down the Russians on what Litvinov and Roosevelt had agreed in regard to prerevolution debts and the activities of the Comintern.[11]

FDR, like other Western leaders in these depression years, feared Soviet influence on domestic politics. Nazi Germany had sympathizers in the United States, there was a fascist movement of note in Great Britain, and across Eastern Europe reactionary regimes dominated; but the appeal of "socialist"

Russia to sections of the working class and, perhaps especially, to intellectuals was a greater cause for worry. Diplomatic recognition of the Soviet Union removed a supposed cause of complaint in those circles and cost Roosevelt very little.

Domestic politics, then, the opportunity to increase trade, the possibility (but *only* a possibility) of cooperation with Russia to check Japanese ambitions in the Far East, determined Roosevelt's Russian policy in 1933. Bullitt had gone to Moscow with great hopes, but the president (in a pattern he would repeat during World War II when the stakes were much greater) cut him adrift to fend for his own with the State Department, whose Russian experts had always doubted anything could (or, more important, *should*) come of diplomatic relations with a Marxist regime.[12]

Unable to get anywhere with Litvinov on unresolved issues, Bullitt joined the ranks of those who believed that behind the distractions of Russian opportunism loomed always the grim single-mindedness of ideological zealotry. The participation of American communists in the 1935 Moscow Comintern meetings set off all the alarm signals. Here was a brazen example of how little the Kremlin cared about its promise to refrain from interfering in American domestic politics.

The Comintern resolution of August 20, 1935, did not call for revolution in America, however, but postponed the millennium to put the struggle against fascism in terms all foreign communists could understand. "In the face of the towering menace of fascism," it read, "it is imperative that unity of action be established between all sections of the working class . . . even before the majority of the working class unites on a common fighting platform for the overthrow of capitalism and the victory of the proletarian revolution."[13]

Bullitt, however, interpreted the Comintern resolution as an order to Western communists to work for war with Germany. "Russia's great wish," Bullitt told a British diplomat, "is to provoke a general conflagration in which she herself will play but little part, beyond perhaps a little bombing from a great distance, but after which she will arise like a phoenix ... and bring about a world revolution."[14]

All of Litvinov's efforts to find a common ground, a basis for collective security, met with similar expressions of distrust and antipathy in Western capitals. Throughout Eastern Europe, however, fear of the Soviet Union was not ideologically driven; it took a more elemental form: dread at the thought of Russian occupation. From the Baltic to the Balkans, national leaders struggled to find a way, somehow, to prevent themselves from being crushed within the closing vise. This fear did not prevent some Eastern European countries from trying to increase their own *lebensraum*, as for example Polish pressure on Lithuania in the aftermath of the *Anschluss*.[15]

The Polish foreign minister, Colonel Beck, also dreamed of being cut in on the division of Czechoslovakia. Goering had assured him, he boasted, that the Germans would not do anything in the Polish "area" of that country without informing him. "They will not present us with any surprises."[16] A more realistic appraisal of what the future held for all Europe was given to Ambassador Joseph Kennedy in London by the Czech minister to Great Britain. If Hitler lasts, he said, the Russians and the Germans would get together, and the old Berlin-to-Baghdad dream of prewar days would become reality. Western Europe would become an enlarged Portugal.[17]

Given this maelstrom of fears and ambitions, Litvinov's chances for a positive response to his calls for collective security in either Western or Eastern Europe were slight indeed. He knew that the Halifax conversation with Goering prefigured the Anglo-French reaction to the annexation of Austria, the Russian foreign minister told Ambassador Joseph Davies (Bullitt's successor), but in the days that followed he nevertheless launched a bid for an international conference to consider ways to stop Hitler's drive east.[18]

Unlike Roosevelt's January 1938 proposal for an all-encompassing conference, Litvinov's invitation excluded the three fascist powers, Germany, Italy, and Japan. The world *was* divided, he was saying. The only question was on which side of the line each power stood. Yet while Litvinov was the official spokesman for Soviet foreign policy, there was actually no agreement in Moscow about where Russia would finally take its stand. Old Bolshevik fears of compromising the revolution by associating with the West, now intensified by Stalin's personality and his determination to eradicate real (and imagined) opposition to his rule, prompted strong isolationist sentiments inside the Kremlin.

In truth, Litvinov was fighting a losing battle—not unlike the struggle Eden had waged in his country. Nor was he entirely able to divorce his appeals to the West from the Marxist argot used by Stalin and others to justify the unconscionable brutality of the Terror and the Inquisition-like atmosphere of the Moscow purge trials, where famous revolutionary leaders and high-ranking military officers accused of "Trotskyist" deviations and espionage abased themselves with public confessions of crimes against the people.

The American embassy reported that Litvinov, in a speech in Leningrad, for example, warned of the tendency to forget that "with the preservation of the capitalist system a long and enduring peace is impossible." While the Soviet Union did not consider one system of capitalist imperialism superior to another, and had no wish to participate in the struggle between them, it could not ignore the reemergence of militant German imperialism because of its unlimited ambitions and its direct interest to the safety of the Soviet Union. His country was the decisive factor in the outcome of this struggle, Litvinov suggested. Without Russia the balance would swing to the former Central Powers.

Instead of analyzing this speech in the context of current Kremlin politics, however, Chargé Alan Kirk saw Litvinov's carefully phrased remarks as simply an "unusually frank" recitation of Soviet "principles."

> It announces, in effect, that the Soviet Union does not consider itself an integral part of the present world system of states except for practical considerations of national policy and charges

the world with notice of the fact that, if the countries with which it has hitherto consented to cooperate do not pursue policies in accordance with the desires of the Soviet Government, even this slight cooperation may be withdrawn.[19]

Litvinov had enjoyed a more sympathetic hearing from Ambassador Davies, but his reports to the State Department were largely dismissed as the wishful thinking of a gullible amateur. In any event, it is unlikely that a more astute analysis of Litvinov's various appeals, clouded neither by Bullitt's exaggerated concern over communist cleverness nor Davies's penchant for hearing a well-intentioned appeal to the West to recognize common interests, would have made much difference.

In Washington, Under Secretary of State Sumner Welles responded negatively to an inquiry from the Czech minister about Litvinov's proposal for an international conference, leaving no room for further discussion. "The policy of the United States, which I was sure the Minister knew, as supported by the majority of the people of this country, was to remain completely aloof from any involvement in European affairs."[20]

Welles had used very nearly the same words, of course, during his presentation to Sir Ronald Lindsay of Roosevelt's January 1938 proposal. The United States would not concern itself with European frontiers, not for the British, and certainly not in response to any appeal from Moscow. However skeptical Roosevelt professed to be about Anglo-French appeasement policies, then, or however much, on the other hand, he claimed to resent the constraints public opinion placed on his ability to conduct foreign affairs, the president adopted a wait-and-see attitude throughout the spring and summer of 1938.[21]

Hitler's menacing accusations about Czech mistreatment of ethnic Germans in the Sudetenland served ample notice that he intended to repeat the Austrian coup whenever his inner voices told him the time was right. The trick with appeasement was to outguess those voices and, by so doing, somehow deprive the German fanatic of a chance to bring down European civilization in a suicidal war no one could survive. In both public and private statements, French and British spokesmen suggested that the best solution for peace was the partition of Czechoslovakia somewhat along the lines of Switzerland. Neither Paris nor London denied, moreover, that such an "offer" was simply an opening bid for Hitler's attention. The best that could be hoped for, French Prime Minister Edouard Daladier told Bullitt, is that the dissolution of Czechoslovakia "will take place without bloodshed in such a way as to save the face of France and England."[22]

The first Czech crisis occurred at the end of May 1938 when German troops were reported to be massing near the border. Neville Chamberlain warned Berlin that London would stand behind the French if Paris, under its treaty obligations, came to the aid of the Czechs. Chamberlain's message apparently resulted as much—indeed, probably more—from irritation that Hitler had not given him enough time to disengage the French from an awkward commitment as from readiness to stand firm. Within a few days the British ambassador in Berlin sought to make amends for having offended the Germans. And within a few days more, London had resumed its policy of attempting to force compromise on Prague.[23]

Bullitt was more frightened about the likelihood of war than even the French or British. From the Paris embassy he cabled Roosevelt, imploring him to renew his call for an international conference. There must be a way, he said, to relieve the French from their moral commitment to Czech territorial integrity. It could not be done through the sort of general conference Roosevelt had proposed in January. Instead the president should send for the ambassadors of Germany, Italy, Britain, and France. In the White House he should tell them that if they agreed to send representatives to the Hague, the United States would participate in a conference over Czechoslovakia.

Americans were, after all, heirs to the various "civilizations of Europe." Then the president should say something like,

> just as we are grateful for Shakespeare so are we grateful for Beethoven, that just as we are grateful for Molière so we are grateful for Leonardo da Vinci et cetera, that we cannot stand by and watch the beginning of the end of European civilization without making one last effort to stop its destruction; that you are convinced that the only result of general European war today would be an Asiatic despotism established on the fields of dead.[24]

Even a less xenophobic regime in Russia, holding a weaker ideological worldview, could not fail to notice the many "hints" being dropped in not-so-diplomatic fashion that Russia did not belong among those listed by Bullitt as the "civilizations of Europe." Of course, the Soviets had done a splendid job of alienating the Western democracies; but as the Stalinist regime could not refrain from preaching revolution (even if revolution postponed), neither could capitalist leaders abandon equally profound convictions, heightened now by domestic instability, about communist intentions.

At the end of August 1938 Litvinov took the initiative again, sending word through various spokesmen that Russia would not fail to keep its treaty obligations to Czechoslovakia, conditioned, however, on the West's willingness to fulfill its responsibilities.

Russian "responsibilities" to Czechoslovakia were contained in a military treaty between Moscow and Prague. France also had a treaty with Czechoslovakia. And there was a treaty between France and Russia. Fearing the entanglement with Russia would lead to an unwanted war over Czech territorial integrity, French Foreign Minister Pierre Laval had made the Franco-Russian pact nearly inoperable by adding stipulations that required approval of the League of Nations before France could take action in concert with the Soviets. Anticommunist French generals, moreover, had refused even to hold staff talks with their Russian counterparts. So when Litvinov spoke of the

West's willingness to fulfill its obligations, he was referring not merely to the letter of the treaties but to the studied reluctance of Paris and London to act with the Soviets on any matter.

Robert Vansittart wondered, therefore, if Litvinov's pointed comments actually reflected the beginnings of a move toward isolationism? Yes, said Ambassador Ivan Maisky, there was an incipient move in that direction. He hoped it would not go too far. But if it did, who would be to blame? Britain had consistently ignored Moscow, conveying the impression that the Russians were always to be kept at arm's length no matter what the issue. "Such an attitude was bound to tell its tale in the end."[25]

While Maisky complained about the British cold shoulder, Chamberlain was beginning to devise a method for bringing himself face-to-face with Hitler. At first he had thought he might simply take off from a British airport, he told the cabinet, and let Herr Hitler know he was coming only after his plane departed. But then he thought: Hitler might say he had a cold. "This would be humiliating, and, moreover, result in a serious situation." Yet the basic idea, "Plan Z" he called it, was sound.

He would go to Hitler with a proposal for a plebiscite to determine the fate of the Sudetenland. Actually, of course, it was understood that the plebiscite would only confirm the detachment of the area and its submersion into the German Reich. What Chamberlain was offering, in the spirit of pre-empting Hitler's inner voices, was a new *Anschluss* without the danger of ugly military incidents leading to a conflagration. He would point out to Hitler that if he was to have the "goodwill of the British people" he would have to do it this way and not by force. He would say to Hitler, finally, that he could now win lasting fame for himself as the man responsible for maintaining peace in Europe.[26]

It took three trips to Germany, three face-to-face meetings with Hitler, to complete Plan Z. Confident in his ability to set the agenda and determine the outcome, as British statesmen had done for generations, Chamberlain went practically alone the first time to meet Hitler at his Berchtesgaden retreat. No meddling Foreign Office experts went along, no beribboned military aide, not even an interpreter.[27] When he arrived, Chamberlain found himself surrounded by symbols alien to everything he had known. Bourgeois man, prudent, dressed for the City in dark suit and Eton collar, looked into a forest of swastika armbands and jackboots and saw martial man, awaiting him like Blake's tiger of the night. Hitler teased his prey with flattering words, calling Chamberlain a "man" with whom he could do business. After the conferences ended the chancellor smiled his grim smile. "Thank God," he said as he went around the German countryside, "we have no umbrella politicians in this country."[28]

At each session the Nazi leader's demands became more minatory; yet after each confrontation Chamberlain returned home with encouraging messages. "He liked the rapidity with which I had grasped the essentials," Chamberlain wrote to his sister in a stunning example of willful resistance to reality.[29] And that was not the whole of it. After the first meeting the prime minister advised his cabinet that he had "formed the opinion that Hitler's objectives were strictly limited." Despite the ruthless hardness he saw on Hitler's face, he noted privately, "I got the impression that here was a man who could be relied upon when he had given his word."[30]

When Hitler made it clear what the essentials were—that nothing would satisfy him save an immediate transfer and military occupation of the Sudetenland—Chamberlain began to have problems in the cabinet. His presentations to his colleagues became exercises in partial concealment, in one instance suggesting, for example, that the idea of granting Hitler's latest demands originated with the French and was not translated by Chamberlain from the German leader's contemptuous words. The more Chamberlain concealed, the more impatient he became with dissent in the cabinet. The record of these manipulations would no doubt provide psychologists with much to chew on, but it is enough to say that Chamberlain was as immersed in listening to his inner voices as was Hitler. He had "established an influence over Hitler," he insisted, and the chancellor now trusted him. The Czech problem was the only remaining obstacle to a resolution of Anglo-German differences. If that were so, and he believed it was, then the crisis had become a wonderful opportunity "to put an end to the horrible nightmare of the present armament race. That seemed to him to be the big thing in the present issue."[31]

Chamberlain did not stop there:

> That morning he had flown up the river over London [on his way home from Germany]. He had imagined a German bomber flying the same course. He had asked himself what degree of protection they could afford for the thousands of homes which he had seen stretched out below him, and he had felt that we were in no position to justify waging a war today, in order to prevent a war thereafter.[32]

After reconvincing the cabinet, Chamberlain had to persuade the French to do what they wanted to do anyway, accede, and to tell the Czechs what they must do, surrender. French Premier Daladier knew very well—better than Chamberlain, certainly—that Hitler sought the humiliation of every nation on earth, Bullitt reported, but this attitude was sheer folly for everyone concerned, including Germany. Germany would be defeated in a war. France would win, said Daladier, but only the Bolsheviks would gain, with social revolutions in every country of Europe the inevitable result of war. "The prediction which Napoleon had made at St. Helena was about to come true: 'Cossacks will rule Europe.'"[33]

The Czechs simply had to be told that their position was untenable. Nothing any nation could do, Chamberlain lectured the Czech president, "will prevent this fate for your country and people."[34] He could not, therefore, encourage Prague to believe that military action offered any hope.

Yet Chamberlain's work was not finished. Hitler had set a deadline of October 1 for Czech capitulation. The prime minister could not understand why Hitler would not simply wait for him to complete these tasks when the substantive issue had already been settled between them. "How horrible, fantastic, incredible it is," Chamberlain began a speech to the British people,

> that we should be digging trenches and trying on gas masks here, because of a quarrel in a far away country between people of whom we know nothing. It seems still more impossible that a quarrel which has already been settled in principle, should be the subject of war.[35]

What Hitler would have done had France and Britain stood firm cannot be fully answered. Denied the opportunity to use his army, or pretending to be denied, Hitler undoubtedly enjoyed the sight of a British prime minister jumping through the hoop at his command. He may, on the other hand, have been aware of rumblings and rumors of plots in the military against his regime, and played his hand accordingly, allowing a fretful Chamberlain also to do the work of convincing German military commanders that Der Führer knew best.[36]

The Czech crisis ended in a Munich hotel at 2 a.m. on September 30, 1938. Chamberlain had asked for Mussolini's help in keeping Europe out of war. The French were also represented at this final scene of the Czech tragedy. Hitler agreed that after his occupation of the Sudetenland, an international commission composed of the four powers and a Czech representative would determine the final boundary. In an annex to the agreement, the British and French offered to guarantee the remainder of the country against unprovoked aggression. Germany and Italy were to join in the guarantee once the Polish and Hungarian minority question had been settled.[37]

Chamberlain and Hitler met privately the next day to begin, the prime minister fervently hoped, clearing away the detritus that had fallen in the path of an Anglo-German understanding. Chamberlain had a memorandum setting forth the essentials of the new relationship. Hitler appeared in a jovial mood. It seemed a propitious time. The prime minister began the conversation in a curious vein, given that the paper they had signed the night before supposedly ended the threat of war. Would Hitler refrain from bombing Prague if war came? he asked. Hitler responded that "he hated the thought" of bombs killing little babies. He reminded Chamberlain that he had been in the Great War and knew about such things firsthand. Were they ready to settle the issue of foreign troops in the Spanish Civil War? Chamberlain went on. Germany had no territorial ambitions there, Hitler replied. He had supported Franco against the Bolsheviks only out of concern that if Spain went communist, the infection would spread to France, Belgium, Holland, and beyond. He would be delighted to withdraw his troops just as soon as others did.

Chamberlain moved on to Southeastern Europe. There was "no truth" in the idea that Britain wished to be involved in that region politically. But he did hope to see the area remain open to British trade. German interest was the same, Hitler remarked. "We have only economic relations but no political ties." Germany was an exporter of industrial products to the Balkan countries and a large consumer of its raw materials. "Our greatest difficulty," the chancellor went on, was in German-American trade. Germany needed American raw materials, but the United States could not accept German industrial imports because of its twelve million unemployed. For his part, said Hitler, he favored the elimination of artificial barriers to trade. "There must be a continuous flow," he concluded, between food producers and industrial exporters.[38]

These were the sorts of words the British prime minister had waited to hear for so long, words that made the sacrifice of Czechoslovakia not a shameful episode in British history but a redeeming moment on which could be built a lasting peace. Chamberlain brought forth the memorandum, and Hitler signed. This was the memorandum that Chamberlain would wave to cheering crowds and movie cameras, proclaiming that he had returned from Germany bringing "peace with honor... peace for our time," a scene that captivated a later generation of cold war policymakers to the end of the Vietnam War and after. The paper declared that Britain and Germany were resolved to find ways to remove possible future sources of differences, and were committed to making a joint contribution to assuring Europe's peace.[39]

From the dominions—Canada, Australia, South Africa—came warm congratulations. The whole world owed Chamberlain its thanks, said dominions prime ministers. "On the very brink of chaos, with passions flaming, and armies marching," praised Mackenzie King, "the voice of Reason has found a way out of the conflict which no people in their hearts desired, but none seemed able to avert." It was a turning point in world history.[40]

Roosevelt's message was only two words: "Good Man."[41] He sent this briefest of encouragements, however, not when the Munich accord was signed but earlier to support Chamberlain's efforts to maintain the peace. At the height of the crisis, when the next radio broadcast might bring shattering announcements of war, the next newspaper accounts of bombs falling on cities, Roosevelt sent an appeal to Hitler. It did not go as far as Daladier's invocation of Napoleon's Russophobia, but it was unusually critical of past crusades to make the world safe for democracy: "Resort to force in the Great War failed to bring tranquility. Victory and defeat were alike sterile. That lesson the world should have learned."[42]

Munich did not lack historical precedents. Some saw it as the final ruling of the old Congress of Europe, when the great powers dictated boundary adjustments to keep the peace. Others saw in Munich the ironic fulfillment of Wilsonian self-determination. The "Munich Analogy" became the watchword, on the other hand, for Americans throughout the cold war years.

For the Russians the "Munich Analogy" had a much more immediate meaning. Moscow suspected that Anglo-French diplomacy at Munich—dominated by Chamberlain—schemed at a war between Germany and the Soviet Union. Such suspicions were accurate only in the sense that *if* a war came, Paris and London would prefer it to come in Eastern Europe. But the sacrifice of Czechoslovakia was to avoid war and the communization of Europe that would follow, a different motive, if one equally worthy (from Moscow's viewpoint) of condemnation. There is evidence, some of it contradictory, that Moscow was prepared to act independently if Czechoslovakia chose to defend itself. All of Litvinov's appeals for collective action had gone unanswered. But before the crisis began in mid-September, the Soviet foreign minister had informed the French ambassador that Russia would live up to its obligations and was ready for military discussions on a tripartite basis with the Czechs. He reminded the ambassador that France was obliged to come to Prague's aid, and remarked that the Soviets therefore had a rightful interest in French intentions. "On condition France renders aid, we are fully resolved to fulfill all our obligations according to the Soviet-Czech pact, utilizing every means at our disposal to this end."[43]

French Foreign Minister Georges Bonnet met with Litvinov later in the month at Geneva, questioning the Russian closely as to how Soviet aid to Czechoslovakia would manifest itself. Both men came away from this conversation confirmed in previous suppositions about the other's intentions. Litvinov was sure that Bonnet wanted an answer only in order to justify French unwillingness to defend Czechoslovakia, a message to take back that the Russians were not serious. Bonnet, on the other hand, believed that Litvinov's game was to get France committed, then find an escape clause to let Moscow off the hook.[44]

Neither nation had much use in pursuing that oblique dialogue further. Litvinov, with Stalin's backing, then concentrated on demonstrations of Russian seriousness. The Poles provided an opportunity for such a demonstration by threatening Czechoslovakia over the Polish minority—albeit in the name of Wilsonian self-determination—in a fashion similar to German bullying over the Sudetenland. When Polish troops moved toward the Czech border, Russia mobilized its own forces in the

Byelorussian and Kiev military districts. The Polish ambassador in Moscow was then summoned to hear from Litvinov's deputy, Potemkin, a blunt warning that if Poland attacked Czechoslovakia, Russia would renounce the nonaggression pact between Warsaw and Moscow.[45]

Russian military preparations continued right up to the signing of the accord. And then they ceased. When Ambassador Bullitt talked with Bonnet a few days later, the French foreign minister dismissed Russia as a serious military factor—in the crisis and for the future. All his information indicated a serious internal crisis had begun in Russia. Litvinov, he said, had actually been in hiding in Paris during the critical days of the Czech decisions. He had had a secret conversation with Litvinov and had asked point-blank if Russia would attack Poland. "Litvinov had replied that the Soviet Government would do nothing in support of Czechoslovakia."[46]

Hitler's enemies had succeeded marvelously, succeeded in calling one another's bluff—a safer risk, presumably, than war for Eastern Europe. But something had been turned around. "Czechoslovakia, from having been a dagger pointed to the heart of Germany," a British diplomat entered in his diary, "is now rapidly being organized as a dagger into Russian vitals."[47]

Ruminating over tea with Ambassador Joseph Kennedy in front of his fireplace a short time after Munich, Lord Halifax suggested that Hitler did not want a war with England. And England certainly did not want a war with Germany unless she faced an attempt to interfere with the dominions. England's best course was to strengthen its air power. "Then after that to let Hitler go ahead and do what he likes in Central Europe." Hitler would likely go for Danzig and Memel, and probably Rumania as well. He was an uncouth fellow, to be sure, not the sort "one would like to go around the world with on a two-wheeled bicycle," but England should tend to its interests in the Mediterranean and elsewhere, stay friendly with the United States, and let Hitler go his own way in that part of the world.[48]

Halifax's musings took as a starting point the Hitler-Chamberlain memorandum, and no doubt as well what he had heard from the prime minister about the *tour d'horizon* Chamberlain had conducted in the German leader's rooms when the memorandum was signed. His chief aide, Alec Cadogan, also mulling over the situation, not surprisingly came to a similar conclusion from an economic analysis of German capacity. The natural sphere for the Nazi autarkic system was Southeastern Europe. But Germany could not go much further. "She cannot eat her way into markets whose produce she cannot assimilate."[49]

Letting Hitler go his way had already become policy as German and Italian diplomats presided over the further partition of Czechoslovakia, standing by as Poland seized Teschen, and carving out territory in the south for Hungary. This was a clear breach of the terms of the Munich agreement regarding the supposed work of the international commission on Czech frontiers, but no protests were sent to Berlin.[50] In mid-November Chamberlain reported to the cabinet that King Carol of Rumania believed Hitler was planning to repeat the minorities ploy to establish an independent state in the Ukraine. He wanted to know more about the current French attitude toward Russia. "The Prime Minister said that our attitude would be governed largely by the fact that we did not wish to see France drawn into a war with Germany on account of some quarrel between Russia and Germany. . . ."[51]

Lord Halifax took up the question with Georges Bonnet the next day and happily discovered that the French wished to get out of the Russian connection altogether! Russia had wanted war in September, Bonnet told him, but would have remained largely aloof, hoping to profit from the general confusion. Clearly it was important for His Majesty's Government to avoid a situation, said Halifax, where it was asked to take action with France and Russia against Germany and Italy on behalf of a state it could not effectively defend.[52]

The most disturbing aspect of the situation, however, was Berlin's apparent indifference about getting on with the process of genuine appeasement. Chamberlain had hoped that his private conversation with Hitler could be promptly translated into practical understandings and specific economic arrangements. The basis for this hope rested in assumptions about supposed German "moderates" whose influence would be felt once an appealing offer had been placed on the table—Chamberlain still believed the colonial issue held such attractions—and upon the complementary belief that the German economy was Hitler's weak spot. He might try to make Germany self-sufficient, but even with dominance in Southeastern Europe he would not succeed.

Over and over again, Chamberlain would say later, Hitler had missed the bus. He had outsmarted the German—prevented him from launching a war to solve his problems—but it was tiresome waiting for him to wake up to the true situation and act accordingly. On December 15 one of the German "moderates," economics expert Hjalmar von Schacht, met with Frank Ashton-Gwatkin at the Foreign Office. Ashton-Gwatkin, a strong supporter of appeasement, expressed disappointment with the German inaction. After the Munich agreement, he said, there was "some hope" that the way had been opened to Anglo-German cooperation in rebuilding Europe.

What followed left Ashton-Gwatkin stunned. Von Schacht asked if he wished to know what Hitler had told him about this "agreement." Ideas about such things were out of date, Hitler had said. This was a dynamic age. No agreement was valid once it ceased to be useful. "Mr. Chamberlain is such a nice old man," von Schacht quoted Der Führer, "and I have signed so many photographs and books, that I thought I would give him my signature as a pleasant souvenir."

But, protested Ashton-Gwatkin lamely, were there not people around Hitler other than those who wished to spoil cooperation? In other words, where were the moderates? Von Schacht wondered in return why Ashton-Gwatkin talked about people around Hitler. "There are four great men in Germany today.

They are Hitler, and Hitler and Hitler and Hitler. No one has any influence on him."

Then it is no use? Ashton-Gwatkin asked. "It is no use."[53]

Chamberlain's long-time adviser and his recent intermediary with Hitler at a crucial moment in the Czech crisis, Sir Horace Wilson, saw this record of the von Schacht conversation and read Ashton-Gwatkin's bleak conclusion: "absolutely no confidence whatever can be placed in Hitler."[54] Yet Chamberlain continued to believe otherwise. The German ambassador had told him, he wrote privately at the end of January 1939, that Hitler was planning no aggression but was chiefly concerned about his economic position and about finding ways to increase German exports. There could be no doubt the Germans were in difficulty over their standard of living.[55]

In the Foreign Office, however, new stirrings reached all the way to Lord Halifax. John Wheeler-Bennett's book, *Brest-Litovsk: The Forgotten Peace*, which had recently appeared, struck Harold Caccia as a fitting text for reexamining British attitudes toward Germany and Russia. Caccia began from the premise that Hitler had spurned post-Munich efforts to reach a general Anglo-German settlement, and that in itself removed one of the reasons for the arm's-length policy toward Russia.

But the relevance of Brest-Litovsk—the peace which Lenin and Trotsky had negotiated with Germany after the Bolshevik Revolution—held another lesson for Caccia. With rumored German designs on the Ukraine, it seemed that Stalin—and still more a successor government—would be likely to reach an accommodation with Hitler in the absence of a "clarification" of British policy. There had been a moment, Wheeler-Bennett reminded his readers (and Caccia his colleagues), when Lenin suggested he would be willing to accept the "assistance of French imperialism against German brigands." But there had been no offer. "We could not of course promise anything," Caccia noted, "but for us too 'Russian murderers' might in certain eventualities be a lesser danger than 'German brigands'!"

No great harm would be done, Caccia concluded, if an attempt were made to find out what Stalin's attitude might be.

A refusal on his part to talk about "clarifications" would prove useful against Labor party critics of the government's current policy.[56]

Caccia's note went the rounds in the Foreign Office, with lengthy commentaries being added to it at each stop. Most of the queries had to do with what, in the final accounting, Britain had to offer the Soviets. Just getting the British ambassador an audience with Stalin (difficult in itself, for the Russian was the most reluctant of the three dictators to talk with foreign representatives) would not be enough. Caccia had recognized that a formal defensive alliance was out of the question. An audience to say that the British would not help Hitler directly in any of his adventures would produce the Russian equivalent of "Thank you for nothing." Cadogan's comment was the bluntest: "We should very soon have to disclose the emptiness of our cupboard."[57]

And what would Stalin have to say of his own intentions? "If by any chance he is toying with the possibility of buying Germany off without a fight," said a doubtful colleague, "he would not be such a fool as to admit it, even for the pleasure of making our flesh creep." Among these comments, about the only positive recommendation was that a higher priority be placed on untangling negotiations for a new commercial agreement with the Russians. At the moment, even those negotiations followed the arm's-length prescription for the right attitude to take toward Moscow.[58]

Caccia's initiative apparently moved Halifax to reconsider what he had said to Joseph Kennedy over tea, and to recall Sir Robert Vansittart from "Coventry" to active duty again. There was much to be said for improving relations with Russia, the foreign secretary said to Chamberlain's old *bête noire*, but he shared the doubts of Caccia's critics—at least as to methods. What did Vansittart suggest? Here was an opportunity Vansittart did not let pass. It was "an incontestable fact" that relations with Russia were bad because "we practically boycotted them during 1938." That was what accounted for the drift toward isolation in Russia. "That fact and that tendency we ought to correct and correct soon." But an ambassadorial interview was not at all the right way to tackle it. If he got an interview with Stalin he would probably be riddled with questions he could not answer. Best to send a cabinet minister, even one whose ostensible mission was simply to sign a trade agreement. Vansittart was sure Germany would take notice, and the visit would have a proper deterrent effect on Berlin—without requiring a political alliance.

"I should like to discuss," Halifax noted on Vansittart's recommendation.[59] An incipient debate between Chamberlain and Halifax thus began to take shape. The prime minister used a speech in his home city of Birmingham to repeat in public what he had been arguing in private: German economic difficulties were the salient factor in the current situation. Hitler's next speech—which appeared to American policymakers as an attempt to blackmail the West into economic concessions—Chamberlain took for evidence that the moderates had at last gained the Nazi leader's full attention.[60]

Support for this view now emerged in an odd place—from Russian Ambassador Ivan Maisky, who suggested to a Foreign Office official that Hitler's speech signaled the chancellor's need to calm matters. Perhaps now was the moment for the French and British to offer proposals on the colonial issue, lest Hitler assert at some later date that he was sorry, but as no proposals had been made, he must now put on the screws. This fascinating piece of diplomatic artwork by Maisky might have been sheer flummery, designed only to tempt an unwary listener into revealing secrets, or, more likely, a hint that Soviet Russia would not disapprove buying off Berlin in Africa any more than did capitalist Britain.[61]

For a few more weeks the heady illusion that he had won enabled Chamberlain to hold all his critics at bay. He looked very well, Ambassador Kennedy reported, and felt "stronger now than he has ever been." A coal agreement with Germany had already been signed, Chamberlain fairly exclaimed to the ambassador, and things had been set in motion for an exchange of commercial negotiators. It looked as though things were clearing up across Europe, he wrote to Nevile Henderson. People were still all "het up" and frightened, but with care the atmosphere would soon be such "that we might begin to think of colonial discussions."[62]

Secretary of State Cordell Hull was not at all enthusiastic for these trade arrangements with Germany that promoted special bilateral agreements negotiated by states directly. The United States had rejected similar ventures earlier in the decade in favor of the reciprocal trade agreements program, and Hull wished to remind the British that they had agreed on the need to take the long view instead of picking up bits of immediate advantage.[63]

Secretary Hull would have frowned as well on Foreign Office notions of using a narrow trade agreement with Russia to gain political advantage. But the slow progress of that idea into something concrete gave almost no one cause for concern about an Anglo-Russian rapprochement. When Maisky was told that a decision had finally been made to send the minister of trade, Robert Hudson, to Moscow, he quipped sarcastically that it was "too good to be true." Oh yes, Hudson was going, said his interlocutor, and it demonstrated a British desire for friendly relations. If so, that was good news, replied the ambassador, even if it was hard to see how that fit in with appeasement of Germany. But the Soviet government was ruled by its head, not its heart, said Maisky, and would wait to see how things developed.[64]

The day after this testy conversation, on March 10, 1939, Stalin addressed the XVIII Party Congress in Moscow. He attacked Britain and France for rejecting collective security. They had done so, he said, despite their superior forces, in part because they feared "the revolution which may break out" afterward. Rather than deny that possibility, Stalin gave Western critics more meat to chew on: "Bourgeois politicians know that the first Imperialist War has made the revolution victorious in one of the greatest countries. They fear that a second Imperialist War may lead to the triumph of the revolution in one or more countries."[65]

Even more important, he went on, the bourgeois nations had failed to act because they hoped to incite a German attack on Russia and destroy the revolution there as well. The commotion in the Western press about the Ukraine, said Stalin, was designed to enrage the Soviet Union against Germany, "to poison the atmosphere and provoke a conflict with Germany without any evident grounds." Enumerating the party's tasks for the future, Stalin left other clues. He saw a need to strengthen "businesslike contacts with all countries" and to "observe caution and not let our country be drawn into conflicts by warmongers urging others to take the chestnuts out of the fire."[66]

When German legions moved on Prague on March 14, in violation of the Munich agreement, Russian reactions were muted. A protest note was sent to Berlin, but there were no new calls to action. Chamberlain, in the House of Commons, observed that since the Czech state had broken up, a British obligation to Czechoslovakia no longer existed.[67] But Halifax and other Tory members were not at all satisfied with the response and pressed the prime minister to say more. He did so in a speech in Birmingham two days later. Halifax used it as a springboard in the next cabinet meeting to urge an approach to France, Poland, Turkey, and Russia about a guarantee to Rumania. Halifax had been influenced in this instance by Ambassador Kennedy, who told him that American opinion would be much stronger for Great Britain if some steps were taken about Rumania, rather than waiting until the Germans or Italians moved on Greece, where only imperial interests were at stake.[68]

When Litvinov replied with a suggestion for a four-power conference at Bucharest, however, Halifax quickly backed away. There was no one to send, he told Maisky. And who could say where such a conference would end? His counterproposal was for a joint declaration: if aggression against Rumania occurred, the four powers would consult. Again Russia accepted. But the Poles refused. From this point on, the principal sticking point in Anglo-Russian negotiations would be Polish and Rumanian resistance to participation in a joint guarantee with Moscow.[69]

But Chamberlain had no intention of pressuring those countries to go along. His Birmingham speech, he wrote his sister, was really designed not to challenge Hitler but to put on the brakes, to gain time, "for I never accept the view that war is inevitable." Polish reactions only strengthened his resistance to a move toward Russia. It would frighten the wits out of the smaller states, he rehashed an old argument, provide Hitler with an excuse to go to war to resolve his increasingly difficult economic problems at home, and leave Britain and France alone to face the consequences.[70]

Chamberlain was right that Hitler was under pressure at home, but the prime minister's view seemed to be that his policy would lead to one of two ends, both preferable to war. Either the so-called Nazi moderates would finally make their leader see sense, or Germany would move east. Chamberlain may have been gambling that his own domestic opponents would come to their senses, even if Hitler would not, and through some terribly difficult maneuvering (he would compare himself at one point to a man driving a careening coach around a mountain bend) accept German hegemony in that part of the world. The smaller states were at Hitler's mercy, anyway, Chamberlain added in another letter, suggesting that their fear of Russia was really of little concern to him except as a rationale for inaction. Urging them to resist Hitler, he said, would be like sending someone into the lion's den. "'Never mind,' we would be saying, 'Never mind if the lion does gobble you up; I intend to give him a good hiding afterwards.'" Perhaps, Chamberlain sighed, something might happen to break this awful German spell. Hitler might realize that the defenses against him ultimately were too strong. He might die![71]

As the prime minister interrupted these dreams to host a dinner for the king and queen on Wednesday, March 29, Lord Halifax telephoned to say that he wished to bring round Ian Colvin, a reporter just back from Berlin. Colvin brought urgent news. Hitler was ready to "swoop" down on Poland. Part would be annexed, the rest turned into protectorates. Then Lithuania and other East European states would be easy prey.

And after all these dramatic events loomed the most unsettling possibility of all, a Russo-German alliance.[72]

Prodded by the foreign secretary, Chamberlain decided the British must guarantee Polish independence. Could he not couple this initiative, the prime minister asked the cabinet, with an offer to mediate German-Polish disputes? No, was the answer. His dreams dying, he still tried to maneuver by drawing a distinction between defending Poland's "boundaries" and its "independence." He was at least able to get the London *Times* to pick up on the point and interpret the guarantee in the "right" sense. If Hitler was only after Danzig, it might still work.[73]

Yet Chamberlain did something else, either by design or inadvertence, that was too clever by half. The prime minister had "consulted" Maisky about the Polish guarantee. Given Stalin's recent statements about Soviet willingness to aid victims of aggression, Chamberlain asked, could he tell the House that Russia approved of the guarantee? Maisky was flabbergasted. Here, just two hours before the prime minister intended to go before Commons, Maisky was being asked such a momentous question. His government could not possibly react in that time. The reply was probably what Chamberlain expected, or even hoped for, to hush supporters of a Russian "alternative" to appeasement.

When Moscow did react later, it was in bitter terms. Chamberlain would never have treated another nation so cavalierly. Having ignored Litvinov's repeated attempts to organize collective action against the fascists, he now asks for help on two hours' notice. What was there to make of this arrogant behavior?[74] Russian *amour propre* aside, the Soviets thought they discerned an attempt by Chamberlain to neutralize his domestic opponents while channeling German expansion to the Baltic states.

The prime minister had certainly hoped to quiet the rising clamor for an alliance with Russia. This "hysterical passion" he believed was promoted by old opponents, like David Lloyd George, who had no idea of what it would mean. He had presented a guarantee to Poland and exposed Russian unwillingness to join in the cause, thus making Moscow appear to be the stumbling block. But try as he might, Chamberlain could not control the outcome of his own words. He could not limit the guarantee.[75]

In early April 1939 a formal alliance was signed with Poland providing for reciprocal guarantees. But the arrangement, without military muscle, did little to deter Hitler—or even Mussolini. Seven days after the prime minister gave his promise to Poland, Italy moved against Albania. The Foreign Office continued to hope that Russia could be induced to join in the pledge to Warsaw, and also to Rumania, as Halifax had proposed, without forcing the issue of a formal alliance. The foreign secretary's urgings were more serious than Chamberlain's quick consultations, but Maisky's government reacted the same to both.

Sir Robert Vansittart feared the worst from such ambiguous maneuvers that left the Russians guessing. "If Russia goes into isolation," he warned, "this will mean a period of the sulks, which may very well be succeeded, and indeed probably will be succeeded, by closer relations with Germany. That I regard as absolutely fatal."[76] But from Berlin came Nevile Henderson's counterwarning that Stalin was playing a double game. He had heard from Alan Kirk, the strongly anti-Soviet former American chargé in Moscow, that Stalin's purpose was to sit on the sidelines "and do nothing while Europe destroyed itself and communism spread."[77]

Chamberlain's choice between such conflicting advice was obvious. But there were some new voices in the cabinet. The new minister for defense coordination, Lord Chatfield, argued that even in terms of Russian expansionism, more was to be feared from a *failure* to reach agreement with the Soviets than otherwise. Russia would be in a far better position to demand concessions from the West after an exhausting war. The military chiefs were very anxious, he went on, about Russia allying with Germany. If we "channel that country into the German camp we should have made a mistake of vital and far-reaching importance."[78]

At almost the same time Chatfield urged negotiations for an alliance, the Russian chargé in Berlin was emphasizing to German officials that "there were no conflicts between Germany and the Soviet Union" and hence no reason for enmity. The Germans responded to this overture with a suggestion for economic talks, but the new Soviet foreign minister, V. M. Molotov, countered that economic negotiations must have a political basis.[79]

Molotov replaced Litvinov on May 4, 1939, a signal that the debate inside the Kremlin had been decided against Litvinov's insistence that "peace was indivisible," and the policy that followed from it. In the historic swings of Russian policy from the time of Peter the Great and the "Window on the West," Stalin's replacement of the strongest advocate of collective security with his brusque second-in-command could scarcely have gone unnoticed. But Molotov did not withdraw previous Soviet proposals for a triple alliance to cover not only guarantees to Poland and Rumania but all of Eastern Europe from the Baltic to the Black Sea.

By putting the "cost" of such an alliance so high it certainly appeared that neither London nor Moscow really wanted agreement. Chamberlain and Stalin knew very well they had little to talk seriously about, hence they restricted their agents to proposals that were unacceptable on the face. Behind the diplomacy of both powers was a barely submerged desire for a peaceful partition of Europe. Only Hitler could give them that—so they put aside, first Chamberlain and now Stalin, all the warnings from Litvinov and Vansittart, and plunged deeper into the darkness. Not everyone in London wished to go that way. Chamberlain suggested to critics that those who warned of a possible Russo-German alliance actually strengthened the argument that Russian policy was unreliable, even "sinister." He still needed a positive answer, however, to the challenge that he was allowing a genuine possibility to go by default. At the end of May, after consultations with his favorite source for new ideas, Sir Horace Wilson, Chamberlain settled upon a scheme for an alliance that was not an alliance. Britain should offer only to sign something whereby it declared an "intention" in certain circumstances to fulfill its obligations under Article XVI of the League of Nations Covenant. "It really is a most ingenious idea," the prime minister assured his sister Hilda. Best of all, it was nothing like a formal alliance, and only of a temporary nature for as long as the crisis lasted. Moreover, he was sure that Article XVI would be amended or even repealed, "and that should give us the opportunity of revising our relations with the Soviet if we want it."[80]

Once he had this idea worked out, he added, "I recovered my equanimity." He still believed that Hitler, or Hitler's generals, would not permit him to risk a major war. "But I can't yet see how the détente is to come about as long as the Jews obstinately go on refusing to shoot Hitler."[81] For some time now Chamberlain had stalled the cabinet with Micawber-like promises that something would turn up. His half-serious complaint about the Jews was of a piece with his belief that Eden and Vansittart had "obstinately" blocked his efforts at appeasement, that the moderates had "obstinately" refused to try to influence Hitler, that his domestic critics had "obstinately" refused to see how unreliable was the United States and how untrustworthy the Soviets.

When the Kremlin responded to the latest British proposals by reiterating demands for a formal alliance, and insisting that it cover the Baltic states as well as the other countries under discussion, Chamberlain threw up his hands in frustration— directed, however at his critics. It was impossible to come to any agreement with such people. But Lord Chatsfield was now seconded by the highly respected General William Ironsides. Agreement with Russia was the only thing Britain could do to save the situation, he told the prime minister in mid-July. Angered, Chamberlain rounded on the general: that was the "only thing we cannot do."[82]

While Chamberlain stalled his critics, Molotov actually helped the prime minister fend off advocates of the Russian "alternative" by his insistence on bringing the Baltic states into the discussion. In direct dealings with those small nations, moreover, Moscow had already used ominous threats. The Soviets had, for example, put Estonia on notice that they claimed a right to intervene if any other nation sought special privileges there, whether or not by invitation. When Moscow then pressed for a definition of "indirect aggression" so that it would give Russia a free hand in the Baltics, even those who favored agreement in Britain and France were given pause. Talks on such a basis were out of the question.[83]

Halifax, who had been out in front of Chamberlain on Russian policy, and who had at least listened to Vansittart's arguments, drew back. "What the Russians are at present asking," he wrote to a famous historian of that country, "is that we should virtually give them a warrant to interfere in the internal affairs of these States and go to war if this leads to trouble." Quite apart from the "immorality of the whole proceeding," the Baltic states and Finland were quite exercised at the prospect of receiving such an unsolicited guarantee.[84]

Even as Halifax answered queries about the delay in negotiations with Moscow, another cabinet minister, R. S. Hudson, was telling a German emissary once again that London recognized German economic supremacy in Southeastern Europe.[85] At length, British and French negotiators agreed to include the Baltic states in a proposed treaty with Russia, but they could not agree on "indirect aggression." British and French military experts arrived in Moscow in early August—not, it soon became clear, expecting to come to terms on the issues, for they had no powers to commit their governments. "They would like to tie up Russia," Ambassador Kennedy cabled home after a conversation with Halifax, "so that there is no possibility of the Russians considering a deal with Germany."[86]

But on the third day of the military talks, August 14, 1939, Defense Minister Kliment Voroshilov bluntly asked if the British and French general staffs believed that Soviet forces would be allowed to enter Polish and Rumanian territory to make contact with the aggressor. There was no reply. The German government, on the other hand, informed Molotov that same day that there was "no question between the Baltic Sea and the Black Sea which cannot be settled to the complete satisfaction of both countries."[87]

The Nazi-Soviet pact was signed nine days later. Toasts were drunk to the resumption of an old relationship and, incredibly, to the absent Hitler. "I know how much the German people love their Führer," Stalin said, raising a glass of champagne. "I want to drink to his health!"[88] The pact removed German fears of a two-front war and was therefore crucial to Hitler's decision to risk attacking Poland. Close observers, while they may not have known that Stalin had attempted to keep lines open to Berlin as an alternative to Litvinov's policy, had been predicting this rapprochement even before Munich. Clearly, the greatest shocks were suffered by Communist party members in foreign countries. None of the reasons given for the pact— Anglo-French duplicity, Stalin's genuine fear of a two-front war against Germany and Japan, a maneuver to gain time—ever sufficed to heal the wounds completely.

The Nazi-Soviet pact pledged the two nations to remain neutral if either became involved in war. A secret protocol partitioned Poland and awarded Moscow Estonia and Latvia, the Rumanian province of Bessarabia, and dominance in Finland. The Germans reserved Lithuania for their own sphere of influence. When Russian Foreign Minister V. M. Molotov visited Berlin in 1940, Hitler congratulated him in a sort of backhanded fashion for driving a good bargain. "Well, you are putting together Ukrainians, Belorussians, all right, Moldavians, that's quite reasonable, but how are you going to explain Baltic States to the whole world?" "We'll explain," Molotov shut off discussion. The leaders of the Baltic states had been summoned to Moscow to hear their fate. "You won't go back," Molotov told the Latvian minister of foreign affairs, "until you sign an annexation with us."[89]

Did Stalin's Marxist orthodoxy, then, make it impossible for him to see that Germany under Hitler was not just another "imperialist" nation but something that, while it grew out of a long-term crisis in the capitalist world, transcended all norms, repudiated all limits? Or did the opportunity to reestablish the Russian Empire, in the name of state security, simply prove impossible to resist?

The secret protocol was to remain secret for a long time. Soviet policymakers denied its existence until near the end of the cold war, despite full revelations found in captured German archives. Stalin's choice was obvious, wrote a British diplomat years later:

> Even if we had agreed to every Soviet demand, even if we had sacrificed the Baltic States and forced Poland to accept Russian troops, in the last resort we could only offer the satisfaction of Russian aspirations at the risk of war. The Germans, on the other hand, offered the Soviet Government complete and immediate satisfaction with no risk of war. The Russian choice was obvious.[90]

One of Stalin's sharpest critics, Roy Medvedev, concluded that the West was responsible for the breakdown of collective security. "Under these circumstances the Soviet Union had to look after its own interests. In 1939 the nonaggression pact with Germany served that purpose."[91]

Stalin's "blunder," continues Medvedev, was thus not the pact but the psychological and political atmosphere he created to justify it. For all the logic of the pact, Medvedev cites the writer Konstantin Simonov, much that accompanied it took away an important sense of the self, "connected with such a concept as 'the first socialist state in the world.' ... That is, something happened which was in a moral sense very bad."[92]

Munich and the Nazi-Soviet pact undid the Versailles settlement and took away the charter which the newly formed states of Central and Eastern Europe had gained after the Great War. The war that began on September 1, 1939, did not restore it. Ironically, Stalin's successful wartime diplomacy to retain the profits of the Nazi-Soviet pact finally made possible the "détente" Chamberlain had sought at Munich between a dynamic Germany and the West. "Translated into nonemotive terms," wrote Claude Cockburn after the war, "what Hitler called 'living space' for Germany could become what would now be called a Common Market or Economic Community...."[93]

Chamberlain was right. The Allies had put themselves in the unfortunate position of saying to the small nations, "Never mind if the lion does gobble you up; I intend to give him a good hiding afterwards."

3

DARKEST HOURS

We have not at any time adopted, since this war
broke out, the line that nothing could be changed
in the territorial structure of various countries.
On the other hand, we do not propose to
recognize any territorial changes which take place
during the war, unless they take place with the
free consent and goodwill of the parties
concerned.

Prime Minister Winston Churchill,
Statement in the House of Commons,
September 5, 1940

No ONE DOUBTED the Nazi-Soviet pact meant war in
Europe. It came within days, on September 1, 1939. Relieved
of the threat of a two-front war, Hitler fabricated an excuse to
attack Poland. Apparently he was shocked when the British and
French honored their pledges to Warsaw. Had Hitler delayed a
bit after his pact with Moscow, or allowed Russia to take the
lead in partitioning Poland, Chamberlain might have tried to
prevent a British declaration of war. The prime minister had
counted on Germany's economic weaknesses finally forcing
Hitler toward moderation. Instead his ambitions and fears, not
least of the soundness of the agreement he had signed, directed
him to the battlefield.

Chamberlain needed much bolstering to go through with the
actual declaration of war. Close observers thought that during

the crisis he passed from "middle age into decrepitude."[1] "I feel like a man driving a clumsy coach over a narrow crooked road along the face of a precipice," he had written to his sister Hilda only a few days before the outbreak of war. "You hardly dare look down lest you should turn giddy and there come times when your heart seems to stop still for minutes together until you can somehow round the next corner and find yourself still on the track."[2]

Hitler was not the only one shocked by the British decision to accept war over Poland. Some historians have suggested that the Munich agreement was so much in the British tradition that the question should not be "Why Munich?" but rather "Why war over Poland?"[3] For Ambassador Nevile Henderson in Berlin, a persistent sympathizer with German revisionist claims, the final answer had nothing to do with boundary lines or the existence of an independent Czechoslovakia or Poland. "The shifting sands of Eastern Europe are not our real concern," he later wrote. "We are crusaders, at war on behalf of Christian ideals versus pagan doctrines...."[4]

What now faced the liberal capitalist West was the final denouement of the terrible decade that began with the Great Depression and witnessed the rise of Nazi Germany, the spread of autarkic trading blocs dominated by restless powers, and the corresponding loss of confidence in the economic and political institutions of the West—a loss of confidence that could only be restored by putting the challenge in absolute terms as Henderson had done: Christian ideals versus pagan doctrines.

Such an approach helps to explain why Britain abandoned the appeasement "tradition" and how American views evolved during the months between the prewar partition of Europe and the Nazi invasion of Russia. For American policymakers, whether Hitler united Germany and Russia by peaceful means or by military force made less difference than the intolerable state of affairs now capped by the Nazi-Soviet pact. Across the Atlantic on the day war began, a State Department expert on European affairs wrote in his private diary, "The issues involved are so terrible, the outlook so cloudy, the probability of ultimate Bolshevism so great, and the chances of a better peace next time are so remote that if one stopped to think one would give way to gloom."[5]

For Americans, however, the war's immediate danger was not German military success or the spread of bolshevism but "the alternative prospects of post-war economic chaos or a world economy dominated by the dictatorships." As Roosevelt, Hull, Sumner Welles, and other top aides saw it, if Germany prevailed (or the war simply lasted long enough), the dictatorships would hold sway over the world, leaving the United States, as Adolf Berle put it, in "the unfortunate position of an old-fashioned general store in a town full of hard-bitten chains."[6]

Connecting bands of economic and political (and ultimately military) force were tightening around the American way of life, threatening to undo the work of an entire century. It was a "ghastly deceit," a War Department aide to Henry L. Stimson wrote, to contend that "we could preserve the United States as an island of free enterprise in a totalitarian world economy." The worldwide threat was one of political economy: forced to spend billions for defense, the United States would have to curtail consumer spending and fetter individual freedom with restrictions it abhorred. "In short, the fruits of the economic gains which we have made in the last century would be lost."[7]

In every instance, it seemed, political negotiations in the late 1930s involved a rearranging of economic relationships that channeled trade and finances into closed tunnels. London had been trying to come to a credit and trade agreement with Germany until a few weeks before the war; and the Nazi-Soviet pact had been made possible by an economic agreement. Germany had extended a credit of 200 million marks to seal the economic pact with Moscow, and had promised to facilitate arrangements between Soviet state enterprises and German suppliers. *Pravda* had hailed the commercial pact, saying it was "summoned to relieve" the strained political atmosphere and would lead to improved relations generally.[8]

Secretary of State Cordell Hull had always suspected that the

"New Dealers" around Roosevelt were only waiting for an opportune moment to reassert themselves. With the world being parceled out, he was sure they were ready with new schemes for national planning, self-containment, and eventually socialism. "If they really get in the saddle," Hull said of his supposed enemies in the administration, the hated New Dealers, "they will adopt a closed economy and will not even try to prevent Britain pursuing a policy of bilateralism."[9] It was essential, therefore, to use the State Department's influence to discourage the British from falling into a "Munich-style" pattern of accommodating spheres of influence, or closing off the empire because of wartime exigencies.

Some Americans suspected that with the imperial preference system Great Britain had abandoned economic liberalism for good, and that London had no intention of ever going back to the predepression, prefascist, pre–New Deal world. The war would only make it harder to overcome British determination to save the empire whatever the costs for other capitalist nations. On the other hand, some Americans merely feared that without a strong American lead, British policymakers would accept the world as it was and not join in Washington's efforts to realize, finally, Thomas Paine's 1776 promise that the power was there to begin the world anew. "There is no question that Mr. Hull's Trade Agreements program is completely out of the window," Ambassador Joseph Kennedy wrote to Roosevelt during the second week of the war. "England is as much a totalitarian country tonight from an economic and trade point of view as any other country in Europe—all that is needed is time to perfect the organization."[10]

"From the very outset of the war," concludes the historian Warren Kimball, "Roosevelt was thinking of the structure of the postwar world." He did not intend to build it upon bilateralism, however close the "special relationship" with Great Britain might be, but to use that relationship to lever the world back onto a liberal track. When the administration's Lend-Lease Bill passed Congress eighteen months later it required negotiations to insure that such arrangements as the imperial preference system did not survive the defeat of the Axis nations.[11]

Britain welcomed the Lend-Lease Bill not simply for the immediate succor it offered but for its promise of a long-term commitment to Anglo-American cooperation. A suggestion was made to Prime Minister Churchill by one of his advisers that he might wish to take notice in the House of Commons of that commitment. He could say, "The Americans have written a new and greater Magna Carta. They have told the world that the great society of nations cannot exist half slave and half free; that America will tolerate nothing less than a free and friendly world in which to develop her way of life."[12]

Churchill did praise Lend-Lease in the House, but he was not quite so ready to turn over world leadership to the Americans. Lend-Lease was a new Magna Carta, but it only set the example and duty for "free men and free nations, wherever they may be, to share the responsibility and burden...."[13]

London's immediate concerns in September 1939 were to keep Russia a genuine neutral in the war. A Foreign Office adviser had remarked that any approach to Moscow was dangerous because the British cupboard was bare of anything the Russians might want. Besides, the Nazi-Soviet pact had stirred deep passions. Chamberlain had wanted the Labor party convinced of Moscow's untrustworthiness, and now they were convinced. Government advocates of cooperation with Russia were also convinced and reviled the Russians in surprisingly vehement fashion. None more so than Robert Vansittart. "I hope we shall nibble no more at any Russian bait," he noted on a proposal for a new try. The only thought should be how to beat Germany. "If we can do that, we can then deal with Stalin and his pseudo-Communism, which it is just as necessary to destroy as Nazism."[14]

The rub was how to beat Germany. Explorations of Russian intentions, however distasteful, were still necessary, beginning with a resumption of trade talks. They were most likely to produce some result and least likely to suggest that London was standing in line as a supplicant for Moscow's favor. Vansittart's position appealed to many, both intellectually and emotionally, but not just at the moment. Thought would be given to supporting Finland in its efforts to resist Russian demands, even to launching attacks on Russian positions in the Caucasus, but these were always rejected in the end.

Lord Halifax, on the other hand, seemed more open than before to suggestions for exploring the Russian situation. He was now joined in the cabinet by the new first lord of the admiralty, Winston Churchill, who went so far as to argue that a Russian presence in the Baltic and in Finland was to Britain's advantage. Throughout the war Churchill would waver on the general question of "spheres of influence," but when he turned over the issue during a cabinet discussion in November 1939 it produced some surprising statements.

No doubt it appeared reasonable to the Soviets, he began, to take advantage of the present situation "to regain some of the territory which Russia had lost as a result of the last war, at the beginning of which she had been the ally of France and Great Britain."[15] It would certainly be a mistake, he went on, to encourage the Finns to resist making concessions to Moscow, because a Russian presence would limit German domination in the area. In general, he concluded, it ought to be our policy to secure as much support as possible from Russia as well as from China and the United States. What remarkable statements from this ancient foe of bolshevism, this man who had often boasted that he sought to strangle Marx's Russian offspring in its cradle! Halifax, whose High Church views had not kept him from praising Hitler's methods before the war, expressed shock at Churchill's blatant *realpolitik*. He was interested in exploring matters with the Russians, but this was too much to accept. Certainly, he responded, with fullest indignation, His Majesty's Government could not advise the Finns to make concessions which "they themselves regarded as vital to their national independence."[16]

The discussion ended there—for the moment. Whether or not Churchill would have brought up Chamberlain's "advice" to the Czechs about their vital interests, Halifax felt he must respond privately in a more convincing manner. Prompted by another former "pro-Russian," Laurence Collier, the foreign secretary wrote Churchill that a Russian presence in the Baltic would not diminish German influence but increase it. It was probably the case, moreover, that the Germans were egging on the Russians in order to frighten the Scandinavian countries into granting Berlin more concessions, particularly in economic matters. There was no reason to believe the Russians could ever be induced to take a hostile attitude toward Germany.[17]

As we have seen, Halifax was not as rigid as this letter implies. Between Vansittart and Churchill, where the foreign secretary stood, was a broad area of agreement that any new approach to Russia must be undertaken carefully, with an eye on the long term as well. Sir William Strang, who had headed the British delegation in the failed Moscow trade negotiations, put it bluntly during a Foreign Office discussion of Allied war aims. "The danger to be avoided," he argued,

> is a turnover of Germany to Bolshevism and close alliance with Russia, with or without Hitler. The best solution might be a non-Nazi Germany, weakened but not crushed, losing territory, or at any rate influence, to Russia in Eastern Europe, and forming a Four-Power Agreement with Great Britain, France and Italy for the defence of Western Europe.[18]

But what had happened after World War I, when Central and Eastern Europe had been left to the temptations of the powers bordering the region, could not be tolerated after this war ended. Some form of cooperation among those small countries must be encouraged if they were to survive and the world spared yet another military conflict. "For this purpose," read a draft statement on war aims, "it would be wise to encourage at once closer cooperation between the Balkan states and closer cooperation between the various refugee groups of Poles, Czechs, Slovaks and Austrians."[19]

The noted economist John Maynard Keynes, now in a Treasury post, argued much the same point in a December 1940 position paper. It was dangerous, he maintained, to aim British propaganda at "a revolutionary sentiment in Europe." In response to Germany's claims to have founded a New Order, a competing plan must be offered, responding to the craving for social and personal security. Germany's role after the war was essential because of its geographic and economic position.

> I cannot see how the rest of Europe can expect effective economic reconstruction if Germany is excluded from it and remains a festering mess in their midst; and an economically reconstructed Germany will necessarily resume leadership. *This conclusion is inescapable, unless it is our intention to hand the job over to Russia.*[20]

Keynes's paper elicited enthusiastic support in the Foreign Office. Anthony Eden, who had replaced Halifax as foreign secretary, made a number of marginal comments indicating his agreement, and he encouraged Keynes to take the matter up with Roosevelt's special adviser, Harry Hopkins. Strang's and Keynes's view of the issues at stake fit closely with Nevile Henderson's conclusion as to why war was finally necessary; and all three centered not on German efforts at partition, which London had already dealt with as acceptable, but on the Nazi-Soviet pact, which was not acceptable. The pact surely meant war—but what if it hadn't happened, what then? The lesson for the British was to design spheres of influence in a different fashion, so as to exclude a Russo-German combination under any leadership.

For Americans, however, the question of spheres of influence took a more sinister form. At the outset of the war they could not see any purpose except an evil one in pursuing such a goal. Hopkins's initial reaction to Keynes's ideas did not provide British policymakers with much guidance. Before anything like Keynes's proposed statement was given out, he said, the president must have an opportunity to study it. "The President on these questions was rather touchy as he regarded the post-war settlement so to speak as being his particular preserve."[21]

Reckoning with Roosevelt's "touchy" feelings would have to come later. For the British, the immediate problem was still Russia. And the mood in the Kremlin was suffused with a self-righteous defense of the Nazi-Soviet pact, accompanied by scolding lectures directed at Western diplomats. Neither tactic helped to repair the damage done to Communist party standing in the West. The Popular Front tactics of the 1930s favored by Maksim Litvinov had been abandoned. At least temporarily, Stalinist Russia found itself in ideological isolation—which, the Soviet dictator had obviously decided, was better than military isolation.

On September 17, 1939, the Red Army occupied eastern Poland, claiming it had a duty to protect Byelorussian and Ukrainian minorities who, by a "whim of fate," had been "left defenseless." But the note to the Polish ambassador in Moscow concluded that the Soviet high command had been instructed to "take under their protection the life and property of the population of Western Ukraine and Western White Russia," a more far-reaching assertion about the future.[22]

When Halifax pressed Ambassador Maisky about the "surprising changes" in Russian foreign policy, he was told that the demarcation line with Poland was only provisional—but Maisky would say nothing about the future. What he would say was that the Red Army had driven out landlords and liberated an oppressed peasantry. It did not seem to him odd, a sardonic Halifax noted, that these "needed social reforms" were being carried out on someone else's territory. When the foreign secretary then observed that the Red Army had gone beyond the old boundaries of tsarist Russia, Maisky appeared oblivious to that incongruity as well. That might be true in some places, he said, but on "average the line was not so favorable as that existing before the war."[23]

Maisky's somewhat tortured efforts to recoup the world mission of communism, and to combine it with a mild defense of tsarist Russia's pre–World War I borders, was not Foreign Minister Molotov's style. On October 31, 1939, he delivered a vitriolic speech which all but equated the "missions" of Nazi Germany and the Soviet Union. "Governing circles in Poland," he began, "took no small pride in the 'toughness' of the Government and the 'power' of their army. However, a short shock against Poland, first from the German army and then from the Red Army, proved sufficient to remove every trace of this deformed progeny of the Treaty of Versailles, which had lived by oppressing its non-Polish nationalists." Two days later, on November 2, the areas occupied by the Red Army were incorporated into the Soviet Union.[24]

Molotov also lashed out at critics of Soviet pressure on the Baltic states and Finland. Even the President of the United States, he said, had seen fit to interfere in Russo-Finnish negotiations over the cession of naval bases and parts of the Karelian peninsula.

> It might be thought that insofar as the United States is concerned matters are better let us say, [than] with the Philippines or Cuba which have long demanded from the United States their freedom and independence and have been unable to receive them, than with the Soviet Union and Finland which long ago received from the Soviet Union its freedom and state independence.[25]

Baltic states representatives were soon summoned to Moscow to hear what the Kremlin had decided about their fate. The Estonian minister in Moscow was told that present boundaries in the area had been forced upon Russia when it was weak, and now must be amended "in consonance with her rightful position as a Baltic power." Estonia could agree to the demands or submit to more drastic solutions. Stalin explained to the Latvian foreign minister in less minatory terms, "I tell you frankly a division of spheres of interest has already taken place. As far as Germany is concerned, we could occupy you whenever we wish." But he justified his threats as merely a defense against a possible German attack on the Soviet Union, an odd combination of reasons.[26]

In London Maisky complained that the British press was making too much of supposed Russian designs on such far-off places as India. The British must not allow the "press to revert to a 19th Century atmosphere of 'Big Bad Wolf' suspicion between our two countries. Let us, he said, use our wartime privilege to curb our press and keep it from unfriendly comment." The Russian military attaché was somewhat more candid. Wherever Moscow turned, he told "Rab" Butler, the shadow of the British Empire fell across "her designs." The Soviet Union had never received a straightforward approach from London. Butler replied that they both had enough territory and troubles without going for each other. The military attaché was gratified with this comment. But, he said, England always treated the Russians as outcasts. If London continued to behave in a feudal manner, they would never get any nearer Russia. Butler's response was classic: "I declared that we were now both Empires, at which he smiled, and that no doubt the best avenue of approach would be the commercial one."[27]

A barter exchange of rubber and tin for lumber made sense. But when the British gingerly advanced the idea, along with the caveat that none of the goods must find their way to Germany, the response was always that "if any trade arrangement was made, it would be from regard to their own interest that the Soviet Government would enter into it."[28] Vansittart was furious at the tone of this response. No one should go to Russia to iron out these matters, he blustered. "The Russians should come here. No one from here can go there—after the long and dismal queue of victims—without appearing to go to Canossa." It would be disastrous for British prestige—and a boost for Russia. "Think of the effect in Europe."[29]

All thoughts of continuing trade discussions, let alone sending a special mission, were put aside when the Russians, using an "incident" similar to the one Hitler had employed to launch his assault on Poland, opened hostilities against Finland. Finnish-Soviet negotiations had broken off in mid-November, with the Finns displaying no apparent fears of action by Moscow. The "Winter War" lasted three months, and though Helsinki finally had to yield much more territory in the truce agreement—again up to an old tsarist line established by Peter the Great in 1721—the war proved to be a diplomatic disaster for the Soviets, and nearly a military one as well.[30]

Ambassador William C. Bullitt in Paris, delighted that he

could at last "get back at" his old enemies in the Kremlin, pushed and prodded officials at the League of Nations to expel the Soviet Union—and succeeded. He did this, he wrote President Roosevelt, in obeyance to old instructions FDR had given him. In the wake of failed Soviet-American negotiations, the president had told Bullitt in 1934 to make it clear that it "was better for any nation to have really friendly relations with the United States rather than unfriendly relations."[31]

Roosevelt had not intended by these rather innocuous in structions to give his representative freedom to ostracize the Soviets. Bullitt's manipulations would cause Roosevelt trouble later in the war, when the president hoped to convince Stalin to join him in establishing a new organization to replace the defunct League. Stalin referred to Moscow's expulsion from the League as a reason for limiting the powers of the organization by giving each of the Big Three veto authority. What bothered him more than diplomatic embarrassment in 1940, however, was the poor showing of his armies in trying to overcome Finnish resistance. After the first month a Soviet general observed bitterly, "We have conquered just enough Finnish territory to bury the dead."[32]

Washington imposed an arms embargo against the Soviet Union which lasted until the German invasion in June 1941. There was grim satisfaction in Allied capitals with the Red Army's performance in Finland. The Russians had to use torrents of artillery and shock waves of troops to overcome an army better schooled in the techniques of winter war. Admiration for the Finns as the only small country to stand up to the dictators did not, however, include a willingness to send military aid, despite the expulsion of the Russians from the League. Ambassador Maisky was almost contrite in asking that London try to put the Finnish situation "into a compartment by itself," as he and Eden had agreed to do with the Spanish Civil War.[33]

He understood, Butler recorded, that the British might object to what the Soviet government was doing in Finland, "and might even help the Finns; but we must not be too spectacular, and... both sides must try to maintain their diplomatic relations." As analogy, Maisky recalled a hair-raising experience he had suffered while in exile before the Bolshevik Revolution. He had been thrown off a sledge in northern Siberia and left alone in the snow for many hours. "He sometimes felt as lonely [in London] as he did on that occasion; but he always remembered that his driver and the reindeer had returned to pick him up again."[34]

As the "Winter War" came to an end, Prime Minister Chamberlain—of all people—saw an opportunity to rescue Maisky from his isolation. He had never seen such opportunities in the years before the war, but now he told American Under Secretary of State Sumner Welles that the events in the Baltic might actually restore Russian freedom of action and lead to certain policy differences with Germany.[35] Roosevelt had sent Welles on a peace mission to the capitals of the warring nations, to see if there was any chance for the economic and disarmament proposals Washington had been promoting for the past two years. Welles had an impression of Russo-German relations very different from Chamberlain's. It was supplied to him by Foreign Minister Joachim von Ribbentrop, who had repeated several times that Germany and its Russian ally were determined never to allow any third power to decide questions affecting Eastern Europe.[36] Welles had also gathered from conversations in Berlin, he told the prime minister, that the Germans expected a privileged position in adjoining countries. Chamberlain replied that he had never seen any great difficulty about a German effort to make arrangements with "her neighbors which might in some degree be held comparable to that between Great Britain and parts of the British Empire."

Well, of course, Welles responded, "all these preferential agreements" were really undesirable, "but it was difficult to resist them in one area if they prevailed in another."[37] Here was the usual conundrum for American policymakers. Welles's response may have seemed almost sympathetic of Britain's plight, but that was scarcely the case. Statements like the prime minister's implied a willingness to bargain away Eastern Europe to protect the empire—before the war with Germany, and now with Russia? However unlikely that might seem at the moment, it was not farfetched given decisions since the creation of the imperial preference system.

Chamberlain's comment made it easy for even Anglophile Americans to connect "appeasement" with the forsaking of liberal principles and the defense of colonialism. What a baleful influence these outdated concepts from Victorian days had on national character!—so Americans, both New Dealers and Hull free-traders, were wont to think. At one time the empire had made Britain economically strong; now, it was clear, it made it politically weak. Appeasement was the result. The infirmities of British policy would certainly not get better as war strained financial resources. What if London faced a similar situation in dealing with Russia?

If one assumed that the United States would have to go to war to save England, it was really to save England from repeating the mistakes it had made in the 1930s. Quite simply, the British couldn't be trusted. The United States, unencumbered by formal empire (or not much of one, anyway) was the natural successor to the heritage of the Pax Britannica. That was what had to be protected. That was what Welles took home with him from his 1940 mission. Great Britain was no longer strong enough to maintain the healthy climate it had once furnished for "material development and the evolution of a [decent] social order," a private citizen, Dean Acheson, was telling an audience at Yale University. The Russo-German and Japanese spheres of influence divided the world "along oriental lines." If those lines were made permanent, America's future as a liberal democracy was endangered.

Acheson did not expect a military invasion of North America. Few imagined anything like that, despite Roosevelt's efforts to suggest that the Germans were seeking to secure bases from which to attack South America. What worried him were the "oriental lines" that would shut out ideas and goods. When Welles told Chamberlain that it would be hard to resist spheres of influence in one place if they existed in another, that was what he meant. And when Acheson described the perils of an isolationist answer to the war, that was what he feared: socialism or fascism growing from the binding effects of "oriental lines" wrapped around America. "I am not saying that morals are a matter of economics," Acheson concluded, "but rather there is high authority for the belief that if we are not led into temptation we may be better delivered from evil."[38]

The Welles mission had failed to delay the German spring offensive against France. As the *blitzkrieg* began the Chamberlain government fell, the result of accumulated discontent over its conduct of the war. It was replaced in early May 1940 by a coalition cabinet headed by Winston Churchill. The new prime minister's bulldog defiance of Berlin reassured those who worried that London might sue for peace. His attempts to rally the French to counterattack failed, however, as their forces simply came apart in the face of the German armored attack. General Maxime Weygand, who urged his government to ask Hitler for terms, quipped bitterly in response to Churchill's pleas, "You have a very good anti-tank trap in the Channel."[39]

The French collapse had an immediate impact on diplomatic relations between the powers. For some time Lord Halifax had been mulling over a new initiative toward Russia. In the wake of all the futile "trade missions" to Moscow, Sir Stafford Cripps, a left-wing Laborite, had had a talk with Molotov in the early spring of 1940. He came away feeling that a new British overture might produce results. The Foreign Office was not impressed. But Halifax, supported by "Rab" Butler, thought otherwise—if only because there seemed very little more to lose.[40]

At a cabinet meeting on May 18, 1940, it was decided to send Cripps on a special mission to Russia. The Russians agreed to accept him only as a regular ambassador, however, out of concern not to offend the Germans—hardly a confirmation of

Sir Stafford's optimism. Efforts were made to convince Ambassador Maisky that Cripps's appointment demonstrated "a new spirit here, a firmer will and a much stronger drive to win the war, and a keen desire to get rid of all the stale old misunderstandings on both sides between his country and ours."[41]

Cripps finally arrived in Moscow in mid-June 1940. The Russians were obviously interested to see if his appointment did, in fact, signal a change in British attitudes as a result of the French debacle. They sought to do so informally. On June 18 the chief London correspondent of the Russian news agency Tass called at the Foreign Office to suggest that Churchill send for Maisky to ask of him what the USSR thought of the present situation—"whether the spectacle of Germany straddling over Europe commended itself to Moscow."[42]

As the Tass correspondent spoke, Russian armed forces were moving into the three Baltic states, Estonia, Latvia, and Lithuania. "Conjectures regarding the future are pessimistic," cabled the American minister in Riga, Latvia. "It is possible that the new governments in the Baltic States will be so constituted that *Anschluss* with the U.S.S.R. can be voted in due course in an endeavor to forestall any Hitlerian 'new order' in Eastern Europe."[43]

A few days later Moscow gave Rumania an ultimatum, demanding the return of Bessarabia and Bukovina, adjacent to the Ukraine, which had been taken at a time when Russia was militarily weak—"an unfortunate state of affairs which no longer exists." The ultimatum was followed by military occupation. The German minister in Bucharest told his American counterpart that "Hitler will never forget" the Russian action.[44]

The Rumanian foreign minister insisted that his country's capitulation was not the last word on the matter. The army would remain intact, always hoping for an opportunity to attack the Russians and regain the territories. Their best chance would come when Germany, resigned for the moment about Moscow's action but also deeply annoyed, made peace in the west and would thus have "a freer hand to deal with Russia."[45]

The foreign minister's comment, with other reports from the

Baltic, suggests how profoundly France's rapid defeat changed political calculations. The Russian moves could be interpreted either as defensive, to outflank any possible German offensive, or as hurry-up actions (like Mussolini's declaration of war on France on June 11) to keep from being left behind in the scramble to rake in as many as possible of the "loose" pieces of Europe.

Thus by the time Cripps secured an audience with Stalin on July 1, 1940, practically everything had changed since he set out for Moscow. He brought with him a letter from Churchill in which the prime minister in effect responded to the earlier request to ask the Soviets about their attitude toward Germany's bid for hegemony over Europe. His Majesty's Government, said the message, was ready to "discuss fully... any of the vast problems created by Germany's present attempt to pursue in Europe a methodical process by successive stages of conquest and absorption."[46]

Stalin's reactions to the prime minister's letter were nothing if not candid. He did not see Germany desiring or, more important, being able to establish hegemony in Europe, which, he agreed, would enable such a power to dominate the world. As for the origins of the Russo-German nonaggression pact, the prewar negotiations with Britain and France had demonstrated that those two nations wished to preserve the "old equilibrium" for which they stood. Russia had wanted to change the equilibrium. "Germany had also wanted to make a change..., and this common desire to get rid of the old equilibrium had created a basis for the rapprochement with Germany.... If the Prime Minister wishes to restore the old equilibrium, we cannot agree with him. On the whole I must say that however much it may be desired fully to restore the equilibrium in Europe the task will be very difficult."[47]

Cripps was nonetheless encouraged by Stalin's assurance that Russia had no further demands on Rumania. Russia had no desire to rule anywhere in the Balkans, Stalin said, replying to Cripps's suggestion that he *ought* to take the lead there. Such a policy, Stalin said, would be "incorrect and very dangerous."

Sir Stafford was convinced that Russia's moves had all been defensive, and he was ready to accord Moscow full recognition of the incorporation of the Baltic states into the Soviet Union. It would bring a change for the better for the peoples of those regions, Cripps asserted in reports to London. Like Stalin, he expected a new equilibrium after the war, within as well as among nations, and Russian policy, as he saw it, fit that prophecy.

Cripps's unsolicited opinions commended themselves to no one in the Foreign Office. What transpired between the ambassador and Stalin was precisely the sort of dialogue that officials in London feared—both as to what the Russians demanded and what the West was expected to yield. The notion that Soviet occupation of the Baltic states represented a "new equilibrium" foreboded serious consequences regardless of which side won the war.

Washington had no Cripps to worry about, but the Kremlin's "devious processes" in legitimizing the Baltic annexations brought a stinging declaration from Sumner Welles. The United States opposed all "predatory activities," read his public statement, whether carried out by military force or achieved by threats. Small nations had to be protected under the rule of law or "the basis of modern civilization itself . . . cannot be preserved."[48]

The administration froze the assets of the Baltic countries, refused to withdraw diplomatic recognition, and in every way it could opposed Russian policy. But even Welles did not lose sight of the need to maintain flexibility. Expediency was not a good guide for policy, read an internal State Department memorandum on the Baltic situation, nor could there be two standards, one for the Axis and one for Russia. "Our failure to recognize the Soviet conquests just now," it went on in a somewhat different tone, "although not pleasant to the Soviet Government, may possibly place another card in our hands when, if ever, a conference regarding the future of Europe takes place."[49]

When Roosevelt suggested he wished to retaliate by closing certain Soviet consulates, Welles persuaded him it would be a futile gesture. The fall of France made it imperative not to shut off communications with Russia, however abhorrent Soviet behavior. Hence the under secretary met with Russian Ambassador Constantin Oumansky to persuade him that the "new equilibrium" that everyone was talking about could not rest on foundations that undermined the security of small states. "Mr. Welles was making statements of real importance and looking ahead," Oumansky admitted during one of these sessions, but his country preferred first to discuss specific issues, such as Baltic assets.[50]

Here was the first real exchange in a Soviet-American dialogue that would follow these lines for more than three years until at Teheran Roosevelt found himself face to face with Stalin over the fate of Eastern Europe. In London, meanwhile, Halifax took note of Welles's denunciation of the forced annexations, and listed it among the reasons why the cabinet should not be "premature" in recognizing the Russian action. Besides, in what Stalin said to Cripps there was no indication that recognition would now be a sufficient "inducement" to Moscow to change its general attitudes. "In short, expediency in this case recommends the same course as morality." The formula should be, therefore, that while refusing recognition in the present, His Majesty's Government should not tie its hands for the future.[51]

Cripps did not like the formula, not at all. It was, of course, for London to decide if putting Anglo-Soviet relations at risk for the sake of American public opinion was worth it. But the consequences to be reckoned with on all levels, including the hoped-for trade agreement, ought to be given very serious consideration.

> The United States of America can still no doubt afford to antagonize the Soviet Government by adopting a moral attitude upon the question of the incorporation of those States, though I am inclined to believe that any major State faced by the danger of German attack, as is Russia to-day, would have adopted some expedient to occupy the Baltic States before Germany could use them as a base for attack.[52]

Halifax yielded—so far. He was willing to grant de facto recognition to Russian administrative control over the Baltic states, but not to extend to the right to lodge claims to their assets in Britain. "I therefore leave it to your discretion to play the hand as best you can...."[53]

It was a poor hand, Molotov in essence declared at the next interview with Cripps. What did London have to offer, aside from a trade agreement of little consequence? The British had complained about the "inequality" of Russian neutrality as between Germany and their country. But the pact with Germany had yielded agreements of "vital importance." "For instance, we were able to secure our interests in the Western Ukraine and White Russia." There was certainly no indication here that the Soviet Union regarded the Polish annexations as temporary war expedients. Another instance, said the Russian foreign minister, was "the adjustment of our relations with the Baltic States."[54]

What Stalin meant about a new equilibrium was now pretty much clear: recognition of the boundary lines as set forth in the Nazi-Soviet pact, and as the Russians had seen fit to enlarge upon in their own way. Cripps understood all that. While he argued his position in various ways, the heart of it always came down to his belief that Russia's moves were essentially defensive against Germany, which any geopolitician could appreciate. And the Foreign Office ought to understand as well that Britain faced a solemn choice: either go all out for better Anglo-Soviet relations, with the chance of gradually divorcing Moscow from Berlin, or risk military defeat. The first alternative demanded "some sacrifices and a thoroughness equal to that of Germany," but put against the danger of a Nazi victory, it was certainly the better choice.[55]

But were those really the only options? Halifax was not sure. His aides were almost unanimous in opposing further gestures that involved surrendering the rights of small nations in the vague hope of influencing Soviet thinking. Sir Alec Cadogan insisted that the Russians would change when it suited them, not sooner. "It won't matter if we've kicked Maisky in the stomach. Contrariwise, we could give Maisky the Garter and it wouldn't make a penn'worth of difference."[56] The Scandinavian countries, particularly Sweden and Finland, were worried about any change in British policy. And, finally, the Americans were dead set against recognition of the annexations.[57]

By October 1940, however, there were new weights on the other side of the scale. The signing of the Axis Tripartite pact in September, for example, indicated not only a closer coordination among Germany, Italy, and Japan, but also the possibility that Russia and Japan would embrace, further endangering China and British interests in the Far East. Hence it was deemed advisable to give Sir Stafford new instructions. But what a tortured, convoluted set of instructions they were, reflecting the deepest British anxieties about the future. If Moscow promised to pursue a "benevolent neutrality" instead of its pro-Axis stance, and if it promised to continue sending aid to China, and if it agreed not to assault Turkey or Iran if they became involved in the war, and if the Russians signed the trade agreement and negotiated an Anglo-Soviet nonaggression treaty, then, after all these "ifs," His Majesty's Government would, *if* it emerged victorious from the war, "consult fully" with Moscow—and other nations that had similarly practiced a benevolent neutrality (i.e., the United States)—about the postwar settlement in Europe and Asia. Such an undertaking, however, was not to be understood as a promise to agree beforehand with Russian opinions.

If the Russians accepted all these conditions and subclauses, London would also agree not to form any alliance after the war directed against the Soviet Union, and to recognize "until the consultations" the de facto sovereignty of the Soviet Union in the Baltic states, Bessarabia, Bukovina, "and those parts of the former Polish State now under Soviet control." Finally, Britain would agree to give Russia available commodities or expert assistance, subject to other commitments, required for Russia's defense against foreign attacks. When Cripps presented this "offer" to the Russians, he was first told that it contained suggestions of the greatest importance. But after asking for clarifications, the Soviets declined to talk about it further.[58]

Cripps had been unable to see Molotov personally to present the plan, being shunted off to his deputies. Molotov was unavailable, apparently, because he had been preparing for a journey to Berlin. The American ambassador in Moscow, Laurence Steinhardt, believed the trip had been at German insistence, in large part because of the publicity about British efforts to drive a wedge between the two countries. Cripps had in fact told Steinhardt about the "political offer," though he did not at first mention the paragraph about wartime recognition of Soviet territorial gains—a pattern that would continue in the war years, further fueling suspicions of British backsliding into appeasement.[59]

Cripps was shocked and deeply discouraged by the news of Molotov's visit to Berlin, fretting that it might make British conservatives seek a separate peace with an anti-Soviet bias. Steinhardt's "informants" in Moscow told him that the talks were on a "frankly imperialist basis and that Molotov and Hitler in effect discussed the division of certain areas of the world." The Russian foreign minister had gone to Germany working from the premise that "the only agreements of any value in international affairs were those providing for the acquisition of territories of strategic or economic importance."[60]

Steinhardt's informants were not entirely correct. In the Berlin discussions, Ribbentrop and Hitler sought to direct Molotov's attention to the glittering prizes awaiting the Soviets in the Middle East and India once England was defeated. Russia was also invited to join the Axis Tripartite pact. For his part, Molotov did believe that specific agreements were the only important thing in diplomacy, but all his remarks were directed toward German actions in Finland, most recently the agreement with Helsinki to transport troops to Norway, and the threat of German action in the area of the Black Sea.

The discussions did not go smoothly at all. Ribbentrop and Hitler predicted England's defeat as a foregone conclusion, but the talks were several times interrupted by British air raids which required a retreat to underground quarters. When Ribbentrop insisted yet again that Britain was finished, Molotov delivered a final thrust. "If that is so," he said, "then why are we in this shelter, and whose are those bombs which are falling?"[61]

Molotov's willingness, even bravado, in challenging Hitler, and his refusal to be bought off with promises of untold riches to be shared out from the British Empire, did not mean that Stalin had decided to confront Germany with an ultimatum (indeed, his efforts to avoid war continued until the eve of the German attack), or that he was ready to shift to a pro-British policy. Molotov's answer to the invitation to join the Axis Tripartite pact was, as Hitler described it, a "cunning" piece of work. The Soviet Union would be happy to join, said the foreign minister after returning to Moscow, when certain conditions had been met. These turned out to be the guarantees he had asked for in Berlin, put in even stronger terms—for example, a complete German evacuation of Finland. Berlin never responded.[62]

When "Rab" Butler questioned Ambassador Maisky about the fate of the "political offer" Cripps had made in October, the Russian ambassador remarked that it would be better for Anglo-Soviet relations if there were no response. The offer had no substance in it, Maisky continued. When Butler protested that it contained real indications of British attitudes, the ambassador scoffed. "We were now living 'in the jungle;' 'drawing room' language was of no value." The part Great Britain chose to play in future "consultations" about the peace settlement, Maisky said, "reminded him of St. Peter in sole charge of the gates of Heaven. It was no use for... [Britain] to aspire to play the part of that Saint. Did we think we were going to settle the world alone after the war?" All Maisky would yield was a promise to tell his superiors about their conversation. Butler recorded, "I summed up the conversation by saying that things appeared to me to remain much as they were...."[63]

Halifax no doubt breathed a sigh of relief when Churchill replaced him at the Foreign Office with Anthony Eden. He would no longer have to confront Maisky or instruct Cripps what he could or could not do. Sent to Washington as ambassador, Halifax would soon, ironically, be trying to convince American skeptics to follow a British lead in recognizing Russian annexation of the Baltic states.

Eden began his tenure as foreign secretary by asking Cripps to remind Soviet officials that his past record demonstrated no prejudice against Moscow. But even Cripps advised going slow in the wake of Molotov's Berlin trip. And Eden agreed that the only policy for the moment must be one of reserve. "I feel that we can only possess our souls in patience until such a time as we have sufficient success in our military operations to inspire in the Soviet Government some of the fear and respect which they now feel for the Germans."[64]

At the moment Anglo-Russian relations were stalemated in the Baltic: Moscow's refusal to accept Cripps's conditional offer for wartime recognition of the annexations, versus British refusal to release the gold assets of those states to the Soviet Union. Molotov told Cripps on February 1, 1941—in terms similar to those he had used in Berlin—that he did not expect London to "express pleasure" over what had happened in the Baltic, but neither had the Swedes, and they had accepted the situation. British obstinacy in this regard did not demonstrate "any desire" to improve Anglo-Russian relations.[65]

Sweden's likely reaction to the annexations had in fact been earlier cited by Foreign Office advisers as one reason for not accommodating Soviet wishes. But even if Stockholm now accepted the situation, as Molotov had put it, the Americans plainly did not, and with the Lend-Lease Bill in Congress, anything that upset Britain's friends across the Atlantic must be avoided. America, moreover, had been able to maintain a dialogue with the Russians. Finally, there were now the concerns of the exile governments to worry about. Germany's sweep across Europe, east and west, had left Britain to host a swarm of refugee officials who buzzed around Whitehall at the least hint of diplomatic deals at their expense. The exile Polish minister for foreign affairs, for instance, had pointed out to

Eden that recognition of the annexation of the Baltic states would compromise the case against Soviet seizure of eastern Poland.[66]

Washington's attitude was perhaps even more important to the British, for the outcome of the war now seemed to hinge on such things as the passage of the administration's Lend-Lease Bill, introduced in Roosevelt's January 6, 1941, State of the Union Message. A fierce debate in Congress was expected, and materialized. It would not do to supply anti-British isolationist newspapers with evidence of a British deal with Russia to turn over the Baltic states to Moscow's rule. The bill passed on March 11, but Lend-Lease offered the British economic relief at a high cost—political independence. Churchill might describe Lend-Lease as the most unsordid act in history, but he hoped to put off settlement issues until Britain had regained its expected strength after the war. At times, moreover, and however fleetingly, he even hoped to use a "special relationship" with Stalin to sidestep certain American pressures.[67]

Stalin, meanwhile, had decided that the state of Russo-German relations had reached a highly dangerous point. From his own intelligence sources, as well as from Churchill and Roosevelt, he learned of Hitler's plan to march east. Why, then, did he not move closer to the British? Churchill gave his answer in his memoirs, written at the height of the cold war. Stalin and his colleagues, he declared, were "the most completely outwitted bunglers of the Second World War."[68]

Stalin's "odd" behavior in the spring of 1941, the ill-prepared state of the Red Army, and his apparent breakdown in the days following the German invasion, all point to such a conclusion, if not quite so finally as Churchill would insist. Yet there is much in the contemporary record to dispute that judgment. Chamberlain had often justified appeasement by pointing to the unsatisfactory state of British rearmament, or, alternatively, by warning that major arms spending would bankrupt the country. Stalin had the evidence before him of what the German lead actually meant: the rapid collapse of France and the far more dramatic success of the Wehrmacht in Yugoslavia and Greece.

French defeat could be put down, in part, to psychological reasons, but not what happened in the Balkans.

Russian military weakness, on the other hand, had been demonstrated in the winter war with Finland. But Stalin also calculated that he could continue to maneuver the diplomatic situation—again as Chamberlain had assumed—to his ultimate advantage. British intelligence appraisals of the state of Russo-German relations as late as May 1941 reached much the same conclusion, if one somewhat less flattering to Stalin's diplomatic acumen: "Germany would have more to gain by negotiation than war." Churchill also believed that was the way things would play out. On May 20 he observed that a German attack "does not seem to enter into consideration."[69]

Stalin's refusal to countenance British and American warnings of an impending German attack takes on a different aspect in this context. Weren't these warnings part of a clever game to lure the Soviets into war? he would insist to Kremlin aides. Stalin's deep suspicions of British diplomacy were not necessarily Marxist preoccupations. American officials were likewise wary of London's skill at behind-the-scenes manipulations. Assistant Secretary of State Adolf Berle, for example, frequently described the "English view" as conceding that there were only two civilized peoples in the world, English and Americans. And, Berle added, "I am not sure that they let us in, except when they are talking to us."[70]

Berle's Anglophobia was well known in Washington, but even those who wished to be seduced by Britain always remained vigilant that the final outcome of the affair not leave London in control of postwar planning. From the nineteenth-century "great game" that Russia and Britain played out in the Middle East and Central Asia, to these maneuverings on the brink of the German invasion, the stakes were immense. If he guessed wrong Stalin faced an invasion and the possible destruction of his country; the Americans, if they guessed wrong about the British, would always have another chance. That was a very big difference indeed.

Sir Stafford had come to Moscow describing himself as a

diplomat from the "new" school, but his behavior seemed to reveal its roots in Lord Salisbury's coolly calculated defense of imperial interests. Cripps had made plenty of noise about his political offer, and British newspapers were filled with rumors of German preparations for war. These were understood in Moscow as "plants" to stir up trouble. "Don't you see?" Stalin explained to confidants. "They are trying to frighten us with the Germans and to frighten the Germans with us, setting us one against the other."[71]

The question remains whether Stalin, in his innermost thoughts, dismissed the warnings and intelligence. His actions suggest that he hoped, as had Chamberlain, that a combination of defensive formations and timely concessions would put off the day of reckoning. Thus, for example, he made quite a show of negotiating a nonaggression pact with Japan in April 1941. The pact appeared to demonstrate solidarity with the Axis alliance, but it also protected him against the danger of a two-front war.

Prompted once again by Sir Stafford Cripps, Eden made a new try in the aftermath of the Russo-Japanese pact to find common ground with Maisky. Eden invited the ambassador to join him in a frank discussion of Anglo-Soviet relations. He was absolutely convinced, the foreign secretary began, that Germany intended to attack Russia. Hitler's ambitions were boundless. For that reason Eden wished to see if there was any chance of a rapprochement before the blow fell. Maisky declared that he, too, wanted progress, but on even the smallest things the British had nothing to offer. Eden brushed that aside. If they were to make an effort to improve relations, "it must be on a scale which was worthwhile." Was it true the main stumbling block was the Baltic states?

Maisky said it was. If that obstruction were removed, progress could be made. Very well, if there was to be a concession on the issue, Eden rejoined, there must be a comparable Russian contribution. Maisky accepted this and asked that London formulate its requirements. "He knew that M. Stalin had always held the view that Russian policy must be on a basis of reciprocity."[72]

The next day Eden cabled Cripps in Moscow that he was ready to recognize Soviet absorption of the Baltic states as part of a general rapprochement. But he must have definite evidence of Soviet willingness to cooperate with the British in other areas.[73]

Eden's resolve to begin afresh—on a worthwhile scale—faded almost immediately in the face of near unanimous opposition to any new overture to the Russians among his Foreign Office advisers. Churchill likewise disapproved. He could not follow Sir Stafford Cripps's advice and clear the way with the Americans, Eden said, because the whole initiative remained "hypothetical."[74] Instead of a formulation of British requirements in exchange for recognition of the annexation of the Baltic states, the Russians were left to stew in the "hypothetical."

Then came the sudden news that a top German official, Rudolf Hess, had parachuted into England with a peace offer! Soviet intelligence knew a great deal (and suspected all sorts of other things) about Hess's "fantastic voyage." Some of them were true. He was anxious to bring the war with England to an end. He conveyed information about Hitler's planned attack on Russia, though how vital this information was remains controversial. The question that gnawed at Stalin all through the war was whether Hess had been "lured" to England as part of a complicated plan to make the Germans believe they would have British support in a war with Russia, or, if once there, he unwittingly became part of a propaganda campaign to frighten the Russians with the threat of a separate peace.[75]

Even Sir Stafford Cripps was willing (indeed eager, for it was his suggestion) to exploit the Hess affair to encourage Soviet fears of a separate peace. Eden wanted nothing to do with that ploy, fearing it would backfire and drive the Russians straight into German hands. But London remained strangely silent about the meaning of the Hess mission and the intelligence the Führer's lieutenant had provided.[76] Against this background, it was scarcely surprising that Anglo-Russian relations reached their nadir on the eve of Hitler's attack.

On June 2, 1941, Eden and Maisky resumed their dialogue over the Baltic states. Nothing had really changed since their discussion in mid-April. Eden repeated his certainty that Germany would attack; Maisky "found it very hard to believe that Germany contemplated taking military action against the Soviet. . . . After all, that would be a very big undertaking." Eden believed the ambassador was trying to convince himself, but the discussion quickly turned to the Baltic states. The foreign secretary now said he did not "believe in a policy of appeasement." But he pressed, all the same, for some indication of what the Russians would do if Britain recognized the takeover in the Baltic—what "corresponding concessions" would Moscow offer? Maisky replied that it was up to London to draw up a plan. "It might then be possible to make progress."[77]

Eden and Maisky met once more before the German invasion. The foreign secretary offered the Soviet Union military aid in the event the attack took place. Maisky simply reiterated his earlier points: (1) he did not believe in "the possibility of a German attack"; and (2) the message would be better received in Moscow if it were accompanied by British action demonstrating a desire for "more friendly relations with the Soviet." At that, Eden simply shook his head. We are dealing with a situation, he said, of the utmost urgency.[78]

Observing Eden's fruitless efforts to begin afresh with Maisky, American policymakers were nonetheless worried where all this was leading. Cripps had held back information about the conditional recognition of the Russian annexation of the Baltic states in his original political offer, but it would have taken a very dull diplomatic imagination not to grasp the essentials of the British predicament and the steady erosion of London's opposition to Russian pressure. Sumner Welles thought it high time to talk this over with Lord Halifax. As Hitler prepared to march, the under secretary was lecturing the ambassador on the grave responsibility of holding the moral line in the Baltic. Soviet psychology, Welles affirmed, "recognized only firmness, power and force." It reflected "primitive instincts" devoid of "the restraints of civilization."[79]

On the night of June 21, 1941, meanwhile, a German deserter made his way to the Soviet lines. He was from Berlin, he told his Russian interrogators, a communist laborer. And when he heard the instructions to his unit, he decided to cross over. When Stalin heard of the deserter he ordered him shot forthwith as the purveyor of malicious disinformation—a sentence not carried out only because the attack began at dawn the next morning.[80] At 4:30 in the morning of the 22nd, the military high command met with the Politbureau and Stalin. The Russian dictator's face had gone white; he sat at a table cradling a tobacco-filled pipe. Then Molotov strode in: "The German Government has declared war on us." Stalin sank into his chair, deep in thought. There was a long and pregnant silence. Only when his military chiefs insisted that orders must be given to the army did Stalin respond. But the directive to counterattack was not issued for nearly three hours.[81]

It was Molotov who spoke to the Russian people. "The government appeals to all of you, men and women, citizens of the Soviet Union, to rally as never before around our glorious leader, Comrade Stalin. Our cause is just. Our enemy shall be defeated. Victory will be ours."[82]

Stalin did not break his public silence for nearly two weeks, when he finally addressed the nation. Maisky and Eden, meanwhile, began talking about the terms of Anglo-Russian collaboration. The foreign secretary offered no political plan, no commitment to the restoration of prewar frontiers. On June 30 Eden said he could not discuss wide-ranging political issues, Maisky reported, owing to the "position of the USA and its diehards." The last words between them before the German attack, and almost the first after it began, then, were about postwar spheres of influence.[83]

4

THE ATLANTIC CHARTER

I thought the Atlantic Charter was directed against those people who were trying to establish world dominion. It now looks as if the Atlantic Charter was directed against the U.S.S.R.

Joseph Stalin to Anthony Eden,
December 1941[1]

ANTHONY EDEN WAS first to hear the good news. He had been summoned to Chequers, the prime minister's country home, on the weekend that began Saturday, June 21, 1941. Discussion centered on the Russo-German negotiations. They were likely to end in a new pact, an abject surrender to Berlin's stepped-up demands, or a lightning German military assault. Those present agreed that Russia probably could not last more than a few weeks in the event of an attack. At half-past seven the next morning, the prime minister's valet appeared at Eden's bedroom door holding a silver salver on which rested a large cigar: "The Prime Minister's compliments and the German armies have invaded Russia."[2]

According to various accounts, Churchill spent that Sunday working on a message he would deliver promising aid to the Russians. One potential "great risk"—the American reaction—turned out to be no risk at all, Lord "Max" Beaverbrook

recalled, because Ambassador James G. Winant had also come
to Chequers that weekend. And he brought with him Roosevelt's assurances to back the prime minister to the hilt if he
announced such a plan.[3]

Churchill was nevertheless torn by conflicting emotions.
Those present recall he was restless, moving back and forth
from the garden to his study. At lunch he castigated the
Russians as "barbarians," further declaring that "not even the
slenderest thread connected Communism to the very basest
type of humanity." After dinner, however, the P.M.'s view had
turned right around: the Russians were "innocent peasants
[who] were being slaughtered; and we should forget about
Soviet systems or the Comintern and extend our hand to fellow
human beings in distress."[4] So it would go throughout the war.

Later that evening he broadcast a message over the British
Broadcasting Company:

> No one has been a more consistent opponent of Communism
> than I have over the last twenty-five years. I will unsay no word
> that I have spoken about it. But all this fades away before the
> spectacle which is now unfolding. The past, with its crimes, its
> follies, and its tragedies, flashes away.[5]

Washington did not much care what Churchill said for or
against the Soviets during tabletalk at Chequers or over the
BBC; it did care a great deal about what he might agree with
Stalin. On the day before the German attack, the State Department's Division of European Affairs set forth the position with
characteristic firmness:

> We should steadfastly adhere to the line that the fact that the
> Soviet Union is fighting Germany does not mean that it is
> defending, struggling for, or adhering to, the principles in
> international relations which we are supporting.[6]

Secretary of War Henry L. Stimson believed that Germany's
attack changed everything about the war. Hitler's "mistake"
offered the United States its best-ever opportunity to achieve
the world leadership that had eluded Wilson's generation. For

the immediate future, he wrote Roosevelt on June 23, it relieved fears that America might be dragged into major operations prematurely. For "the past thirty hours" Stimson had done little else, he continued, but reflect upon the significance of Germany's decision. His advisers estimated it would take Hitler from one to three months to "beat" Russia. During that respite, America could put itself in a position to win the battle of the North Atlantic, "while at the same time your leadership is assured of success as fully as any future program can well be made."

> By getting into this war with Russia Germany has much relieved our anxiety, provided we act promptly and get the initial dangers over before Germany gets her legs disentangled from the Russian mire.[7]

Like Roosevelt's other advisers, however, Stimson was concerned about political commitments to the Soviet Union, and about increased danger from American communists as a result of the president's decision to consider Russia at least a semially.[8] On July 14, two days after the signing of the first Russo-British agreement, Roosevelt warned the prime minister that it was "much too early for any of us to make any commitments" regarding the peace. In a remarkable sentence for a nation still at peace, the president added that such commitments were to be avoided "for the very good reason that both Britain and the United States want assurance of future peace by disarming all troublemakers...." And then this:

> I am inclined to think that an overall statement on your part would be useful at this time, making it clear that no post war peace commitments as to territories, populations or economies have been given. I could then back up your statement in very strong terms.[9]

In these first hours and days after the Germans launched their *Barbarossa* assault on the Soviet Union, Churchill was not worried that he could be coerced or cajoled into such a compromised situation. As Eden made clear to Ambassador Maisky, the British political offer had narrowed down to one promise: no separate peace with Hitler. "It follows therefore that we shall give whatever help we can to Russia and the Russian people."

Maisky's concerns had also narrowed. What kind of help for the Russian people could Moscow expect? Was it to be something beyond Royal Air Force activity over France? The German onslaught had already driven far into Russian-annexed Poland and the Baltic states. Was there no other intervention Britain could undertake, such as "attempting any form of landing on any part of the German occupied coasts now that a large part of the German Air Force was away in the East?"[10]

As Maisky continued pressing Eden for a "land" operation—if only for its psychological effect—Stalin sent a message requesting a formal treaty with England. The war cabinet agreed that the request should be answered with a proposal for an "agreed declaration" on war policy. This declaration should simply set forth a joint statement following what the prime minister had said in his BBC broadcast: all forms of military assistance and no separate peace.[11]

Churchill had wanted to go even further, however, and try to exploit Russian fears of a separate peace with an accompanying explanatory note in this vein:

> You [Stalin] will of course understand that at the victorious Peace Conference in which the United States will certainly be a leading party, our line would be that territorial frontiers will have to be settled in accordance with the wishes of the people who live there and on general ethnographical lines, and secondly that these units, when established, must be free to choose their own form of government and system of life, so long as they do not interfere with the similar rights of neighboring peoples.[12]

Eden dissuaded the prime minister from making this statement that would not only refuse recognition of the Baltic states' annexation and the Russian gains elsewhere but risk the main purpose of the response, a mutual no-separate-peace pledge. The foreign secretary feared that even a joint declaration might not be enough to keep Russia in the war, however, and asked

Ambassador Winant what he thought about an alternative to a joint declaration that was not yet a treaty of mutual assistance. Considering public opinion in his own country, said Winant, it was best not to call the Anglo-Soviet pact a "treaty." "A treaty had a specially serious sound in the United States," he explained, "in view of the constitutional provision which insisted on any treaty made by the United States being approved by two-thirds of the Senate."[13]

It also had a specially serious sound of permanence, and closeness. Harry Hopkins arrived in London a few days later, unaware of Churchill's strong opposition to a bargain with Russia. Hopkins was to make preparations for the first Roosevelt-Churchill meeting of World War II, to be held a month later off the coast of Newfoundland. Roosevelt's instructions to his aide put at the top of the list a cautionary note: "Economic or territorial deals—NO."[14]

Churchill's response to Hopkins's various questions about military and political strategy circumvented the main issues, establishing a precedent that would characterize British diplomacy throughout the war. This was hardly unexpected. As the only member of the future Grand Alliance with a great stake in the status quo ante, the British had to "get by by their wits" and to maneuver as best they could between the would-be heirs to the Pax Britannica.[15]

When FDR's special emissary hinted at fears the British were considering "appeasing" the Russians, for example, the prime minister told Hopkins dismissively that he was not interested in the peace; if Hopkins felt unduly concerned about British diplomacy, he should see Anthony Eden to be reassured. The prime minister, having climbed down from his original intention of putting Stalin on notice, no doubt wanted the foreign secretary to handle this task as well. Hopkins probably was not unhappy with this answer. It was not for him to challenge the prime minister, even with Roosevelt's warrant in his pocket. Besides, the primary subject for consideration was how best to aid the British to resist the likely German onslaught once the Russians were defeated. For that matter, Roosevelt's message could be put in plainer words to the foreign secretary than one would use with Churchill, and thereby given more emphasis. And as Eden recorded their meeting in his diary, that is exactly what took place. Roosevelt "was most eager," the president's representative began, that there be no British commitments to postwar frontiers in Europe. The United States did not wish to come into the war only to find out later that "we had all kinds of engagements of which they had never been told."

Eden then explained the British position. "I was eager to keep my hands free as anybody," he said. But he also recorded in his diary what he was thinking as he gave this less (a good deal less) than binding pledge. "The spectacle of an American President talking at large on European frontiers chilled me with Wilsonian memories."[16]

Wilsonian memories also chilled American policymakers, but for very different reasons. The debacle of the Treaty of Versailles in the United States Senate, when Wilson and his loyal followers found themselves unable to disentangle the League of Nations from the "secret treaties" made by the Allies in World War I, had haunted everyone connected with the making of foreign policy—and especially the Democrats—ever since. Only the opening of the Kremlin archives by the Bolsheviks finally exposed the complete network of treaties between the Allies (Britain, France, and tsarist Russia) that parceled out the spoils of the Ottoman Empire to the victors.

Roosevelt needed no warnings not to allow himself to be caught up in a new secret treaties "scandal." But it was not only fears of this "isolationist" power to block postwar political plans that worried policymakers. Americans had already concluded that British appeasement, dating from their efforts to come to terms with Germany, had to do with both protecting the empire and, worst of all, solving their economic and trade problems in bilateralism. It all went together: appeasement, colonialism, economic blocs.

The government-to-government economic negotiations with Germany, while they had failed to seduce Hitler, exemplified this tendency toward bilateralism, as did Sir Stafford Cripps's proposals for barter exchanges with Russia. Germany might be defeated, but Secretary of State Cordell Hull feared that if the United States was unable to tie down a firm commitment to multilateralism, "the Hitlerian commercial policy will probably be adopted by Great Britain."[17]

British experts were in Washington discussing terms for economic talks under the requirements of the Lend-Lease Act at the same time Hopkins was asking pointed questions in London about political arrangements with Russia. In neither capital were American policymakers reassured that their British interlocutors were fully committed to the U.S. view of the postwar world. Lord Keynes's reluctance to commit Britain to multilateralism—which he described at one point as "the clutch of the dead, or at least moribund, hand" of the past—was particularly discouraging to State Department negotiators. They fully agreed with Hull that the alternative to the recipro-cal trade agreements program and multilateralism was more New Deal, more regulation, and, eventually, something like socialism.[18]

Roosevelt's concern about political commitments to the Rus-sians had led him, as already noted, to ask Churchill for a public statement that no such thing was contemplated. He had assured the prime minister there was "no hurry" about this, but then he subjected him to considerable prodding. Although the text of the Anglo-Russian pact of July 12, 1941, pledging mutual assistance, contained no secret protocol, American con-cern lingered. It traveled with Roosevelt and his advisers in early August on the cruiser *Augusta* to Argentia, off Newfound-land, where the *Prince of Wales*, with the prime minister and Harry Hopkins on board, came to meet the American party. Hopkins had made a speedy trip to Moscow from London and back again in time to join Churchill for the trip across the Atlantic. He had come away from a meeting with Stalin convinced that the Soviet Union would not be overwhelmed by Germany and forced to sue for an early peace. Ultimately, however, he reported to Roosevelt, Russian survival (and vic-tory in the war) depended upon Western aid. Once a stable eastern front had been established, Hopkins had told Stalin, a large-scale aid program could be discussed under the general provisions of the Land-Lease Act. Roosevelt thus went into his meeting with Churchill believing that he held in his hands the destiny of both Russia and Great Britain.[19]

Under Secretary Welles lost no time in "reminding" his British counterpart, Sir Alexander Cadogan, that it had been six weeks since Roosevelt had requested a public statement from Churchill affirming that no postwar commitments had been made—six weeks and no reply.[20] Lord Salisbury might have taken umbrage at such arm-twisting, but it was not the 1890s, it was 1941, the year Churchill would call the hinge of fate. Cadogan offered to produce the texts of all current British agreements, assuring Welles there was nothing in any of them to cause concern. The American said he was "heartened" by this information and passed on to another issue. What were the British going to do about getting rid of imperial preference? "I did not see how we could possibly undertake divergent policies" on postwar economic questions, concluded Welles, having in mind Keynes's disparaging words about Cordell Hull's program for returning the world to the sane principles of liberalism in international trade.[21]

Out of this first summit meeting of the war came an Anglo-American declaration of war aims known as the Atlantic Charter. Roosevelt was less concerned about getting specific pledges from the prime minister than he was to get the British "on record" before America came into the war. Neither Churchill nor Roosevelt wished to be pinned down to a particular definition of what the Atlantic Charter actually meant; both were satisfied they could defend the declaration at home.[22]

Looking back after the war, Churchill took great pleasure in pointing out to readers of his memoirs that he, not Roosevelt, had produced the first draft of what became famous as the Atlantic Charter. "Considering all the tales of my reactionary, Old-World outlook, and the pain this is said to have caused the President, I am glad it should be on record that the substance and spirit of what came to be called the 'Atlantic Charter' was in its first draft a British production cast in my own words."[23]

After several language changes, this first Allied statement of war aims contained eight "common principles" which summed up "their hopes for a better future for the world." Point Three declared their commitment to "respect the right of all peoples to choose the form of government under which they will live; and . . . [their] wish to see sovereign rights and self-government restored to those who have been forcibly denied them."

As it turned out, the most difficult discussions at the Argentia meeting centered on American efforts to persuade the British to agree to Point Four of the proposed declaration. In it both governments were to agree to help all states enjoy equal access to trade and raw materials. Here Keynes was pitted against Hull, the imperial preference system against the reciprocal trade agreements act, the British past against America's tomorrow. Roosevelt checked Welles from pressing too hard when Churchill pleaded he could not sign such a statement without including the qualifying words "with due respect for their existing obligations." That would have to do for the moment. Roosevelt felt he had said enough to make it clear there must be a meeting of the minds on this question somewhere down the line.[24]

At the end Sir Alec Cadogan finally asked Welles if the Atlantic Charter that Roosevelt and Churchill initialed was enough to satisfy the Americans that no commitments had been made, or did they still wish a separate public statement? "In view of the Eight Point Declaration," replied the under secretary, "that would be entirely superfluous and he was sure that the President would not wish for anything of the sort."[25]

The charter served British purposes, Churchill would claim, by insuring an American declaration of war—"after the joint declaration, America could not honorably stay out."[26] But Churchill hoped to give honor some help at the conference. Russia must be kept in the war, he said. A separate peace on the eastern front at any stage would spell disaster. He must caution Roosevelt, said the prime minister, that "he would not answer for the consequences if Russia was compelled to sue for

100 · *Spheres of Influence*

peace and, say, by the Spring of next year, hope died in Britain that the United States were coming into the war."

The president "had taken this very well," Churchill reported to the war cabinet, "and had made it clear that he would look for an 'incident' which would justify him in opening hostilities." Whether Churchill accurately reported FDR's words in this instance is of less interest to us than the context, and this early concern about a separate peace in the east. It is especially significant that the threat was employed in this instance by the British prime minister in hopes of increasing his leverage with Roosevelt, a complicated beginning for World War II diplomacy.[27]

With so much at stake, no doubt Brest-Litovsk and Russian withdrawal from World War I were on Churchill's mind. All the more so because his "peripheral" strategy would depend upon a tricky balance on the eastern front. As Churchill had outlined it before the Atlantic Conference, and would do so again and again, the peripheral strategy rested upon time-honored British methods of naval blockade, supplemented now by air bombardment.

In themselves these steps might bring about a German collapse, he suggested to Roosevelt. "But plans ought also to be made for coming to the aid of the conquered populations by landing armies of liberation when opportunity is ripe." This projection of a second front, or a series of small second fronts, to aid local uprisings "when opportunity is ripe" appealed very little to American military planners. Stimson once derided Churchill's strategic planning as limited to stopping up rat holes. Even less did the Americans fancy the correlative North African campaigns that the prime minister kept urging on Roosevelt.[28]

Churchill's and Roosevelt's "letter" to Stalin from the Atlantic Conference promised the Russian leader "the very maximum of supplies that you most urgently need." It called for a conference to discuss "long-term policy" and sought to establish a connection between distribution of Western aid and strategic planning. "The war goes on upon many fronts, and before it is over there may be yet further fighting fronts that will be developed."[29]

Churchill asserted later that he and Roosevelt drafted this message together; but the nicely ambiguous language about "yet further fighting fronts" suggests the prime minister's deft hand and his delicate sensitivity to the issue of "balance" in wartime diplomacy. If the eastern front were to be maintained, he imagined, it would require a balanced effort by the West, a skillful combination of reassurance and material aid. As long as America was not in the war, little could be done to wrest the strategic initiative from Churchill, nor to counter his head start in establishing relations with the new ally, Stalin's Russia, nor, finally, to keep him from pouring ideas into Roosevelt's ear.[30]

The United States had no corresponding relationship with Stalin, a deficiency Roosevelt would try to remedy later in the war. However dubiously Americans regarded British military planning, there was no framework for Soviet-American relations. In his first press conference after returning from Argentia, Roosevelt said the meeting had been in the works since the previous February, that it was "primarily an exchange of views," and that no thought had been given to implementation of the charter's eight points. Did he and the prime minister reach a complete understanding on all aspects of the world situation, including the Far East? Well, came the response, they discussed all areas of the world. One reporter was quick to pursue the possible significance of Roosevelt's purposeful ambiguity:

PRESS: Mr. President, is Russia bound to subscribe to this eight point program?

THE PRESIDENT: No.

PRESS: Will she be?

THE PRESIDENT: Nobody ever suggested it until you did.[31]

This was a slight bending of the truth, to be sure, but the Soviets had not been asked to join in the drafting of the charter, either. When, despite FDR's remarks, it was presented to them by the British as a *fait accompli*, Ambassador Maisky reacted predictably. It seemed, he complained to Foreign Secretary Eden, "as if England and the USA imagine themselves as almighty God called upon to judge the rest of the sinful world, including my country. You cannot strengthen the alliance on such a basis."[32]

Persistent British efforts to secure Soviet adherence to the charter raised the question of "blackmail" in Moscow. Were the Americans and British holding back on deliveries of supplies to force acceptance? Molotov thought there might be some such design, and he informed Maisky that the Soviet Union had not been consulted in advance about the declaration. "Our comrades are very much irritated that plans are afoot to rivet the USSR to the chariot of other countries."[33]

It also annoyed the Russians that the British wanted a special signing ceremony to be attended by representatives of the exile governments as well. "The British and Americans," wrote a deputy foreign minister, "would like to reduce us to the status of governments in exile in London and Dominions of the United Kingdom."[34] The Russians had not quite got it right. Churchill wanted to exclude the empire from the Atlantic Charter, but he also wished to push Russia into line with the exile governments, to make them equal on a political basis. Eventually his effort to maintain two separate worlds—the world of the English-speaking peoples and the empire, and the world of the Atlantic Charter—came unstuck. After returning home from Argentia, the prime minister had responded to questions about his dichotomy by declaring that the progressive evolution of the empire and commonwealth were quite separate from the problems of nations deprived of freedom by the Germans. But the desire to check Russian expansionism meant that he could not restrict the rule of the Atlantic Charter to Europe. The Labor party leader and deputy prime minister, Clement Attlee, told an audience of West African students in London that the charter applied to "all the races of mankind." The prime minister's protestations that he and the president had confined their promises to the "national life of the states and nations now under the Nazi yoke" only called attention to the issue of war aims.[35]

Still holding to the view that the world could be divided into spheres *under* and *not under* the rule of the Atlantic Charter, British policymakers continued to press the Soviets to sign the Anglo-American declaration. Finally the Russians agreed. Maisky brought with him a lengthy statement to be read at the Allied conference proclaiming the Soviet Union's agreement, adding a caveat that included this key paragraph:

> Considering that the practical application of these principles will necessarily adapt itself to the circumstances, needs and historic peculiarities of particular countries, the Soviet Government can state that a consistent application of these principles will secure the most energetic support on the part of the Government and peoples of the Soviet Union.[36]

Several signals emerge here, especially the phrases "consistent application" and "most energetic support." They clearly indicated not only that the Russians reserved the right to adapt the charter to their surrounding "circumstances," like Churchill, but also that their observance of the Anglo-American rules depended upon the West's actions in its own sphere.

Maisky's statement also placed heavy emphasis upon the need to "bring about the speediest and most decisive defeat of the aggressor."

> For the full accomplishment of that task they must assemble and devote all their strength and resources, and determine the most effective ways and means of reaching their goal.

These were coded phrases referring to the trilateral conference Hopkins had promised during his visit to Moscow in July, just before the Roosevelt-Churchill summit. While the conference had not been postponed to force Soviet adherence to the Atlantic Charter, Lord Beaverbrook, who headed the British delegation to the Lend-Lease talks in Moscow at the end of September, found Stalin in a suspicious mood. Beaverbrook's efforts to ease those feelings prompted some rueful reminders that caused Stalin to smile but cut to the bone. Amidst pointed discussion about either a second front or British troops in Russia, Beaverbrook asked Stalin if he really thought an Allied invasion of France was possible. He would leave that to Churchill's judgment, Stalin replied, but why not send troops to Archangel or the Ukraine? Churchill was once for sending an army to Archangel, Beaverbrook quipped. This produced some "laughing comments" about the "incidents of the previous war."[37]

This reference to the British intervention in Russia in 1918 went down lightly, but Stalin then asked about peace objectives in this war. Both Beaverbrook and his American conegotiator, Averell Harriman, replied that the Atlantic Charter's eight points were a peace program. Beaverbrook argued that Stalin would win many friends in America by signing the charter, because those goals were important to American public opinion. Here was an opportunity for Stalin to use the American press to build a better understanding of Russia. Roosevelt, added Harriman, wanted more "information" to come from the Soviet government, because many groups in America "had strong prejudices against the Soviets."[38]

Did he have any other ideas? Harriman then asked. Stalin looked at Beaverbrook. "Are the Eight Points going to satisfy you?" Churchill's normally loquacious friend seemed bemused by the question. Harriman stepped in to seize the initiative. Did Stalin have something specific in mind? he asked. Stalin did indeed have something in mind: "What about getting the Germans to pay for the damage?" Beaverbrook dodged an answer: "We must win the war first."[39]

At the next meeting Harriman produced lists of materiel that the United States could make available to the Soviet Union under Lend-Lease. After they went through the lists, the American asked Stalin if he did not wish to cable Roosevelt routinely, as Churchill had done for some time. As many issues would arise in the future, it was important to develop a "close interchange of thoughts between the three of them." Beaverbrook suggested that Stalin ask Churchill to come to Moscow. Encouraged by this Anglo-American display, the Soviet leader pressed his case about Finland's behavior. Its troops were now in Russia, he claimed, fighting Germany's war. He also asked if a treaty, an alliance not only for war but for peace, could not be signed between Russia and England?[40]

Harriman was quite pleased with all of this. "I left feeling that he had been frank with us and if we came through as had been promised and if personal relations were retained with Stalin, the suspicion that has existed between the Soviet Government and our two governments might well be eradicated."

To Stalin's several messages over the late summer and fall of 1941, demanding specifics to go with what had been promised since the August and September meetings about long-range planning, Churchill returned messages praising the heroism of Soviet fighting forces. These did little to assuage the Russian leader or to soften the language of his increasingly minatory "requests" for the opening of a western front.

Churchill's basic argument was that the forces simply were not available, nor the means to get them to France, to accomplish anything on the scale Stalin envisioned. A premature assault on the heavily fortified French coast would instead end in a major disaster, postponing victory for months if not years. In private (and sometimes to Ambassador Maisky) the prime minister displayed considerable anger that Stalin thought he had any business to remonstrate with the British over any front at all.

Only four months ago, he told Maisky on one occasion in early September, His Majesty's Government did not know which way Russia would jump. Indeed, it was thought likely Stalin would choose Hitler again. "Even then we felt sure we should win in the end. We never thought our survival was dependent on your action either way. Whatever happens, and whatever you do, you of all people have no right to make reproaches to us."[41]

References to the 1939 Nazi-Soviet pact always brought Maisky's rejoinder, "What about Munich?" Churchill was perfectly willing to talk about Munich, however, and to lay that noxious wreath on poor Neville Chamberlain's grave. (Chamberlain had died in November 1940, six months after leaving office.) He was not willing, on the other hand, no matter what Stalin's messages implied about John Bull's weak stomach or a separate peace in the east, to initiate Anglo-Soviet high-level military consultations.

Neither Ambassador Sir Stafford Cripps nor the British military attaché, General Noel Mason-Macfarlane, was given permission to return to London to present the case for greater consultation and coordination with Russia. Churchill personally dictated the denial of Mason-Macfarlane's request, a piece of farrago about how the general could not leave his post during the critical days of the battle for Moscow. Stalin would much rather have him in London for all that Mason-Macfarlane could contribute peering through field glasses at the German advance.

And the general agreed, cabling his superiors that the British could not hope to beat the Germans by "fighting separate wars." It was illogical, he went on, to try to coordinate Lend-Lease supplies if the United States was to be asked to deal with two fronts "fighting uncoordinated wars."[42]

The increasingly acrimonious Stalin-Churchill correspondence continued into the fall. As German armies pressed closer to Moscow and southward toward the industrially vital Donets Basin and the Caucasus regions, there seemed to be no clear response to the various Russian proposals. "I can't understand what Stalin wants," Churchill complained.[43] The letters that passed between London and Moscow during this period could hardly disguise the troubling reality of mutual suspicion. War or no war, Anglo-Soviet relations had not grown much closer than the arm's-length military discussions of the summer of 1939. What Stalin wanted, it was clear enough to others, was satisfaction that London did not intend to keep matters in play on the eastern front, militarily and politically, so as to exploit the situation at an opportune moment. For what were the promises made about no separate peace? To allow Russia and

Germany to exhaust themselves? To deprive the Soviet Union of its gains from the Nazi-Soviet pact?

While in Moscow, Harriman had another special assignment from Roosevelt. He was to put himself in touch with representatives of the Polish army that was being trained in Russian territory. His original instructions on this point suggested that, as the exile government of Poland had already been declared eligible for Lend-Lease (and Russia actually had not), he should deal directly with the Poles. The second reason for opening this issue was fraught with political complications for the future:

> It is believed that it would be in conformity with our policy of maintaining so far as possible Polish prestige and influence in Eastern Europe for us to deal direct with the Poles with respect to the supplying of the Polish forces in Russia since such direct negotiations would be likely to enhance the prestige and stress the individuality of those forces now as well as in the future.[44]

Harriman's specific instructions were remanded two days later by Harry Hopkins, but both Harriman and Beaverbrook discussed the arming of the Poles with Foreign Minister Molotov, who surprisingly offered no objections to Anglo-American efforts.[45]

All the maneuvering about the Atlantic Charter, the reluctance of the British to talk about opening a second front, and then Churchill's refusal to declare war on Germany's allies, brought a crisis in the Stalin-Churchill correspondence in early November. Both Maisky and Eden became concerned about a possible break. Stalin had asked for twenty to thirty divisions to be sent to Russia to join the fight on the eastern front, while Maisky raised several times on his own the question of a British declaration of war on Germany's allies, Finland, Hungary, and Rumania. At a time when it was not possible to give more material aid, it was all the more important, he said, to meet Moscow's political wishes. "'*Please* do it,' the Ambassador said."[46]

There had been no clear response from London on either of these issues. Then, in early November Stalin received a letter from the prime minister, phrased in almost patronizing terms. Did the Russian leader think it "really good business" for Great Britain to declare war on Germany's allies? After all, it might give the impression that "Hitler were the head of a European Grand Alliance solidly against us." As for British military plans, Churchill could say no more than "rest assured that we are not going to be idle."[47]

Eden showed the Churchill message to Ambassador Maisky shortly after it had been dispatched to Moscow. What if his government, after receiving the cable, still asked for a declaration of war on the three pro-German countries, Maisky asked. The foreign secretary indicated that if Stalin regarded the question as "one of major importance," the war cabinet would make every effort to meet him. It was a question of emphasis.[48]

Stalin answered Churchill's message within twenty-four hours of receiving it, indicating what he thought was important.

> First, there is no definite understanding between our two countries concerning war aims and plans for the post-war organization of peace; secondly, there is no treaty between the U.S.S.R. and Great Britain on mutual military aid against Hitler. Until understanding is reached on these two main points, not only will there be no clarity in Anglo-Soviet relations, but, if we are to speak frankly, there will be no mutual trust.[49]

The situation with regard to Germany's allies had become "intolerable" for the Soviet Union; moreover, Stalin was upset that the United States had been consulted and that the question had been broadcast in the press. The same day Stalin sent this message, he delivered a broadcast of his own, a radio message on the anniversary of the Bolshevik Revolution. In it he claimed the Red Army's setbacks were the result of the West's failure to come to Russia's aid.[50]

Maisky and Eden were present as Churchill read Stalin's letter, his face going red, his hand opening and closing in a convulsive gesture. There followed, as the prime minister told the cabinet, "some frank speaking." If Russia had let us know they were coming into the war on our side, Churchill began, things might have been different. As for the question of a postwar settlement, His Majesty's Government could not go beyond the Atlantic Charter.[51]

Once Maisky and Eden calmed the prime minister, it was decided to send Eden to Moscow. The foreign secretary knew, he told the cabinet, of Russian fears that the United States and Britain planned to "get together" to settle the peace between them. He wanted to remove those suspicions. When Eden and Maisky then met privately to clear the air, Eden complained about the tone of Stalin's letter and the apparent attempts being made to influence British public opinion against the war cabinet. The Soviet ambassador admitted that the tone of the letter was unfortunate. But Stalin's proposals, he said, were quite reasonable requests. (He might have added that Eden himself had implied that Stalin make known those questions of great importance to him.) The tone could be explained, moreover, by Russian suspicions about those in the British government before the war who had advocated giving Germany a free hand in the east. "As a result when, maybe for very good reasons, we did not form a second front, these suspicions were to a certain extent revived. This was why, as he had previously explained to me, the presence of British soldiers in Russia was of such great political importance, quite apart from their military value."[52]

Maisky also presented Eden with a mollifying verbal message from Stalin, disclaiming any intent to offend the British government. He had raised important questions, Stalin asked his ambassador to say, and he did not wish to complicate the answers by causing personal difficulties. He was particularly upset about the Finnish business because he had been greatly hurt by the way it had been handled in London, putting the Soviet Union in a humiliating position before the world. In spite of his hurt feelings, the message ended, he still had only one object in mind: to reach an agreement on mutual aid and the postwar organization of the peace.[53]

Maisky accompanied the foreign secretary to Moscow on this most difficult diplomatic mission. As they left London by train Maisky sat staring out the window, pondering their likely reception in the Russian capital, while the villages and green fields chased after one another, an endless wallpaper pattern. Then something caught his attention; something was different. At each of the stations they rushed by was a great commotion, people gesticulating and hurrying about, apparently arguing hotly.

"We could not understand what was the matter," he wrote later. Eden ordered the train stopped at the next station, and an aide came back with the shocking answer: Japan had attacked the United States.[54] The foreign secretary was not sure whether he should go on to Moscow, but Maisky told him his mission was more important than ever. Churchill, already preparing to go to Washington, merely wished him Godspeed. But everything had been altered, as both Maisky and Churchill understood. The ambassador was concerned—and these fears were confirmed when they reached Moscow—that Stalin did not fully comprehend the meaning of the attack on Pearl Harbor.

Efforts to force an "either...or" choice on Eden and His Majesty's Government would surely fail now, Maisky knew. The Americans were certain to oppose any political agreement that involved postwar frontiers; and now it was Roosevelt's accent one must listen for in the voices speaking for the West. Upsetting the president would not be in Russia's best interests.[55] Such energies were better spent working through the Americans for an early second front instead of Tory-baiting Eden and Churchill.

The foreign secretary's own agenda for the Kremlin conversations had been worked out well in advance of Pearl Harbor. Foreign Office officials conceded that the Atlantic Charter had made the Russians suspicious of an Anglo-American bloc, but it was still necessary to say to Stalin that His Majesty's Government could not now recognize Russian incorporation of the Baltic states. Eden also planned to postpone any discussion of reparations from Germany, offering instead promises of British aid for postwar Russian reconstruction. Also on the foreign secretary's list of topics was a vague plan for "confederation" of the weaker Central European states, starting with a Czech-Polish agreement that might also eventually include the Balkan states.[56]

"Unless we are able ourselves to propound some acceptable solution for the Balkan peoples," read a Foreign Office memorandum Eden brought with him to Moscow, "there is a danger that the Soviet Government will succeed in gaining a preponderant influence in the Balkans through the medium of Pan-Slav propaganda."[57] Eden's chief aide, Sir Alexander Cadogan, called this plan the "Volga Charter."[58] When Eden presented the project to the war cabinet, he wanted it specific enough to exorcise Stalin's suspicion that we were "prepared to make peace with a Germany controlled by the Army, if they were going to overthrow the [Nazi] Party." Churchill demurred. That was going too far. How was one to know what government would be in charge when war ended?[59]

Taken as a whole, Eden's program for the Moscow talks was not very substantive, filled as it was with speculation and mental hedges like that Churchill put about future dealings with a post-Hitler Germany. No doubt it had occurred to others in the Foreign Office and cabinet that it would be foolish to bind themselves to deal only with a post-Hitler government acceptable to the Soviets. At Moscow, moreover, Eden would not really be alone, for after Pearl Harbor the United States had instantly become a major factor in all policy calculations.

"Don't let Churchill get you into any more specific engagements than those in the Atlantic Charter," William C. Bullitt warned President Roosevelt in a handwritten note on December 5, 1941. The former ambassador to Russia and France, now an adamant opponent of the Soviets, cautioned against having anything to do with Old World diplomacy. "Try to keep him [the prime minister] from engaging himself vis-à-vis Russia.

The treaties—if made—will be as difficult for you to handle as the secret treaties were for Wilson."[60]

This was not new advice. Neither was it an isolated opinion. Secretary of State Cordell Hull sent a cable to Ambassador Winant in London that same day, two days before the Japanese attacked Pearl Harbor. Roosevelt had personally approved such a warning to Foreign Secretary Anthony Eden, en route to Moscow, not to agree to any deal. Russia would receive equal treatment at the peace conference, no more. The Atlantic Charter delineated U.S. attitudes and policies toward the post-war world, Hull said, and it would be "unfortunate" if "any of the three governments, now on common ground in the Atlantic Charter, [were] to express any willingness to enter into specific commitments regarding specific terms of the postwar settlement. . . . Above all there must be no secret accords."[61]

Stalin nevertheless opened the Kremlin talks on December 16, 1941, shortly after 7 p.m., with a bold proposal for what amounted to an Anglo-Russian diarchy to rule postwar Europe. Far from wishing to chase the British back across the channel after the defeat of Germany, Stalin projected a map of Europe that saw them firmly ensconced in military bases in France and Holland. Russia would have similar fortifications in Finland. As Stalin spoke, boundaries moved and blank spaces on the map filled in: British naval bases appeared on the coasts of Norway and Denmark; Russian military and naval bases materialized inside an enlarged Rumania. From east to west, north and south, Great Britain and Russia ruled benevolently over Central Europe.

> It will be necessary to have some military force for this purpose and I think it is desirable that there should be a military alliance between the democratic countries which would be organized under a council of some sort and it will have an international military force at its disposal. If certain of the countries of Europe wish to federate, then the Soviet Union will have no objection to such a course.[62]

Looking around, Eden must have wondered if he was in the right capital. Was Stalin serious about this breathtaking proposal? Eden would ponder the question on his return trip, when he was able to reach some tentative conclusions. Meanwhile, he felt it necessary to slow things down a bit. Stalin was running ahead, far ahead. His proposed treaties, Eden responded, cut across British obligations to the United States under the Atlantic Charter.

"I want to be quite frank about this matter," Eden advised. "Even before Russia was attacked Mr. Roosevelt sent a message to us asking us not to enter into any secret arrangements as to the post-war reorganization of Europe without first consulting him." To the war cabinet the foreign secretary reported that Stalin had been uninterested in further joint declarations. He wanted immediate recognition of his territorial claims in Finland, the Baltic states, and Rumania. He would concede only that the Polish frontier could be left open until later. "His desire was to establish that our war aims were identical as then our alliance would be stronger. If our war aims were different then there was no true alliance." What was he to say to all this? Eden asked the war cabinet.[63]

A quick answer came back: "As you will remember, Sir A. Cadogan assured Mr. Sumner Welles at the Atlantic Meeting that H. M. Government had undertaken no secret commitments which would tie their hands in the post-war settlement." That did not mean, of course, that Britain would necessarily oppose Russian demands at the peace conference.[64] But it did not mean either that Churchill planned to approve them. Now, the war cabinet's message implied, the United States would weigh in on London's side to check Soviet ambitions.

What was the Atlantic Charter, Stalin mused. The difference between mathematics and algebra could be defined as the difference between declarations such as the Atlantic Charter and treaties. "A declaration I regard as algebra, but an agreement as practical arithmetic, and I think in the present circumstances, when Hitler is boasting to everyone of all the treaties he has managed to obtain, it would be wiser to have treaties between the two countries, and our documents are in that form."[65]

Yes, Eden managed to say, but such sweeping proposals had to be considered not only by the United States but also by the dominions... and so on. His protests trailed off. Very well, said Stalin, inform the Americans. Perhaps it would be possible to do it by an exchange of notes? Oh no, said Eden, "I think it would be much wiser for us to tell them about it." Stalin was undaunted: "I would be very glad if the United States would participate."

"I doubt whether they would do that," Eden rejoined, not really knowing what to make of all he had heard, or whether he really wished the Americans would or would not "participate." He was on the defensive, his agenda totally absorbed into Stalin's vast schemes. If this was what Stalin wanted, as Churchill had asked, what sort of response could ever be made? Not only did Stalin continue to press the proposed treaties on Eden, he also wished to "underline" his desire "to come to an agreement with you on this so as to have a united front on these problems."

"Why does the restoration of our frontiers come into conflict with the Atlantic Charter?" Stalin challenged. Eden, completely on the defensive, replied weakly, "I never said that it did." At one point, when the discussion became animated, Stalin became upset with Eden's constant pleas that he could not "go back upon my arrangement with President Roosevelt." Stalin burst out, "I thought the Atlantic Charter was directed against those people who were trying to establish world dominion. It now looks as if the Atlantic Charter was directed against the U.S.S.R."[66]

Shaken by his Moscow interviews, and perhaps doubting British ability to launch a second front in Europe soon enough to head off a potential disaster (military or political) on the eastern front, Eden concluded that it was probably better to settle with Stalin now rather than later.[67]

Stalin's final effort to get a quick agreement at Moscow had been a proposal to amend a draft declaration which the British foreign secretary had hoped he might put across when he arrived. It would read, Stalin proposed, as follows with his amendment at the end: "The two contracting parties undertake to work together for the reconstruction of Europe after the War with full regard to the interests of both parties in their security as well as to *the interests of the USSR in the restoration of the frontiers violated by Hitler's aggression*." Stalin said he suggested this form for their treaty in order to remove fears that the Soviet Union intended to bolshevize Europe after the war. "I would like to have these principles clearly stated to remove all apprehension from people's minds on the point."[68]

Perhaps Eden had this intriguing argument in mind when he reported to the war cabinet and to Prime Minister Churchill in Washington that he believed Stalin considered his 1941 frontiers the "acid test" of British goodwill. When Eden reminded his colleagues that "if we won the war, Russian forces would probably penetrate into Germany, and that at a later day she might well want more than her 1941 frontiers," the foreign minister was given the sort of dressing down a subaltern in India might expect for overstepping his prerogatives.[69]

The Baltic states had come into Russian possession, Churchill cabled Eden from Washington on January 8, 1942, as the result of "acts of aggression in shameful collusion with Hitler." To yield to Stalin's demands would "dishonor our cause." What was the talk of an acid test about? Before Hitler's attack the Russians were utterly indifferent to the fate of anyone besides themselves. Finally:

> When you say... that "nothing we and the U.S. can do or say will affect the situation at the end of the war" you are making a very large assumption about the conditions which will then prevail. No one can foresee how the balance of power will lie, or where the winning army will stand. It seems probable however that the United States and the British Empire, far from being exhausted, will be the most powerfully armed and economic bloc the world has ever seen, and that the Soviet Union will need our aid for reconstruction far more than we shall then need theirs.[70]

At the moment Churchill was riding high. His trip to Washington had been a success on almost every front. Who were the Russians to put such demands on the table? And why did Anthony believe that he must end his visit to Moscow with a "flourish of trumpets"? "The Russians have got to go on fighting for their lives anyway," he cabled Clement Attlee, "and are dependent upon us for very large supplies which we have most painfully gathered, and which we shall faithfully deliver."[71]

Churchill's mood was far distant from that on the day he heard of the German attack. With the Americans in, the war looked very different. If the eastern front held, and it now appeared it would, Germany would likely go for North Africa. Roosevelt agreed with Churchill's estimate of German intentions and assured his English friend that he would send troops as soon as possible, "wherever they could be the most helpful."[72] Was this not the best to be expected? The Russian front was holding, and Roosevelt had demonstrated enthusiasm for the peripheral strategy.

But appearances deceived.

5

PILGRIMAGES TO WASHINGTON

The increasing gravity of the war has led me to feel
that the principles of the Atlantic Charter ought not
to be construed so as to deny Russia the frontiers
she occupied when Germany attacked her.
Winston Churchill to Franklin Roosevelt,
March 7, 1942[1]

JAPAN'S ATTACK ON Pearl Harbor had made Anthony
Eden's forced pilgrimage to Moscow less important; all roads
now led to Washington. At least this was Churchill's view.
"The accession of the United States," the prime minister sent
word to Eden en route, "makes amends for all, and with time
and patience will give certain victory."[2] Immediately Churchill
prepared to leave for the United States. Eden's preliminary
reports from the Soviet Union reached him as he neared his
destination. There could be no thinking about granting Stalin's
territorial demands now. To approach Roosevelt with the Russian territorial proposals, Churchill cabled his foreign secretary,
might lead to "lasting trouble on both sides."[3]

How different the setting in wartime Washington, filled with
bustle and confidence, from the gloomy towers of the Kremlin
in the besieged Russian capital! "There is no need to fear,"
Adolf Berle had written in *Fortune* magazine on the eve of

American entrance into the war. "Rather, we shall have the opportunity to create the most brilliant epoch the U.S. has yet seen. It is entirely feasible to make the country at once more prosperous and more free than it has ever been."[4] It bears repeating, however, that while U.S. policymakers looked forward to having vast military and economic resources at their command for the war and the peace to come, they still feared they might be hobbled by "Old World" diplomacy. To put the matter somewhat differently: if Russians worried about being relegated to the role of stagehands while American heroes and their sidekicks played out the final scene of the war drama as a great pageant, Americans were equally full of misgivings that something would go wrong. What if, at the last minute, their collaborators sprung a new ending?

At times these concerns bordered on the obsessive. "Theoretically," Berle wrote in his diary, "Eden made no commitments [in Moscow], but in diplomacy there is always that half light which can ripen into a commitment or no commitments, depending on the understanding of the parties...."[5] Every move Stalin made was suspect; but so must the British be watched closely. Churchill's frequent references to the Atlantic Charter notwithstanding, there were great dangers inherent in his "peripheral" strategy for the war. During one of their first discussions in Washington, the prime minister argued that if the Russians held out, German attentions would turn to North Africa. It was important for psychological reasons, he observed, that this be a joint Anglo-American venture. Roosevelt seemed eager to go along at this stage. He was anxious, he said, to have American land forces go into action "as quickly as possible wherever they could be most helpful...."[6]

American military planners were unimpressed with the "peripheral" strategy. Their concerns coincided with a growing feeling that the British wanted American troops to fight for the restoration of the British "sphere of influence" in the Middle East, with the inevitable result that Central Europe would be left either to chaos or to Russian domination. With these concerns in mind, the State Department had prepared a Declaration of the United Nations for Churchill to sign with representatives of the other countries allied against the Axis powers.

The declaration was the first of several documents by which the administration attempted to expand the Atlantic Charter into a truly universal constitution that would bring about "One World" after the war. Adolf Berle, again, was one of the principal drafters of the document. When Russian diplomats were shown the draft, they made what Berle regarded as suspicious changes in the wording.

> They included, after the words "the struggle for freedom", the words "in their own countries, as well as in other countries", which might apply to the subjugated countries of Europe, and might equally apply to a forthcoming world revolution.[7]

But Berle was willing to see how the Russians behaved later. On the other "front," it took some arm-twisting to persuade Churchill to allow India to sign as a separate entity and not merely as one of the self-governing commonwealths under a United Kingdom signature (which itself would have been a "promotion"). Roosevelt himself reordered the list of signatories from the original draft, moving India from the list of commonwealths (along with Canada, Australia, New Zealand, and South Africa) to where it belonged alphabetically, between Honduras and Luxembourg.[8]

Back in London Eden had decided that his colleagues in the war cabinet should not ignore Stalin's disparaging comments about high-sounding declarations. The outcome of the war might depend as much on Stalin's good humor as the success of the Red Army. But Eden was also thinking about the Russian's desire to dispel the notion that the Soviet Union was out to bolshevize Europe. An agreement on frontiers now might limit the expansion of communism.[9]

The United Kingdom harbored a good deal of underlying suspicion of Russia, Eden went on. He had invited Molotov to visit London in an effort to overcome such feelings on both sides. The Russian foreign minister had seemed delighted at the invitation. Still in Washington, Churchill would have none of it. There must be no talk of settling frontiers now, he rebuked Eden. "I know President Roosevelt holds this view as strongly as I do and he has several times expressed his pleasure to me at the firm line we took at Moscow." He continued,

> You suggest that the "acid test of our sincerity" depends upon our recognizing the acquisition of these territories by the Soviet Union irrespective of the wishes of their people. I, on the contrary, regard our sincerity involved in the maintenance of the principles of the Atlantic Charter, to which Stalin has subscribed. On this also we depend for our association with the USA.[10]

Ambassador Halifax thought the prime minister was "unnecessarily fierce" in responding to Eden. Anthony was not overplaying it, Halifax wrote Churchill on January 11, 1942, when he stressed Stalin's concern with postwar security. "Quite apart from his great value in winning the war, ... future peace is going to depend very much upon Joe and ourselves being prepared to think and act together, along with this country, afterwards."

> I have a feeling, based on re-thinking over and over again our talks with the Russians in the summer of 1939, that Anthony is not exaggerating how important a place all these ideas of security are going to hold in Stalin's mind, and how much they are likely to influence his judgment in regard to cooperation with ourselves.[11]

Instead of saying that what Stalin wanted "bumped" up against the Atlantic Charter ("which would be a pretty broad hint that he wasn't going to get much change out of us if we could help it anyhow"), Halifax proposed reconciling the charter and Stalin's demands by making protectorates of the Baltic states. But of particular interest here is the ambassador's consideration of the United States as a third party, to come after Russia in the alphabet of postwar diplomacy.

Eden thanked his predecessor for a "most helpful letter" about Russia. It was difficult to say what Stalin's real motives were in regard to propagating communism, he wrote, but there could be no doubt of his concern for Russian national security. "He seemed to me a man with a complete 'Real Politik' outlook and a political descendant of Peter the Great rather than of Lenin." International socialists and communists had a mental outlook that was easy to spot, Eden suggested. "But I can say this, that it never peeped out at any time."[12]

Eden reput the case to the war cabinet: surely it was unwise to pass up an opportunity to settle with Russia because of America's "exaggeratedly moral" posture, "at least where non-American interests are concerned."[13] Eden had asked Stalin for two or three weeks, and time was up. The argument for settling frontiers on a good-fences-make-good-neighbors basis would come up later in the war, most notably at the October 1944 TOLSTOY Conference; but in early 1942 what would change Churchill's mind was the deteriorating British military position and mounting political pressure at home. Singapore fell to the Japanese in early 1942, while in North Africa the prime minister was baffled that his military commanders "should stand idle for so long a period at enormous expense while the Russians were fighting desperately and valiantly along their whole vast front."[14]

Not only did this give German Field Marshal Erwin Rommel opportunity to replenish his supplies in North Africa, as Churchill lectured his commanders, but it produced political fallout in London. Churchill would write derisively of those who scrawled slogans or poked fingers at MPs on their way to Parliament—"Second Front Now!" But he was forced to undertake a "considerable reconstruction" of the war cabinet in mid-February to "accommodate Sir Stafford Cripps, who had new strength to bring...."[15]

Cripps had returned from Moscow to lead the "second front" forces, and Churchill felt obliged to ask him to become leader of the House. Although Churchill wrote that Cripps had new strength to bring, this is partly misleading, for Sir Stafford had long ago separated himself from the parliamentary Labor party. His strength derived almost exclusively from the popular belief that he could bring something of the Russian spirit into the counsels of His Majesty's Government.

He was even being spoken of as a successor to Churchill in a "Peoples' Government." The prime minister was too familiar with Lloyd George's struggle with Arthur Henderson and Ramsay MacDonald in World War I—when, as it now appeared in 1942, the issue was Russia—not to be concerned about the parallel and the threat that the wartime "political truce" would be shattered.

The "Cripps for Premier" movement bore watching, agreed American officials. No threat to Churchill's rule seemed imminent, FBI director J. Edgar Hoover advised Assistant Secretary of State Adolf Berle, on the basis of intelligence information. But there was likely to be a very difficult time ahead for several months. And Ambassador Winant reported that the Cripps appointment as government leader in the House of Commons had been widely hailed in the press:

> Some commentators foresee intensification of efforts for closer relations with Russia as a result of his presence in the War Cabinet, and appointment will please all those asking for greater recognition of Russian role in the war.[16]

Meanwhile, Cripps's old enemy in the cabinet, Minister of War Production Lord Beaverbrook—"Max," the famous Tory press lord—had suddenly become a Russophile! Yes, a second front as soon as possible, he argued; not only that, there must be as well an Anglo-Russian political agreement that would accept Soviet claims to its 1941 frontiers.

Beaverbrook even took his arguments direct to the Americans. A Canadian, he had never trusted the Yankees, but now he was writing Harry Hopkins confidential letters about the failings of his war cabinet colleagues. "Britain has no foreign policy toward Russia," began one letter. "Max" almost went further than Stalin had in denouncing British unresponsiveness to Russian pleas for "military help." Beaverbrook rattled off the list of Soviet complaints like headlines in his newspaper, the London *Daily Express*.

"Stalin says that Britain treats the Russians like natives or negroes." Beaverbrook could see why. The war cabinet seemed not to understand that the only basis of a successful policy was equality—an equal voice in the conduct of the war, an equal voice in what supplies went where, and an "unconditional share" in determining the peace settlement. The Western allies should begin, he concluded, by recognizing Russia's 1941 frontiers without further ado.[17]

Whatever Harry Hopkins thought about Beaverbrook's passionate advocacy, his arguments were beginning to gain ground in the war cabinet. After all, he asked, what was the Atlantic Charter about? Security, wasn't it? Stalin had even said he was willing to leave the postwar Polish boundary question open. Given what the Russians had contributed to the war, compared with what the Americans had done, there should be no doubt about meeting at least some of the Soviet demands.

Beaverbrook went on for some time in this vein. Not only were the Russians bearing the brunt of the war, but His Majesty's Government had failed to accede to many Russian requests, or else delayed, as in the question of declaring war on Finland. Eden picked up the argument at this point, suggesting that one way to reconcile the Americans might be to propose that the Russians be granted postwar military bases in the Baltic states. That was the technique the Americans had used. American bases in the West Indies, the foreign secretary pointed out to Ambassador Winant, had been acquired from Britain in the 1940 Destroyers-for-Bases deal. Eden supposed some might see the arrangement as a violation of the Atlantic Charter. He did not suggest that London had acted under the same duress as the Baltic leaders, but Winant thought he had a point.[18]

Churchill did not like the drift of this argument, but Eden and Beaverbrook had put him on the defensive. Very well then, he insisted, let us put the pros and cons to the Americans in a balanced fashion. But that meant giving Roosevelt the final word, complained the foreign secretary. Churchill could not be moved further. Eden did what he could, through Ambassador

Halifax, to reconcile Washington to some gesture toward meeting Moscow's desires. It was largely the issue of the Baltic states, Halifax began, and British policy there in 1939 that accounted for the breakdown of Anglo-Soviet relations and the Nazi-Soviet pact. Perhaps a "compromise" involving recognition of the Soviet "right" to have bases in the Baltic states might be enough, or a promise that the prime minister would support their annexation to Russia at the peace conference.

When Halifax finished his presentation, Under Secretary Sumner Welles told him his words "evidenced the worst phase of the spirit of Munich."[19] The ambassador no doubt winced at the implied comparison. Welles could hardly have given him a colder shoulder. He would talk to the president, but he "could not conceive of this war being fought in order to undertake once more the shoddy, inherently vicious, kind of patchwork world order which the European powers had attempted to construct during the years between 1919 and 1939."[20]

Two days later Welles reported back to Lord Halifax that he had spent an hour and a half with Roosevelt, providing him with all the telegrams and other materials on the subject. These FDR had studied "in the fullest detail." He had then asked Welles to say to Lord Halifax that "only one word had come into the President's mind and that was the word 'provincial.'"[21]

Beaverbrook refused to take such an answer as final. On February 18 he had sent the war cabinet an "ultimatum." "I ask for a decision by my colleagues," it began. "It is now impossible for the British Government to refuse the Russian claim." And why was that? Using Gilbert and Sullivan logic, Beaverbrook argued that the prime minister's original statement pledging aid to the Russians in defending their "native land" had been given on June 22, 1941, and therefore included Soviet frontiers as of that date. "The British Government will not be fulfilling the Prime Minister's pledge of June 22, 1941, unless it concedes the rightful frontier claims put forward by the Russians."[22]

The war cabinet declined to follow the argument, and Beaverbrook immediately resigned. The last straw, he wrote to Anthony Eden, was Churchill's elevation of the Labor party leader, Clement Attlee, an equally dedicated opponent of an agreement with the Russians, to the symbolic post of deputy prime minister.[23] In his resignation there was even an implicit threat of a full-scale press campaign against the government.

Already there were rumors in the American press about divisions among the allies. Roosevelt tried to deflect efforts to find out what was going on. "Don't you think we might win the war," he remonstrated at a press conference in late February, "before we start determining all the details of geography and of forms of government, and boundaries, and things like that? Wouldn't it be just as well to win the war first, as long as you have principles?"[24]

The president had advised Halifax, meanwhile, that he hoped to see Russian Ambassador Maksim Litvinov to seek agreement on a way to meet Russian security needs other than by wrecking the Atlantic Charter. Roosevelt was too optimistic about his powers of persuasion, observed Eden. Stalin had no intention of arguing rights and wrongs with the president. Borders in Western Europe had been set by treaty, Eden predicted Stalin would say, and the Baltic states had voted themselves into the Soviet Union while the arrangements over Bessarabia and Bukovina had been made by treaty with Rumania. Where was there any wrecking of the Atlantic Charter in these arrangements? Stalin would argue.[25]

But Churchill thought it might in fact be better if Roosevelt did take the lead. The president might resent a British attempt to deprive him of the opportunity. Perhaps he wished to bargain for Russian entry into the war against Japan? Perhaps so, retorted Eden, but the likely outcome was deadlock. Not realizing how important the frontier question was to Stalin, Roosevelt might blunder into an impossible situation. And what would follow?[26]

At length the prime minister reluctantly agreed that Eden should broach the issue with both Maisky and Winant, to see if it might be settled in London. Winant would have to consult Roosevelt about the idea, and meanwhile the foreign secretary would have a talk with Ambassador Maisky to see how he would respond to the notion of tripartite talks. You understand, he told the Russian diplomat, that His Majesty's Government had a "commitment" not to enter into any engagements that affected postwar Europe "without their [American] consent." This was an intriguing hint, because it appeared to reduce the principles of the Atlantic Charter to a negotiating point. But Maisky was unconcerned with such subtleties. It had been eight weeks, he said, since Eden left Moscow. As for the Americans, why should they wish to involve themselves so deeply in Anglo-Russian discussions? He had seen Winant and informed him that, after all, the United States was not being asked to sign anything, only to acquiesce.[27]

Eden knew he had promised the Russians an answer within a reasonable time. He urged Churchill to write Roosevelt a personal note, for unless the frontier issue was settled, full strategic talks with the Russians were impossible. Stalin had made it clear he expected a political agreement as a prerequisite to strategic cooperation. If, for example, Britain wished to raise the question of Russian entry into the Far Eastern war, it could only be after the frontier question was out of the way. "Otherwise Stalin will neither talk nor listen."[28]

None of Eden's arguments was as compelling as the continuing deterioration of the military situation, particularly in the Far East. The Japanese took Burma after a short fight and moved on to the Dutch East Indies. Churchill feared for India and Australia. "We seem to lose a new bit of the Empire almost every day," wrote the chief of the Imperial General Staff to a friend, "and are faced with one nightmare situation after another."[29]

Against this background Churchill felt he must change his position. "The increasing gravity of the war," he cabled Roosevelt on March 7, 1942, "has led me to feel that the principles of the Atlantic Charter ought not to be construed so as to deny Russia the frontiers she occupied when Germany attacked her."[30]

This was the basis on which Russia acceded to the Charter, and I suspect that a severe process of liquidating hostile elements in the Baltic States, etc., was employed by the Russians when they took these regions at the beginning of the war. I hope therefore that you will be able to give us a free hand to sign the treaty which Stalin desires as soon as possible. Everything portends an immense renewal of the German invasion of Russia in the Spring and there is very little we can do to help the only country that is heavily engaged with the German armies.[31]

In writing that there was "very little we can do" to help Russia militarily, what Churchill feared most was that Roosevelt would take his words as a challenge. Stalin's November 1941 letter to Churchill could be read as offering a choice: a second front in 1942 or recognition of his 1941 frontiers. The worst thing Roosevelt could do would be to make a rash promise to Litvinov about opening a second front in the west.

Roosevelt brushed aside Churchill's fears. "This may be a critical period," he telegraphed the prime minister, "but remember always it is not as bad as some you have survived before." Roosevelt's wartime Russian policy had begun with Lend-Lease. His chief adviser on Russian matters, Averell Harriman, had told him that Lend-Lease offered the opportunity to begin anew with Russia, to sweep away past misunderstandings and suspicions. He was now thinking about a natural follow-on to Lend-Lease, and it sent shudders down Churchill's spine. "I am becoming more and more interested," FDR said, "in the establishment of a new front this summer on the European continent, certainly for air and raids." Heavy losses could be expected, but these would be compensated by equal German losses "and by compelling Germans to divert large forces of all kinds from Russian fronts."[32]

Russia was entitled to security and peace of mind at the end of the war, Roosevelt told Ambassador Halifax. But the political settlement and Russian security would depend upon what kind of Germany the allies established, not by passing out chunks of territory to the victors. The Atlantic Charter, the president went on, clearly called for German disarmament. He would personally discuss these matters with Stalin.

Nettled by these constant references to appeasement and Munich, Ambassador Halifax replied tartly that the Baltic states had not been notably successful in their form of self-government during the interwar years. He might sound cynical, but counting the fate of the Baltic peoples higher than assurances of Soviet cooperation in the postwar world was scarcely "realistic."

But perhaps the Russians were attempting to launch their own "second front" behind British diplomatic lines. Word had come to Halifax through Roosevelt's private secretary, General Edwin M. "Pa" Watson, that Soviet Ambassador Litvinov had been seeking an appointment with the president to talk about the importance of opening another front against the Germans. As Halifax noted to London, Litvinov had not said anything about this to him—and it raised the likelihood that the Russians were trying to line up the Americans to put pressure on His Majesty's Government for a second front.[33]

When Roosevelt met Litvinov on March 12, 1942, the president assured the ambassador that the United States was determined not to leave Russia vulnerable to a new German attack at the end of the war. Everything else said that day became the subject of controversy. Roosevelt remembered the discussion this way several months later: "He said that he had stepped in," Vice President Henry A. Wallace recorded in his diary, "and prevented the British and Russians from arriving at an accord that would give the Russians this area [the Baltic states]." FDR also told Wallace that he had advised the Russians to establish close economic relations with those areas but agree to separate political relations for at least five years, at which time a plebiscite might be held. He knew the Russians believed a plebiscite had already occurred, but it was not under fair conditions.[34]

What Halifax learned of this conversation was that Roosevelt had insisted he could agree to no secret treaty nor subscribe to an open treaty until the war had been won. He would, on the other hand, support any "legitimate" steps to protect Soviet security.[35] According to the only extant record in Russian archives, finally, the president supposedly assured Ambassador Litvinov that he did not foresee "any difficulties" about the border issues after the war. But the conclusion of a secret Anglo-Russian agreement troubled him:

> The issue may cause undesirable discussions and the President may be reminded about the Atlantic Charter where it mentions self-determination. He himself had always thought it had been a mistake to separate provinces from Russia after the war and he thought Wilson had also been opposed to this. And therefore he assures Stalin in personal way that he absolutely agrees with us.[36]

With these two very different interpretations before them, Russian and British diplomats were left wondering what American policy in fact was. Maisky said that Moscow read Litvinov's report of the conversation as a full recognition of Soviet security requirements. When Eden pointed out that Lord Halifax's information did not tally at all with such an interpretation, Maisky took note but finally came up with an ingenious solution:

> [Roosevelt] objected to a secret treaty—but there was no question of a secret treaty. He said he could not subscribe to an open treaty dealing with frontiers until the war had been won. But he was not being asked to subscribe to the proposed Anglo-Soviet Treaty. All that was required was that he should approve, or at least acquiesce, in it.[37]

Eden decided he would do as Maisky suggested and simply wait for Stalin's response to Roosevelt to clear matters up. That reply came a few days later. Moscow had decided merely to take note of Roosevelt's position and to place the burden back on the British to move ahead with an Anglo-Soviet treaty containing the political clauses. Maisky made it quite clear that his government believed it was an issue to be resolved between London and Moscow. "They had never asked the President to intervene: on the contrary, he had done all he could through Mr. Winant to encourage the United States Government not to do so." Maisky hoped London would now be able to "make it plain to the United States Government that in the interests of the Allied war effort we considered that we should now conclude our treaty with Russia."[38]

Obviously, Roosevelt had not made the impression he thought he had. "I know you will not mind my being brutally frank," Roosevelt had confidently written Churchill on March 18, 1942, "when I tell you that I think I can personally handle Stalin better than your Foreign Office or my State Department. Stalin hates the guts of all your top people. He thinks he likes me better and I hope he will continue to do so."[39] When Harry Hopkins saw Halifax on March 26, they had a long talk about the growing dangers of impasse. Hopkins, reported Halifax, "is racking his brains for some new bridge-building device that he can suggest to the President."[40]

Roosevelt's trusted aide had much on his mind, including a report he had received from military intelligence, G-2, suggesting a "distinct possibility of a Russo-German accommodation." This danger, according to the head of military intelligence, General Raymond Lee, stemmed in part from the way Lend-Lease had been handled. He concluded:

> Poor Soviet-British relations and our dependence on the British for supply cooperation and information have marred our relations with the U.S.S.R. Information from British sources concerning the Soviet situation must be discounted; direct contact on high policy is desirable. The Russians have exploited our help, but they do not understand our altruism, are suspicious of our failure to get a war plans understanding, and fail completely to cooperate with us.[41]

Military intelligence estimates such as these obviously contributed heavily to the American conclusion that no progress could be made until the United States wrested control of the diplomatic initiative from Great Britain. Sumner Welles might chide Halifax and call him to task for still thinking like a Munich-er, but the clinching argument was that the British appeared to be promoting a territorial settlement because they could not, or would not, deal with the only issue that really mattered: the second front.

Like Churchill's critics in Britain, many American policy-makers thought the prime minister's hesitations were all about preserving the empire. Few would go so far as to say, "Chamberlain wanted to repartition Africa rather than fight for Czechoslovakia; Churchill is ready to send the Baltic states and half of Eastern Europe into Russia's iron grip rather than invade the continent"—but the parallels were there. Where Chamberlain had tried to bring Germany back to its bourgeois character, British policy now seemed aimed at bringing back Peter the Great's imperial Russia. The strategy would not work: it would not save Russia and might in fact encourage a separate Russo-German peace. After all, the old diplomacy had produced the Nazi-Soviet pact. Why shouldn't Stalin take advantage of the highest bid?

General Lee's report was also on Secretary of War Henry L. Stimson's desk. On March 27, 1942, Stimson wrote the president, "John Sherman said in 1877, 'The only way to resume specie payments is to resume.' Similarly, the only way to get the initiative in this war is to take it." The president should send "a trusted messenger" to London with American plans for a European offensive. He should not talk with subordinates. Having done that, Roosevelt should lean with all his strength on those charged with producing landing craft for the ultimate invasion. "The rate of construction of a number of landing barges should not be allowed to lose the crisis of the World War."

The only objection he had heard from the British about an early cross-channel operation, Stimson continued, was this matter of landing craft. It was well within Roosevelt's power to take charge of the situation, "while, on the other hand, so long as we remain without our own plan of offensive, our forces will inevitably be dispersed and wasted."[42]

As Roosevelt pondered, Ambassador Halifax asked for another interview to explain the British position. The war cabinet had decided to go ahead with the final treaty negotiations. The word came back that the president saw no point in seeing Halifax; he had nothing to add to what he had already said. Actually he did, for Welles reported to Halifax that if some sort of arrangement could be made for a reciprocal exchange of populations, American opinion might "attempt to tolerate the transaction."[43]

Halifax was sure that Stalin would turn down any such suggestion, for it would undermine the fiction that the plebiscites had revealed the will of the Baltic states. Roosevelt then cabled Churchill on April 1 and again on April 3, saying he was sending Hopkins and General George C. Marshall to London because he had come to "certain conclusions" about long-range problems and the military situation facing the three great powers. He also advised Churchill that he proposed to ask Stalin to send special representatives "to see me at once." The messages fairly crackled with Roosevelt's square-jawed determination to jolt the British out of the stiff-upper-lip mentality Americans thought still pervaded their war councils.

> Your people and mine demand the establishment of a front to draw off pressure on the Russians, and these peoples are wise enough to see that the Russians are today killing more Germans and destroying more equipment than you and I put together. Even if full success is not attained, the *big* objective will be.[44]

What the "*big* objective" was, Roosevelt did not say. But clearly military success was not the only scale on which to measure the benefits of the operation. At the time he sent these words to the prime minister, Roosevelt knew the British and Russians were preparing to go ahead with their "Baltic Munich" in any event. When he wrote Stalin, therefore, he tried to persuade the Soviet leader to send Foreign Minister Molotov to see him *before* Molotov went to London for the final treaty negotiations.[45]

He had in mind, he told Stalin, "a very important military proposal involving the utilization of our armed forces in a manner to relieve your critical western front. This objective carries great weight with me." As an added inducement for a

Molotov visit, Roosevelt suggested that he needed Stalin's "advice before we determine with finality the strategic course of our common military action."[46]

It was not enough. Molotov's schedule remained unchanged. But at least Hopkins got to London before the Russian foreign minister. He greeted Eden with personal reassurances from Roosevelt that "our main proposal here should take the heat off Russia's diplomatic demands upon England."[47] But what happened after this greeting left everyone confused. At a special war cabinet session on April 14, Churchill promised his American visitors that nothing would be left undone which could contribute to the success of the endeavor they were about to undertake.[48]

Eden chimed in with a statement that the American plan had much more than military significance. "It was, in fact, the great picture of the two English-speaking countries setting out for the redemption of Europe." The publicity would show "our own people that we were not permanently wedded to the defensive." If the Russian front held throughout the spring, it would be tantamount to victory, the foreign secretary went on, "and in that case we should wish to be on the Continent to participate in it."[49]

What was going on here? Had the British agreed to a second front in 1942? Marshall and Hopkins had brought with them several proposals, including a plan for a cross-channel invasion initially set for 1943, and a contingency plan for a landing in France sometime in the fall of 1942. The earlier thrust would be mounted only if it appeared the Russian front was near collapse, or if the German position critically weakened. So what had been agreed? The British sent Marshall and Hopkins home believing all was well, that something concrete had been decided, and that a treaty between Britain and the Soviet Union would now be unnecessary. But the discussion had not centered on the specifics of any of the plans.

Churchill had now gone over completely to the view that recognizing the 1941 borders was better than trying to launch a military invasion in the near future. On a Halifax message repeating the information that Roosevelt was seeking an alternative to an agreement on frontiers, the prime minister commented, "This seems to me a very foolish view."[50]

Preparations went ahead for Molotov's visit. As British officials reviewed what Stalin had told Eden in December, they drew up an eight-point draft (the same number as the Atlantic Charter!) which they hoped would remove at least some of the American causes for concern. Clearly, however, the issue of the Baltic states was only the tip of the iceberg—a point the Americans had been making all along.[51]

The first article of the draft reaffirmed the "principles" of the Atlantic Charter as the agreed basis for peace. The second was a mutual pledge to insure that Germany could not again threaten European security. The third recognized, in hedging fashion, Russia's 1941 frontiers, with the exception of Poland, and with an implied quid pro quo that both parties agreed on no territorial aggrandizement beyond those frontiers nor interference in the internal affairs of "European peoples." Article Four would allow peoples placed under a new sovereignty to emigrate and take their property with them. Interestingly, Roosevelt had proposed something similar to Litvinov in their discussions. The notion of adding to displaced persons roaming around postwar Eastern Europe did not really have much support, however, and the article was dropped early in Anglo-Soviet negotiations.

Article Five proposed a Balkan federation, sure to fuel Russian suspicions of British intent to stay involved in potential anti-Soviet politics in the region. The final three articles had to do with bilateral relations, no separate peace, economic assistance, and the duration of the treaty—obviously easier ground for both sides.[52]

The Russian response to this draft proposed a separate annex to deal with the Polish question, by which the British would recognize any agreement on postwar frontiers reached between Moscow and exile leaders.[53] Eden did not like the "annex." Still less did he like Ambassador Maisky's strained efforts to make the Russian proposal seem reasonable. The British had a special obligation to accede to it, insisted Maisky, because they had offered so little in military aid to stanch the terrible flow of blood on the eastern front that would continue yet another year.

Maisky was not finished. Stalin also desired, he said, a "secret protocol" to the treaty along the lines the Russian ruler had spelled out to Eden in December. He wanted Britain to consent to defense pacts between Russia and Finland, and Russia and Rumania. For his part, Stalin would encourage London to negotiate similar arrangements with Belgium and Holland. Obviously, such an arrangement looked at a formal division of Europe into permanent (insofar as such things were ever permanent) spheres of influence. An Anglo-Russian over-lordship of this type would place Britain in an invidious position both vis-à-vis Eastern Europe, where its support for such arrangements would amount to the same coercion used against Czechoslovakia in 1938, and the United States, upon whom Britain's immediate and long-range future well-being so obviously depended.

It was out of the question for His Majesty's Government to consider such a protocol, Eden told Maisky. What had happened to the British-proposed article for a confederation of the smaller states of Eastern Europe? Now it was Maisky's turn to squirm. In a long and involved "explanation," the ambassador insisted the Soviet government was not opposed to the idea but felt it was the wrong time to decide such a question. To promote the notion of a confederation at this stage would only encourage the activities of the exile governments in all sorts of ways—meaning, of course, anti-Soviet ways. Eden had the last word—at least this time:

> I said this was most disappointing. Many people thought that we were prepared to hand over the smaller countries of Europe to Soviet domination, and, if no reference were made to confederation, in some terms similar to those we suggested, I feared that the effect of the treaty would be very bad in those quarters.[54]

This was blunt talk. The confederation idea was close to Eden's heart. More than any comments from his Foreign Office aides, the Soviet attitude on this question stiffened the foreign secretary's resistance to finalizing the political treaty. To the Soviets, of course, the reconstruction of the post–World War I *cordon sanitaire* which the Allies had constructed with a chain of treaties across Eastern Europe had to be avoided under whatever new guise, perhaps even at a cost of losing the much desired political treaty.

Interest on both sides for signing a treaty was declining. "To my mind," noted the always skeptical Sir Alexander Cadogan, "one object of the Treaty was always to hold the Russians during the dangerous period (now) when the German attack is impending but not yet launched, and when the Russians *might* be frightened into a negotiation. Unfortunately, the Russians will insist on attaching a price we simply cannot pay."[55]

He would like to get a treaty, Cadogan said, but if the price were too high, there was nothing for it but to seek to avoid a break. That might be better in the long run anyway. Cadogan's views, generally speaking, summed up the Foreign Office position as Molotov arrived via airplane in Scotland. But several members of Parliament had also written the foreign secretary about the impending treaty, learning about it from various sources, especially from the Polish government in exile. "There was a great deal of talk in the Lobbies," Harold Nicolson wrote, about the "Baltic Agreement." His own view was pragmatic: if Russia defeated Germany, she would take the Baltic states with or without British consent. If she lost, Russia would make a separate peace, and any arrangements made with other countries would go by the boards. He could not, therefore, see any advantages to an agreement that would shock "liberal minded people."[56] He would have to vote against such an agreement, and might also speak against it.

Eden had advised Halifax, meanwhile, that he should do everything possible to squelch publicity in the United States. It was not just that Americans would not like the treaty, but that "a break just now would be most embarrassing to relations between the three Powers. There is no immediate prospect of signature and we will keep you posted as to developments."[57]

Molotov seemed unperturbed by the uproar in the press. When he arrived, on May 20, 1942, the Russian foreign minister immediately informed Eden that he would be going on to the United States after their discussions. In addition to the draft treaties, therefore, he wished to talk about "the question of a second front." And he advised Eden that "President Roosevelt himself has raised it with M. Stalin."[58] Molotov's demeanor suggested a rather confident and, for him, almost avuncular mood. "We did our best in 1939," the foreign minister said when he met Sir William Strang, "but we failed: we were both at fault."[59]

For five days, May 21 to May 26, Molotov and Eden rehearsed all the familiar arguments over the political treaty. The Russian foreign minister first attempted to persuade his British counterpart that the "secret protocol" was nothing more than a codification of the Stalin-Eden conversations. Failing in that, he suggested it be embodied in vaguer terms in the political treaty itself.[60]

Eden's frequent references to American views, which earlier he had not considered decisive, indicated that Moscow's proprietorial attitude about Polish affairs had made the British diplomat eager for outside help. In these somewhat altered circumstances, Eden was happy to have Ambassador Winant standing by ready to offer Washington's opinion.[61]

Secretary of State Cordell Hull wrote in his *Memoirs* that Molotov's arrival in England led to the strongest protest yet against Anglo-Russian attempts to settle postwar affairs between them. "Our memorandum was so strong that we were in some fear lest the President disapprove it. Mr. Roosevelt, however, quickly returned it with his O.K...."[62] Armed not merely with this protest but with other "important information" for Molotov, Winant telephoned Maisky for an appointment. They met at the Russian embassy at 10 p.m. on May 24.

At the meeting Winant emphasized Washington's interest in an early second front, adding that the State Department had also advised him of arrangements to discuss commercial policy and "a program in the relief field. . . ." Molotov listened with great interest, the ambassador cabled home, and remarked that the president's attitude toward the treaty warranted serious consideration. He would think about postponing discussion of a political treaty until he had been to Washington and heard firsthand what the president had to say.[63]

Two days later Molotov agreed to abandon the political treaty, settling instead for a simple military alliance. Eden was much relieved that he had not had to continue arguing with Molotov over annexes and secret protocols. He thanked Winant for his efforts. He also thanked the exile Polish leader, Wladyslaw Sikorski, for his efforts, giving him "all the credit" for the way things turned out. Sikorski said no, Eden deserved "150%" of the credit for having the courage to take a sharp turn. "Yes," Eden tossed back the honors, "but we succeeded because I took your advice. The Poles evidently know the Russians much better than we do."[64]

Eden knew he had slipped around a dangerous corner. The Russians were not likely to abandon their objectives. At some later moment the Polish question would have to be settled. Meanwhile one must be alert to keep everything in play, including the exiles, whose influence on domestic politics could not be ignored, and who could yet play a role in the postwar balance of power. To assuage Russian suspicions, on the other hand, Eden raised the value of a "nonpolitical" military treaty by proposing that it be extended for twenty years. Both the foreign secretary and the prime minister allowed themselves to believe, finally, that the Russian emissary's willingness to climb down from previous demands boded well for postwar cooperation. "Our relations with the USSR were now on an entirely different and far more satisfactory footing."[65]

What decided Stalin to choose this course? Ivan Maisky would write, "I don't know what obliged Stalin so sharply to change his attitude, but however that might be, the change had been made." Molotov gave his own answer to the question during the series of interviews that have recently become known as his "memoirs." Stalin ordered him to accept the British treaty without the boundary stipulations because of the politics of war, and because it had been enough to open the question at this point.[66] Molotov left promptly for Washington, carrying in his briefcase drafts of the twenty-year military alliance for which he had made this great "concession" on the Baltic states. Even the supposedly perplexed Maisky must have understood that Russia had gained two advantages: a significantly better military alliance from Britain extending into the postwar era, and serious indications from Washington that Roosevelt did not accept the peripheral strategy that the Russians suspected was really designed to allow Germany and the Soviet Union to exhaust themselves. The peripheral strategy had been thwarted, or so it seemed, by Roosevelt's counteroffer to the political treaty: a second front. Thus, as Winant cabled about Molotov's sudden turnabout, "The Russians are deeply interested in establishing a second front."[67] They could get no definite commitments from the British on action in 1942, but now they had forced Roosevelt to take the lead in Anglo-American affairs for fear of an Anglo-Russian political treaty.

Besides, as the Russian historian Vilnis Sipols has noted, the British officially advised Molotov that they recognized Latvia, Lithuania, and Estonia to be integral to the USSR, removing their former representatives from the diplomatic list kept in the Foreign Office. And the wording of the military alliance referred to the defeat of "Germany," not just "Hitlerite Germany." These were significant developments and distinctions, eliminating, for example, the possibility of a successful effort by German generals or politicians to engineer a deal for peace on the western front by staging a coup against Hitler, in the fashion of Prince Max at the end of World War I. Harold Nicolson had said it well—if Russia won on the eastern front it would take the Baltic states anyway; if it lost, no treaty would make a difference anyway.[68]

In Washington, meanwhile, Roosevelt laid out a red carpet for Molotov. During the Russo-Finnish War American attitudes toward the Soviet Union had probably reached their low point.

But now that had changed. Russian-American relations were a *tabula rasa* (especially to the president's White House advisers) on which could be written the heroic deeds of war and the outline for a brave new world.

Hopkins was distressed, then, by the way the president chose to open this new chapter of Russo-American relations. At his first meeting with Molotov late in the afternoon of May 29, 1942, Roosevelt presented the Soviet foreign minister with a gratuitous (if well-meaning) State Department proposal for American good offices in settling Russian disputes with Iran and Turkey, and another somewhat difficult, if not controversial, proposal that the Russians sign or adhere to the 1929 Geneva Convention on the treatment of prisoners of war.

Things got sticky when Molotov suggested the Russians knew a good deal more about their relations with those countries than did the Americans. He also bridled at the apparent equation between Russian and German treatment of prisoners of war. Feeling that Molotov was beginning to think Roosevelt did not really mean business, Hopkins intervened. "The conference seemed to be getting nowhere and I suggested that Molotov might like to rest."[69]

Beginning with cocktails that evening, the climate improved for serious discussions. Roosevelt wanted to talk about the postwar world, inviting his guest to think about great-power cooperation as the basis for a new world order. All other nations must be disarmed, the president insisted, even such a historic world power as France. If there were too many policemen the danger was that they might start fighting among themselves. "The President said he could not visualize another League of Nations with 100 different signatories; there were simply too many nations to satisfy, hence it was a failure and would be a failure."

One can guess what Molotov thought of this talk about the future. He made it clear he wanted to get things back to the here and now. Was the president familiar with the treaty negotiated in London? he asked. Roosevelt replied that he was, and that "it was all to the good." Now was not the time to raise the question of future frontiers. There might come a proper time later. Molotov might have countered at this point that it was difficult to talk about Big Four policemen if no one knew what it was they were to defend. Instead he pointed out that his government had very definite convictions on these points but had deferred to British preference—and to what he had understood to be the president's attitude.[70]

Having made his opening, Molotov launched into a full discussion of the urgent need for a second front. A German victory in the east was not incomprehensible, he said, and that would leave the Western Allies alone to face Hitler's war machine. If an early second front were not launched, Molotov continued, so that at least forty German divisions were withdrawn from the eastern front, a Russian collapse might occur, or at least a withdrawal to the Volga. "If this catastrophe occurred, the Soviets would no longer be able to pull anything like their present weight in the war, and the whole brunt of carrying it on against an appreciably strengthened Hitler would fall on the British Empire and the United States."[71]

The president reminded Molotov that both he and Churchill had to reckon with military advisers who preferred "a sure thing in 1943 to a risky adventure in 1942." But he recognized the force of the foreign minister's argument and the need for offensive action "at the earliest appropriate moment."[72] After Molotov repeated his points in greater detail the next day, in the presence of Roosevelt's chief military advisers, the president turned to General Marshall. Were developments "clear enough so that we could say to Mr. Stalin that we are preparing a second front?" "Yes," came the reply. "The President then authorized Mr. Molotov to inform Mr. Stalin that we expect the formation of a second front this year."[73]

What precisely did that mean? General Marshall was not sure. Roosevelt was not sure himself. But however subtly the president attempted to shade this commitment, substituting at one point the phrase "preparing" a second front for "formation ... this year," he had put himself out on a limb. Marshall tried to intervene, pointing out that serious logistical problems must be overcome. Roosevelt seemed oblivious to the danger, or confident he could finesse the situation. From what happened at the final discussion with Molotov on June 1, it was impossible to tell which was actually the case.[74]

After a prickly exchange on Finland, FDR reverted to the special responsibilities each of the Big Four must accept after the war. Russia, he suggested, should take part in a new trusteeship system for managing the difficult transition of colonial territories to independence. He mentioned French Indochina, the Malay States, and the Dutch East Indies. One wonders what thoughts went through Molotov's mind as Roosevelt blithely rattled off this list of colonies to be put under great-power supervision. The president had opposed any Anglo-Russian attempt to talk about postwar frontiers as compromising the future peace and as inconsistent with the Atlantic Charter. But what he denied could be done piecemeal in London, Roosevelt was now proposing for the Big Four globally. They were to disarm the rest of the world, reorganize the colonial system, and in general oversee things down to a sparrow's fall. Or so it seemed.

Little wonder, after such a recitation, that Molotov pressed one last time for a specific commitment to the second front. Well, Roosevelt hedged, had Molotov considered that an early second front might mean curtailing Lend-Lease convoys to Russia? "With what seemed deliberate sarcasm," the Russian foreign minister asked in return where Russia would be if Moscow agreed to a curtailment of the convoys—and then no second front materialized? Still more insistently he asked, "What is the President's answer with respect to the second front?"

"We expect to establish a second front," Roosevelt replied.[75] He did not say precisely when, but it was a fateful response nonetheless, dictated by a desire to save a particular vision of the future peace even as the war still hung in the balance. Had FDR simply accepted a permanent great-power division of the world, he could have tried to accommodate the State Department's "Wilsonian" vision to the traditionalist methods already evidenced in the draft Anglo-Russian treaty. But how Roosevelt approached the problem, and the evolution of his wartime thought, suggests he was groping all the while for a new method that might achieve Wilsonian ends through a gradual enlargement of trust within the great-power alliance.

Harry Hopkins tried to convey some of this approach in a letter he sent to Ambassador Winant on June 12. Things had gone well with Molotov, he wrote. He and the president got on "famously." "We simply cannot organize the world between the British and ourselves without bringing the Russians in as equal partners." For that matter, the Chinese, if things went well for them, would also have to be considered partners. The days of the "white man's burden are over."

The publicity releases about the second front told the story, Hopkins went on. "I have a feeling some of the British are holding back a bit but all in all it is moving as well as could be expected."[76] Readers of the *Washington Post* for June 18 could have learned from Walter Lippmann the essentials of the bargain struck in London, Washington, and Moscow, which historians have waited four decades to confirm from the archives. Discussing the negotiation of the Anglo-Russian treaty, Lippmann praised what he called the "liberal" policy finally adopted by all three nations:

> Yet it is necessary for us to understand that the liberal policy became a feasible policy only when it was clear that the United States is preparing to act strongly and constructively in the postwar period. If we had not . . . we would have been in no position to express any opinions about what Russia ought to do to make her western borders strategically secure. . . . By combining armaments and diplomacy, by weaving together the conduct of the war and the preparation of the peace, we are marching on our two legs to our goal.[77]

Four days later Hopkins and Ambassador Maksim Litvinov appeared together at Madison Square Garden at a Russian War Relief rally. "And what of our 3,000,000 trained ground troops with their modern mechanized equipment?" proclaimed

Hopkins. "I want to assure this audience that General Marshall, the great leader of our Army, is not training these men to play tiddlywinks. A second front? Yes, and if necessary a third and fourth front, to pen the German Army in a ring of our offensive steel."[78]

Even as Hopkins spoke, however, forces were in motion to deny Roosevelt his chance to build the peace along the lines he wished, and to insure that Europe would indeed be partitioned into spheres of influence. On June 9 the president met with Admiral Louis "Dickie" Mountbatten, whom Churchill had sent to prepare the way for his own visit. The subject of their "long and interesting talk" was the second front. Mountbatten argued the standard British position, that the shortage of landing craft and the presence of twenty-five German divisions in France meant that "no landing we could carry out could draw off any troops. . . ."

In reply, FDR asked Mountbatten to "remind the Prime Minister of the agreement reached last time he was in Washington, that in the event of things going very badly for the Russians this summer, a sacrifice landing would be carried out in France to assist them." In this conversation Roosevelt gave every indication of being torn by suspicions (more than shared by his military advisers) that the British wished to lure him into the "peripheral" strategy and thus deny him an opportunity, even before America's power could make itself felt, to design an American peace. Mountbatten's record of what he told Churchill of this conversation displays all these concerns.

> I pointed out that you [FDR] stressed the great need for American soldiers to be given an opportunity of fighting as soon as possible. . . .
>
> I said that you had asked for an assurance that we would be ready to follow up a crack in German morale by landing in France this autumn. . . .
>
> I pointed out that you did not wish to send a million soldiers to England and find, possibly, that a complete collapse of Russia had made a front attack on France impossible. I said that you

had asked whether we could not get a footing on the Continent some time this year, even as late as December, in which case you would give the highest possible priority to the production and shipping of Landing Craft, equipment and troops. . . .

I pointed out that you did not like our sending out divisions from England while American troops were still being sent in and that you suggested that we should leave about six divisions in England and that the corresponding six American divisions should be sent straight to fight in North Africa. . . .[79]

When Churchill himself arrived, the press talked about "lightning decisions" and the second front. But there were also reports that Tobruk had fallen to the Germans in North Africa. News reports out of Washington began to suggest that the second front would now have to be limited to holding the line in Egypt. No one was more distressed at this prospect than Secretary of War Stimson. He had not anticipated the fall of Tobruk, but he had expected Churchill would arrive with a barrage of arguments against a cross-channel attack. Stimson urged on the president (with his military advisers' full concurrence) that no "new plan should even be whispered to friend or enemy" unless it was so manifestly helpful to the objective of an invasion of France "that it could not possibly be taken as evidence of doubt or vacillation. . . ."[80]

As he feared, however, the objective was slipping away. On July 15 Stimson sent the president a handwritten note with a book on the ill-fated World War I campaign in the Dardanelles. It offered a parallel with present "attempted diversions from Bolero [the proposed cross-channel attack] by our British friends . . . I beg you to read it without delay and *before you decide upon your present action*."[81]

To his diary Stimson lamented, here was a case "of a fatigued and defeatist government which had lost its initiative, blocking the help of a young and vigorous nation whose strength had not yet been tapped by either war."[82]

"I feel damned depressed," Hopkins noted in the aftermath of a final no from the British on a cross-channel attack in 1942.

Roosevelt had sent his special adviser and General Marshall to London to figure out some way to keep the promise he had made to Molotov. He was not entirely surprised at the British refusal, the president cabled his emissaries, but they must find an alternative to use "American ground forces in 1942," whether it be in North Africa, Norway, Egypt, the Caucasus, or even Persia. There simply must be a decision.[83]

Secretary Stimson thought Roosevelt had yielded the main point too easily, however, and sent the president a memorandum implying he had allowed Britain to impose its will on military strategy for the sake of the empire.

> These proposals bear on their face the inevitable results of an attempt to compromise fundamentally opposed principles and policies. The U.S. has been seeking to establish a prompt offensive to ultimately destroy Hitler in Europe and in the meanwhile to keep Russia in the war. The U.K., while professing the same purpose, is equally if not more insistent upon a present attempt to preserve its empire in the Middle East.[84]

Roosevelt was angered by Stimson's suggestion, all the more so because he feared it was true. The secretary's obduracy offered "no help to Russian resistance in 1942," he complained. So Roosevelt settled for an attack on North Africa. American forces would not land in Europe until 1944. There were many reasons to doubt that a cross-channel attack could have been carried out in 1942. But the North African campaign led to the Italian campaign in 1943, and thus pushed strategic thinking away from Roosevelt's original goals, military and political. The British had welcomed Roosevelt's intervention in 1942 to limit the Anglo-Russian treaty to a twenty-year military alliance. They preferred to avoid political commitments of the sort Stalin and Molotov proposed, particularly about Poland. But by 1944 Churchill as well as Stalin would claim that their treaty relationship, however narrow, was wide enough for them to settle the fate of Central and Southeastern Europe.

This outcome came as no surprise to some observers—for example, to Henry Luce's *Time* magazine, which had predicted that the 1942 Anglo-Russian treaty, even devoid of political clauses, was designed as a counterweight to American predominance at the peace table. Roosevelt also understood the stakes, and that was why he was similarly concerned. *Time*'s question weighed on the president's mind as well:

> How much of Britain's impulse toward the pact could be accounted for by recent high Tory feeling that, in a world where the U.S. was daily growing stronger, a pact with Russia was a sound move for the preservation of European weight in the world of the future?[85]

Of all the pilgrimages to Washington in those early months of the war, Molotov's journey was probably the most successful, at least diplomatically. He had succeeded in putting Western diplomacy on the defensive. If he recalled the situation accurately many years later, he had gone to Washington knowing full well that the Western allies were not capable of launching a second front in 1942. The British had been almost willing to grant the frontier question out of inability to fight in Europe; now the Russians had a claim on Roosevelt as well. "It was of great importance for the [Russian] people," Molotov remembered, for morale purposes, "for politics and for further pressure on them." Whether Molotov's latter-day boast about his "triumph" was fully justified, the president felt the pressure. He began reconsidering his opposition to Churchill's Baltic policy soon thereafter, even while insisting he had brought premature political negotiations to a halt.[86]

6

PONDERING THE
RUSSIAN SPHINX

I am impressed with the consideration that
economic assistance is one of the most effective
weapons at our disposal to influence European
political events in the direction we desire and to
avoid the development of a sphere of influence of
the Soviet Union over Eastern Europe and the
Balkans.

Ambassador Averell Harriman, 1944[1]

"AT THE BEGINNING of 1943," wrote Cordell Hull in his
Memoirs, "Russia was a complete sphinx to all the other nations
of the world, except that she stood there fighting heroically."[2] It
fell mainly to Hull, as head of the State Department, to solve
the riddle—specifically, to discover Russia's attitude toward
American postwar planning, and by one means or another
induce the Kremlin to cooperate. Yet Roosevelt would keep
Hull out of Big Three discussions of wartime strategy, as if
what were decided at these sessions did not impinge on postwar
planning. Nominally in complete charge of economic planning
for the peace, Hull had to rely on tidbits of information as FDR
maintained a tight control over any matters that touched upon
Soviet-American relations.

The result was anything but happy. Resentful of the president's attitude, State Department (and other) policy planners were all the more suspicious of what Roosevelt was saying and doing for the sake of the Grand Alliance. Worse still, early on FDR developed an unfortunate habit of "stranding" the special agents he entrusted to pursue Soviet-American relations. Thus it was with William C. Bullitt in the 1930s when the issue was possible collaboration against Japan, and so it was in the middle of the war with Averell Harriman when the issue was a definite plan for American aid for Russian reconstruction after the war.

It would be wrong, however, to conclude that the president and his secretary of state disagreed about the central issue in future Soviet-American relations. As they both saw it, Stalin had two choices, and only two choices:

> one, isolation after lopping off certain territory along Russia's boundaries, accompanied by the maintenance of heavy armaments; two, become part of the world and meet all Russia's responsibilities under a sane, practical policy of international cooperation.[3]

If Russia chose the first option, and took Eastern Europe and the Baltic region out of the world economy after the war, it would not only put an awful burden on reconstruction plans—however they might develop—but it would, in Hull's view, re-create the world of the 1930s with all that implied. It was never the narrow economic question of markets in Eastern Europe that so concerned American policymakers, but the political economy of the postwar order.

The president favored what might be called a two-phased approach to the Soviets. It was his belief that the crucial transition period after the war should be used to build trust among the Big Three. As that trust grew, presumably, the tendency to act unilaterally would fade away of itself. Whatever had to be conceded to reassure Stalin during the war would be redeemed when the transition to a more open world was complete. Admittedly this was all quite vague in Roosevelt's mind. Understanding his two-phased approach helps to explain, nevertheless, why the president could approve of seemingly contradictory stances, for example, on the issues connected with Russia's demands for its 1941 frontiers.

As the time came to start thinking about mechanisms for reviving the world economy, the approach to the Soviets was no clearer. Roosevelt's method depended upon maintaining strong personal ties among the Big Three. What would happen when postwar planning and the need for such harmony conflicted? The president could delay decisions only for so long before facing the possibility of jeopardizing both the Grand Alliance and postwar planning.

FDR was undoubtedly correct, on the other hand, to believe that the "planners" too often disregarded the real world in favor of abstractions. On the crucial issue of spheres of influence, central to both political and economic planning, the president had hedged. He had counterbalanced his public statements against spheres of influence, and his intervention in the Anglo-Russian treaty negotiations, with his own personal statements to Molotov about Big Four responsibilities in a world disarmed except for the great powers. Both Britain and Russia looked on Roosevelt's "elevation" of China to such status with skepticism and concern—skepticism about China's ability to play such a role, and concern that America hoped to use China's "vote" to declare a majority for American wishes on every issue.

Roosevelt liked to produce thumbnail sketches for the United Nations he envisioned. It would contain three bodies, he once told Lord Halifax—a general assembly of all members, an executive committee of the Big Four, and an advisory council elected on a regional basis to meet from time to time with the Big Four to resolve crisis issues. The assembly, suggested Roosevelt, would meet once a year to let "the smaller powers... blow off steam." The executive committee, on the other hand, would "take all the more important decisions and wield police powers of the United Nations." Whether this scheme was compatible with a genuine effort to make colonial areas independent, or merely hinted at a complicated spheres-of-influence arrangement, remained to be seen.

Roosevelt could get quite carried away at these impromptu

"briefings," suggesting, for example, that the French would have to get out of Dakar and Bizerte in Africa so as to allow the United States and Great Britain to act as policemen for the new United Nations. Ambassador Halifax wondered if the president was perhaps being "very hard on the French." Yes, that was so, admitted Roosevelt, but then "France would no doubt require assistance for which consideration might be the placing of certain parts of her territory at the disposal of the United Nations."[4]

During this discussion Sumner Welles reminded the president that he had given promises to return the French Empire intact at the end of the war. Roosevelt parried the remark by saying he thought that referred only to North Africa, but in any event, "in the ironing out of things after the war this kind of position could be rectified."

State Department planners feared that the president was leaving far too many matters to be "rectified" at war's end. There must be some foundation, they argued, beyond what passed verbally between the Big Three. The constant fear in the State Department was that if the transition period were mishandled, the United States would lapse into "isolationism," particularly if America's wartime allies appeared to pursue independent policies. The aftermath of World War I and American disillusionment with "secret treaties" (the counterpart to spheres of influence) was always on State Department minds. Secretary Hull represented the "Wilsonian" wing of the Democratic party, of course, the "internationalist" who had always feared the "New Dealers" would go too far in the direction of economic self-sufficiency and national planning. Hull bided his time. He had survived the first wave of the New Deal—barely—and when war came he felt justified in his fundamental beliefs about the necessary relationship between open channels of trade and a peaceful world.

The camel is a ruminating animal, Hull liked to tell his State Department colleagues after Pearl Harbor, slow of foot and pondersome. But in the end it carried a lot more weight than a whole pack of jackasses! In discussing postwar economic planning, one must never slight this intra-administration fight that ensued with the beginning of the New Deal. That the war stopped "isolationist" talk did not mean—at least not to Secretary Hull—that it would not resurface after victory. Hull would even confront memories of the domestic battle in discussions with V. M. Molotov during the 1943 Moscow Foreign Ministers' Conference. The secretary had introduced a long list of measures to set the foundations of the postwar world on a strong base, and finally was able to "buttonhole" the Soviet foreign minister to ask his opinions. Molotov said he thought agreement was important. Then he paused, as if he suddenly understood why Hull was so determined, before saying,

> Isolation was almost your country's undoing, was it not, Mr. Secretary?
> Yes it was. And isolation was almost your country's undoing, was it not, Mr. Secretary.
> Molotov smiled and admitted it was.[5]

"After the war," Hull went on, seizing the opening Molotov had given him, "you can follow isolationism if you want, and gobble up your neighbors. But that will be your undoing. When I was young I knew a bully in Tennessee. He used to get a few things his way by being a bully and bluffing other fellows. But he ended up by not having a friend in the world."[6]

For Americans this was their second chance to right the world. There would not likely be another. Was it now to be thrown away? It would if the British sought to continue the Ottawa Imperial Preference System after the war.[7] And it might if Russia were to lead others into accepting a postwar world divided into spheres of influence.[8] If either of those untoward things occurred, there would be every reason to fear a revival of economic nationalism elsewhere—even in the United States, in the form of a super New Deal.

In short, unless steps were taken during the war to make sure such things did not happen, policy would never get to Roosevelt's second phase. That was where political and economic diplomacy overlapped. Despite Hull's fears, on the other hand, about Roosevelt's grasp of the connections between political commitments and economic troubles, many former New Dealers agreed with the secretary's analysis.[9] Perhaps the most prominent of the Brains Trusters still in a policymaking position, Assistant Secretary of State Adolf Berle, was adamant on the point. The "organizing principle" of postwar Europe, he wrote in his diary on October 27, 1942, "will either be on Stalinist lines or it will be along liberal and individualist lines."[10]

There was no hope that Russia could be brought to abandon its communist "system" of state trading abroad and government monopolies at home. No one in Washington expected that. They hoped instead to find a formula that would accomplish other ends, namely, Russian restraint in the areas of its "responsibility," and willingness to participate (however passively) in the restoration of the world economy along liberal-capitalist lines.

Experiences from the 1930s told Hull and his aides, moreover, that Russia was not likely to become a major outlet for American goods. The dream of a billion-dollar market that Maksim Litvinov had held out at the London Economic Conference in 1933 had never been realized. Russia's drive for self-sufficiency, the lack of American interest in Russian products, and the continuing dispute over what had been agreed in the negotiations leading to the establishment of diplomatic relations, all had a dampening impact on economic relations. In 1938, the last prewar year, Russia had purchased about $80 million worth of American machinery, a very small portion of the $3 billion the U.S. exported that year.[11]

American diplomats, and especially the once-enamored William C. Bullitt, the first U.S. ambassador to the Soviet Union (1933–1936), placed a sinister connotation on the failure of prewar economic diplomacy.[12] In a 1934 speech to the Philadelphia Chamber of Commerce, Ambassador Bullitt had painted a picture of the Soviet Union as a "continent filled with mineral riches as great or greater than those of the United States, a continent containing 170,000,000 human beings.... There are few products in the United States for which there is not some demand in the Soviet Union."[13]

But in a farewell blast at Soviet leaders and policies, Bullitt warned in a famous dispatch that the time was not far distant when Russia would become "a dangerous factor in the field of international trade."

> It is attempting to make itself as self-sufficient as possible and it will use its monopoly of trade ruthlessly to undersell and injure its enemies and to assist its friends. . . . It will . . . try to promote as much chaos as possible in the economies of capitalist countries in the hope that misery may beget communist revolution.[14]

Cordell Hull summed up prewar State Department estimates of the Soviets in a much shorter epigram: "They are utterly as unreliable as Jesse James."[15] Simply put, the department retained its skepticism about Soviet-American economic relations, either in themselves or as avenues to other objectives, while the White House saw possibilities in such wartime measures as Lend-Lease for establishing a good climate for postwar political and economic relations.

The origins of the American decision to send Lend-Lease aid to Russia have been discussed earlier, but it is worth recalling that Roosevelt had the Soviets on his mind when he rejected attempts to exclude Moscow from the program.[16] In the first weeks after the German attack on Russia, however, the president preferred to find other ways to send help. The first aid Russia was to receive, it was agreed at a White House conference with Ambassador Constantin Oumansky, would come through the Reconstruction Finance Corporation, and would be a mix of barter and credit arrangements.

At this meeting Roosevelt explained to the Russian ambassador his concern about moving too quickly with Lend-Lease "because of the unpopularity of Russia among large groups in the United States which exercised great political power in Congress. . . . If Moscow could get some publicity back to this country regarding freedom of religion it might have a fine educational effect . . . before the next Lend-Lease appropriations bill came up in Congress. . . ."[17]

Before the year was out, though, some of those who administered the Lend-Lease program were talking about "our need for Russia as a real friend and customer in the post-war period." General John Burns, head of the Soviet protocol committee, gave Harry Hopkins a long memo on relations with Russia in October 1942 that concluded:

> Russia's post-war needs for the products of America will be simply overwhelming. She must not only rehabilitate her war losses in homes, industries, raw materials and farms, but she must provide the resources for the inevitable advances in her standards of living that will result from the war.[18]

The rise of this sort of thinking inside the government gave State Department planners the shivers. They saw in it exactly the wrong attitude about postwar relations with Russia. Ambassador Bullitt, who had started out in 1933 as an anti–State Department Roosevelt appointee who was going to get things done in Russia, now argued the case against those who insisted the most important task of American policy was to overcome Soviet distrust. Suggesting that "liberals" who took this line were being duped by a Kremlin propaganda campaign carried on through foreign Communist parties, Bullitt wrote to the president on January 29, 1943, to urge him to seek an early meeting with Stalin.

They had often talked about Wilson's fate at Paris, Bullitt reminded FDR—the result of waiting too long. Once Germany surrendered, he went on, American influence over Russia would disappear, and instead of a postwar balance of power in Europe there would be a Balance of Impotence. Those who saw in Russia a valuable outlet for American goods were going to be disappointed, and doubly so because the Soviets were intent upon withdrawing Eastern Europe, and eventually all of Europe (if their plans succeeded), from the world economy.

> Again and again our diplomatic representatives in Moscow have been assured by the Soviet Government that the absolute monopoly of foreign trade will not be abandoned because its abandonment would mean the collapse of the whole Soviet

system of State-directed economy. We know, therefore, that areas annexed by the Soviet Union, will be withdrawn, as heretofore, from the area of normal trade between nations, which it is our policy to extend.[19]

What was the president to do about all this? He should insist upon an early meeting with Stalin. "By using the old technique of the donkey, the carrot and the club you might be able to make Stalin move in the direction in which we want him to move." Threats to slow down Land-Lease, or to deny aid for Russian reconstruction, could be added to a warning that the United States might have to turn its major war effort against Japan instead of Germany.[20]

Thus far Churchill had been carrying on all the personal diplomacy in Big Three relations. In fact, Roosevelt had scarcely gotten a word in edgewise. The prime minister had come to Washington immediately after Pearl Harbor to win Roosevelt to strategic conceptions, and in August 1942 he made the more arduous journey to Moscow to tell Stalin there would be no second front that year. British military reverses, the shortage of landing craft, and other factors made even the most limited assault on the Continent impossible. As the prime minister went on with his recital, "Stalin's face crumpled up into a frown." There was not a single German division in France worth anything, he grumbled. That remark led to an argument over intelligence sources, and then to other questions. But there would be an attack before the year was out, the prime minister promised, on German positions in North Africa. Operation TORCH, he said, would pave the way for greater things in Europe in 1943. Taking a piece of paper, Churchill drew a picture of a crocodile he called Europe, and directed Stalin's attention to what he called the "soft belly." It would be attacked at the same time that "we attacked its hard snout."[21]

Stalin's interest rose. "He saw it all in a flash," Churchill recorded of Stalin's reaction.[22] "May God help this enterprise to succeed," he said. But what else did Stalin see? He saw first that the prime minister still had Roosevelt's proxy on strategic questions; he saw that Churchill planned to put military forces into Southeastern Europe as events made possible; he saw, finally, that future negotiations over respective spheres of influence would be shaped by military positions. By taking Churchill's promise of a second front in 1943 as a solemn vow, whether or not it materialized that year, Stalin could at least strengthen his moral claims on his Western allies at the peace conference.

In subsequent discussions, therefore, Stalin reverted to the second front many times, often in an insulting fashion, causing the prime minister to wonder at his suddenly changing moods. But the Soviet leader was laying the groundwork for future political demands with these complaints. Churchill had often deflected Russian criticisms by erupting at Maisky about Britain's standing alone during the period of the Nazi-Soviet pact; now Stalin was doing the same with disparaging comments about British reluctance to meet the German army on the battlefield.

Churchill had, in a roundabout fashion, introduced other questions about Southeastern Europe and Turkey during his Moscow sojourn, but the Foreign Office soft-pedaled the question of a Balkan confederation for the remainder of the year. It was likely to irritate the Russians at a bad time. Still, everyone kept a wary eye on the activities of the Soviet ambassador to the exile governments in London. He was thought to be undoing the Foreign Office's quiet diplomacy to promote the confederation.[23]

At the conclusion of the successful TORCH campaign, Churchill and Roosevelt met at Casablanca in January 1943 to plan the next strategic moves in the war. The president had sought to have Stalin present for these discussions, even mentioning the idea of a tripartite meeting to the Russian leader before he sounded out the ever-eager Churchill. Many things might have been different had Stalin responded to FDR's invitation. But he did not, preferring for good or ill to stay home and play to the hilt the role of injured party.

Roosevelt's advisers were also irked at having had to follow a

British strategic lead, and came to Casablanca determined no longer to be a fluttering tail on Churchill's kite. But that was not to be either. The British had brought boatloads of documents, groused an American diplomat, to bolster their proposal for an all-out Mediterranean strategy that would postpone the second front for well over a year.[24]

The most famous statement to come out of the Casablanca Conference was Roosevelt's dramatic pronouncement to reporters at its conclusion that the Allies would accept nothing less than "unconditional surrender" from the Axis nations. It was controversial at the time and continued to be so after the war. Churchill and Roosevelt discussed the statement, the former wondering about excluding Italy from such absolute terms. The president clearly wished to reassure Stalin—who, he told his military advisers before the conference, "has a feeling of loneliness"—that there would be no separate peace in the west.[25]

Harry Hopkins was decidedly upset with the military decisions at Casablanca. "I told him," he reported of a conversation with Churchill, "it seemed to me like a pretty feeble effort for our two countries in 1943."[26] Especially, he might have added, with the news from the eastern front. After five months of battle at Stalingrad, the German army had been forced to surrender. It was the decisive battle of the European war and recognized immediately as such in both Allied and Axis capitals. Russia had survived Hitler's onslaught. Two armies of more than a million men each had fought, and the Russians had won. Stalin wanted an immediate counterattack all along the front, which turned out to be a costly error, but Stalingrad had erased forever the idea that the peace could be an Anglo-American affair.[27]

As military historian John Erickson writes,

> Politically, Stalingrad was a victory full of long-term potency, a slow-burning fuse which worked its way through the subsequent history of the war both on the Eastern Front and at large. If the battle of Poltava in 1709 turned Russia into a European power, then Stalingrad set the Soviet Union on the road to being a world power.[28]

The fuse was already burning too fast for Churchill. Immediately after the Casablanca Conference the prime minister left for talks aimed at persuading the Turks to come into the war under a Western aegis. Foreign Secretary Eden had serious doubts about what would come of this mission to "nip into the Balkans with their [Russia's] old enemy Turkey before they can get there themselves."[29] But he agreed with his associates in the Foreign Office who were now anxious to pursue the Balkan confederation scheme in order to check any Russian forward movement. We may have a card or two to play, noted Orme Sargent, despite Soviet advantages in the area. At the end of the war there might be an Anglo-American army in the Balkans, plowing through the "soft belly" of the crocodile; Turkey might be a belligerent; and "we and the Americans will control the relief organization which will have to feed the starving population throughout...."[30]

So eager was the Foreign Office to get rolling with the confederation idea that an approach was made to Turkey shortly after Churchill's visit. Istanbul took it as a bid for them to lead such a bloc. Word of this leaked to the Russians, and Molotov made it plain that his government did not like the idea. Eden pulled back at once. "Much will depend upon whether we ourselves are in occupation of that area," he said in a memorandum to the cabinet on postwar Europe.[31]

When the foreign secretary came to Washington in early 1943, Roosevelt asked him point-blank to comment on the "Bullitt thesis that the Soviet Government was determined to dominate all of Europe by force of arms or by force of communist propaganda." Eden took a much more sanguine position, replying that the "wise and expedient thing" would be to cultivate "to the utmost extent possible the friendship and confidence of the Soviet Government so as to pave the way for international cooperation...."[32]

It was impossible to say if Bullitt's fears were justified, yet "we should make the position no worse by trying to work with Russia...." Roosevelt agreed, adding that he did not "take exception to the Russian claim to the Baltic states." He hoped for a plebiscite, but no one was "going to be able to turn her out." Neither did he have any difficulty agreeing to Russian demands on Finland, nor about the Curzon line as the future eastern boundary of Poland.[33]

Foreign Office experts noted that Roosevelt seemed "to have come much nearer to our views about the Soviet Union." Perhaps too much so, given the internal debates in London. "It would certainly be impossible to start negotiating with the Russians on these lines," cautioned Frank Roberts of the Foreign Office, "until the western military effort balances that of the Russians in the eyes of occupied Europe."[34]

The Foreign Office's attention to an emerging American debate was further focused by Walter Lippmann's column of April 1, 1943. Many important people paid attention to what the usually well-informed pundit wrote, and in this column he took on Bullitt's hard-line thesis. There were ominous signs that Bullitt's views would prevail, he warned, especially in the State Department. Isolationalism after World War I, Lippmann insisted, had been a reaction to fears that the United States was getting itself involved in a broad commitment to the status quo. Article X of the League of Nations Covenant, with its binding obligation to oppose aggression and aggressors, had made people choose between involvement in every dispute in Europe and withdrawal. Another isolationist reaction was inevitable, he went on, if Washington insisted upon declaring general principles and prejudging all questions according to abstract standards.

Above all, Lippmann then concluded, American statesmen "mustn't mislead other governments by allowing them or encouraging them to think they can adopt a line of policy which can be carried through only with the permanent armed support of the United States.... It is our duty to make it clear to our Allies... that they must find an order which remains in equilibrium without the permanent intervention of the United States."[35]

This was a very different Lippmann from the man who a year earlier had praised Roosevelt for saving the Atlantic Charter from Anglo-Russian diplomacy. And it also appeared to be a different Roosevelt. Whatever had moved the president in the months after Casablanca and Stalingrad, an open struggle now appeared to be going on for his heart and mind. Truly alarmed now, Bullitt returned to the charge in May 1943, repeating his earlier recommendations and adding:

> The most curious phenomenon of the present period is the fact that at a time when our military strength is increasing prodigiously our world political leadership is disappearing. You remember Napoleon's remark that Wellington won at Waterloo because he did not realize he was beaten. We are in the opposite case. We are losing our world leadership because we do not realize we have won power over the world.... [36]

Bullitt's fears seemed overdrawn in the late spring of 1943 when Moscow dissolved the Comintern. We know now that Soviet manipulation of foreign Communist parties did not cease; but contemporary decisions in Washington were not made chiefly on the basis of overoptimism about postwar Russian aims, as Bullitt feared, but on other grounds. To policymakers, an all-out effort to halt the Russian advance in the Balkans might mean the Red Army would overrun Germany, which was the key to postwar dominance in Europe. A confrontation in the Balkans would also involve the United States in the area of least importance to American war aims; staying out, on the other hand, could set a precedent for allowing its partners to settle critical questions in an inherently unstable fashion. [37]

One way of getting through the transition period was along the route originally suggested by Averell Harriman, from Lend-Lease to postwar reconstruction aid. But Hull saw no indications that the Russians were interested in his program for reconstructing the international economic system.

Hull pressed Eden on the issue of Russia's seeming disinterest in postwar cooperation, for example, and tried to impress upon him that many people, not just Bullitt, were saying Moscow would take "what she pleases and confer with nobody."

The foreign secretary appeared almost cavalier, replying laconically that in the meantime Russia was killing Germans. We all know this, Hull shot back, but if Russia showed no interest in joint efforts to promote peace and economic rehabilitation "based on liberal commercial policies, . . . nothing would be gained except that Russia and Great Britain will have succeeded in eliminating Germany."[38]

Roosevelt was still hoping in the early spring of 1943 to convince Stalin that his security needs could be cared for without violating the Atlantic Charter. An inspired article on Roosevelt's plans by Forrest Davis in the *Saturday Evening Post* placed the onus on Moscow for maintaining Big Three harmony. The riddle of the hour was what Russia intended to do with its new military power. Should Stalin choose to collaborate, the foundations of a decent postwar world could be laid; otherwise the Western allies would no doubt be forced back on an American-led balance-of-power system.

Taking a realistic, nonutopian point of view, Davis continued, the president remained confident the great powers could be brought into agreement. The common denominator would be the need for peace in all countries—in Russia which had been living under a war economy for the whole life of the Soviet Union, and in the United States, "uninvaded and relatively fresh." Stalin was going to have to understand, Davis wrote, that he would have to take risks in peace as in war—as they all were.

> Stalin could, it is likely, satisfy his desire for territorial security in harmony with the Atlantic Charter, through a combination of the plebiscite and trusteeship techniques. That carries with it a risk, but he can scarcely hope to have it both ways: standing on a *fait accompli* in Eastern Europe but collaborating elsewhere.[39]

Having made up his mind to try to convince Stalin to accept something like the U.S. position in Latin America as a model for Eastern Europe, Roosevelt redoubled his efforts for a face-to-face meeting with the Russian leader.[40] Apparently much impressed with what former Ambassador Joseph Davies was telling him about prospects for dealing with postwar problems, the president asked Davies to be a go-between with Stalin. That would mean a discussion of matters like Poland's eastern frontier, Davies cautioned. Roosevelt did not demur. Without explicitly authorizing Davies to say that he agreed with Russia's claims to the so-called Curzon line, which approximated what the Red Army had seized in 1939, the president told Davies he could say, "We think you are entitled to the Curzon line, but think it unwise to insist upon it now."⁴¹

Averell Harriman was then assigned the task of persuading a *very* reluctant Churchill of the wisdom of such a meeting. Harriman stressed the point that the American public's reaction to a three-cornered meeting, at which Churchill appeared to be the broker, would harm chances for acceptance of the results. Churchill was deeply alarmed, for he saw where this was leading. Enemy propaganda would make great use, he protested to Roosevelt, of a meeting between Stalin and the president, from which the British Commonwealth and Empire were excluded. "It would be serious and vexatious, and many would be bewildered and alarmed thereby."⁴²

No one more vexed and bewildered than himself, he ought to have said. Roosevelt then told a small white lie. He suggested that the idea for a two-party meeting had come from Stalin via Joseph Davies. But he insisted that he wished to go ahead. Stalin would be more frank with him alone, he cabled the prime minister. He wished to talk with the Soviet dictator about China, about the Balkan states, Finland, and Poland. "I want to explore his thinking as fully as possible concerning Russia's postwar hopes and ambitions."⁴³

So as Roosevelt confided his private musings to Davies on such matters as the Curzon line, he withheld certain thoughts from Churchill. Roosevelt simply did not want the British to set up the United States for a confrontation with the Soviet Union over spheres of influence when, he fervently hoped, there remained other options. If Churchill took the lead in attempting a settlement, the best to be expected was a shaky interim solution that might or might not lead to something better. Harriman had made a good case for what the United States had to offer that Britain did not:

> As you know, I am a confirmed optimist in our relations with Russia because of my conviction that Stalin wants, if obtainable, a firm understanding with you and America more than anything else—after the destruction of Hitler. He sees Russia's reconstruction and security more soundly based on it than on any alternative. He is a man of simple purposes, and although he may use devious means in attempting to accomplish them, he does not deviate from his long-run objectives.[44]

None of this would work, however, if the British and Russians sought an "independent" solution of the matter of spheres of influence. To concern about the psychological damage of attempting to repeat the appeasement experiment—primarily the further undermining of faith in liberal government—was added the conviction that it would not work anyway. And when the attempt failed, and an East-West confrontation followed, what then?

The State Department thought Churchill perfectly capable of diverting political questions after the war so as to produce either an East-West struggle or an Anglo-Soviet accord, in order to protect the empire—exactly the mistake Chamberlain had made with Hitler. Whenever Roosevelt came close to touching upon the empire, the prime minister shooed him off. The president never persisted in his arguments beyond a certain point, but he said enough to impress Churchill. For his part, the prime minister deplored Roosevelt's pursuit of "vague" aspirations to a postwar world order that "cost them nothing to make" and lay open "our whole Empire to great embarrassment." "I have several times informed the President," Churchill said in exasperation at one point, "that I did not accept universal application of the Atlantic Charter."[45]

Roosevelt did not wish openly to challenge either Stalin or Churchill about their "exclusions" to the Atlantic Charter; nor did he wish it to appear that the United States was out to deprive them of reasonable security zones. But neither did he want to permit them to reestablish the conditions that led to war. Roosevelt agreed with Secretary of War Henry L. Stimson: the Balkans loomed much too large in British planning. London seemed to feel, the secretary wrote the president, that Germany could be beaten by a series of attritions in northern Italy and the Balkans, "and that the only fighting which needs to be done will be done by Russia." He added:

> To me, in the light of the post-war problems which we shall face, that attitude towards Russia seems terribly dangerous. We are pledged quite as clearly as Great Britain to the opening of a real second front. None of these methods of pinprick warfare can be counted on by us to fool Stalin into the belief that we have kept that pledge.[46]

Roosevelt met with Stimson and his military chiefs of staff that same day. The discussion began with a Stimson-Roosevelt dialogue on the folly of an expedition into Southeastern Europe, which concluded with this statement:

> THE PRESIDENT said that the British Foreign Office does not want the Balkans to come under Russian influence. Britain wants to get to the Balkans first. He said that personally he could not see the logic of this reasoning. He did not believe the Russians would desire to take over the Balkan states. Their wish is to establish kinship with the other Slavic people. In any event, he thought it unwise to plan military strategy based on a gamble as to political results.[47]

To prevent a diversion into the Balkans, he admonished his generals, the United States must have preponderance in the OVERLORD operation into France, "starting from the first day of the assault." Earlier Roosevelt had gambled on military strategy and political aims with his 1942 pledge for a second front that never opened. Now, with American power reaching its zenith, the president seemed determined to let the Balkans go by default rather than allow either an Anglo-Russian confrontation or an Anglo-Russian political agreement. What was one to make of this complete about-face from his previous positions?

William Bullitt, sidetracked in an office in the Navy Department, wrote to protest:

> War is an attempt to achieve political objectives by fighting; and political objectives must be kept in mind in planning operations. Our political objectives require the establishment of British and American forces in the Balkans and eastern and central Europe. Their first objective should be the defeat of Germany, their second, the barring of the Red Army of the way into Europe.[48]

Far from concern about British adventurism in the Balkans, Bullitt believed Roosevelt must stir up the British to prevent a spheres-of-influence "appeasement" arrangement. "A Europe divided into a Soviet sphere of influence, which would be communist, and a British sphere of influence, which would be capitalist, would produce at best an uneasy armistice but no peace. Europe would be another 'house divided against itself.'"[49]

On the eve of the next Roosevelt-Churchill meeting, the Quebec Conference of August 1943, the question of postwar political forces in former Axis countries and satellites had become a reality in Italy. Handling the touchy matter of a post-Mussolini government was in the foreground, but the more general issue was always present, looming over both military and political discussions.

Harry Hopkins brought with him a memorandum prepared by General J. H. Burns, who worked with Edward R. Stettinius in the Lend-Lease Administration. The gist of the memo was that Russia had borne the burden of the war, and would continue to do so.

> Whenever the Allies open a second front on the Continent, it will be decidedly a *secondary* front to that of Russia; theirs will continue to be the main effort. Without Russia in the war, the Axis cannot be defeated in Europe, and the position of the United States becomes precarious.[50]

Since Russia was the "decisive factor in the war," every effort must be made to obtain her friendship. Even more significant, "since without question she will dominate Europe on the defeat of the Axis, it is even more essential to develop and maintain the most friendly relations with Russia."

At Quebec the discussions about postwar relations with Russia went round and round the sphinx, ending in confusion. Eden and Hopkins were the first to make the circuit. If he went to Moscow for the forthcoming foreign ministers' meeting, said Eden, and made it plain there would be no second front in 1943, and no progress on the issue of Russia's frontier claims, "then I thought the meeting would almost certain[ly] do more harm than good." Hopkins agreed, adding that Roosevelt's views on Russian frontiers were almost exactly the same as Eden's. He had said as much to Litvinov and Molotov.[51]

Roosevelt, Hopkins continued, wanted to see Stalin personally because he could not entrust anyone to say these things to the Soviet leader. At dinner, however, with both Hull and Hopkins present as well as Eden and Churchill, Roosevelt acted as if concessions to the Russians were the furthermost thing from his mind. The foreign ministers could not act as plenipotentiaries, the president observed. If Molotov raised the Finnish question or the Baltic states, the American representative would have to say he had no instructions and would refer home. What good would that be, Churchill interjected, since the United States government would not be able to give an answer? Roosevelt said he could then keep silence, "as the Russians kept silence." Churchill, clearly annoyed at this Rooseveltian gambit, said he did not see how this could improve Big Three relations. Even more annoyed, Eden said that such a position was "wholly unacceptable" as far as he was concerned. Stalin had made plain as long ago as 1941 his requirements for the western frontiers. Hull could not pretend two years later that he was hearing this question for the first time and must therefore refer home.[52]

Later in the conversation, however, Churchill drew back from Eden's position, saying that next year Russia would be relatively weaker than the Western powers. There was no advantage, then, discussing "these matters now." This time Harry Hopkins intervened. Relations with Russia were deteriorating. "We really must make an attempt to improve them now."

But if there was no agreement on a policy on the frontier question, repeated Eden, there was little likelihood of improving Big Three political relations. Roosevelt ended the conversation with vague remarks about his plan for a four-power declaration to establish machinery for organizing the interim peace, before the final peace treaties were ready to sign.[53]

Eden feared going to Moscow empty-handed: no second front, no agreement on postwar frontiers. Roosevelt, unwilling to allow the British to drag him into the Balkans, sent Cordell Hull to present his proposed four-power declaration, complete with a self-denying clause that committed the great powers to refrain from using military force in liberated areas. The Russians had an equally short agenda: military steps to bring the war to a conclusion as quickly as possible. Hull insisted that he was not there to talk about military strategy but only postwar issues. Nevertheless, he yielded to Russian pressure to reaffirm yet another promise that the second front would be opened in 1944.

This pledge won him a hearing for the proposed four-power declaration. The key provisions included a commitment to a general security organization, based on the equality of all peace-loving states, and the self-denying clause, Paragraph 6, which affirmed:

> That after the termination of hostilities they will not employ their military forces within the territories of other states except for the purposes envisaged [to disarm the enemy states] in this declaration and after joint consultation.[54]

Later statements, such as the Yalta Declaration on Liberated Europe, were all derived in one way or another from this pledge. On October 25 the secretary of state brought forward a proposal on U.S. cooperation in the rehabilitation of war damage in the USSR. Once the war emergency came to an end, it read, "our productive capacity will be sufficiently great to enable us to play a substantial part in rehabilitation and reconstruction in the U.S.S.R." It was agreed that preliminary discussions should begin between Soviet representatives and the U.S. mission in Moscow.[55]

Hull's juxtaposing of the four-power declaration with an American "offer" of postwar reconstruction aid was supposed to impress the Russians with where real advantages could be found. Britain could make no such offer. Hull believed the Russians had at last realized what an "isolationist" policy or a bilateral "deal" with the British would cost in terms of American support.

The secretary was positively aglow with what he thought he had accomplished in Moscow. Speaking at a special joint session of Congress, Hull declared that the postwar issue had been resolved: "As the provisions of the Four Nation Declaration are carried into effect, there will no longer be need for spheres of influence, for alliances, for balance of power, or any other special arrangements through which, in the unhappy past, the nations strove to safeguard their security or to promote their interests."[56]

Roosevelt was also excited, as was Churchill, who called the results "prodigious." But the newly appointed ambassador to Russia, Averell Harriman, struck a cautious note. Certain doubts had been laid to rest, he cabled Roosevelt, but the "character of certain real difficulties that exist has been more sharply defined." For one thing, the second-front issue remained crucial; for another, from the way the discussions went, the Russians probably concluded that Washington had agreed not to raise serious questions about the frontier issue. While he doubted the Russians wished to extend their system, "it was indicated that although they would keep us informed they would take unilateral action in respect to these countries in the establishment of relations satisfactory to themselves."[57]

Harriman's report restored a proper note of realism in Roosevelt's attitude toward the postwar world. When congratulations on the Big Four declaration at Moscow came from none other than the skeptical Walter Lippmann, the president wrote back on November 8, 1943, "Moscow was a real success. Sometimes. however, I feel that the world will be mighty lucky if it gets 50% of what it seeks out of the war as a permanent success. That might be a high average."[58]

Despite his reservations, Harriman was more than eager to begin his mission to the Soviet Union. Previous American representatives had gone about things in the wrong way, Harriman told Adolf Berle, using a "policy of soft and encouraging statements" which made it possible for the Russians to maneuver Americans into feeling guilty whenever something went awry in Lend-Lease deliveries. "He feels that to find a formula with the Russians would be of the extremist difficulty," Berle noted, "but says he is incurably optimistic. . . ."[59]

Talking on the record to British and American correspondents on November 4, the new ambassador to the Soviet Union declared that a matter for "the greatest possible consideration" was assistance to Russia after the war.

> The American people have the greatest of sympathy for the Russian people [who] have also suffered so much, and it is in their hearts to attempt to be of the greatest assistance. We will have the plan to produce greatest assistance [sic]. We will have the plans to produce machinery and equipment needed by the Soviet Union and in so doing we will help our own people to convert from war to peace production.[60]

Just before Harriman arrived in Moscow, and before the Foreign Ministers' Conference, the first head of American war production, Donald M. Nelson, spent ten days in the city. He was received by both Molotov and Stalin. Whenever talk turned to postwar economic relations, Nelson's hosts pressed him on the possibility of obtaining American goods on credit. Stalin's enthusiasm for credit impressed members of the embassy. Nelson left promising to present the idea of a joint Russian-American commission to formulate a plan for such an arrangement to Roosevelt.[61]

Harriman undoubtedly heard about the Nelson-Stalin exchanges, and it probably buoyed his "incurable optimism" still higher. One thing troubled him: he did not want the discussions to get caught up in Washington infighting. If that happened, he feared, there never would be a plan to present to the Russians. Nelson's message had apparently triggered action in

Washington, however, as the ambassador discovered that Harry Hopkins was already talking with Soviet officials about "the formation of some kind of committee."

He was in the best position, Harriman cabled Hopkins, to judge whether Soviet requests were really for war purposes. Goods not needed for the war should come under different financial arrangements, Harriman continued.

There is no doubt they want to do the maximum amount [of] business that is possible with us but they are going to be tough in their trading. I believe that a better deal from our standpoint can be made in Moscow. . . . We must not lose sight of the fact that this subject is of great importance in our over all relations with the Soviet Government.[62]

Elbridge Durbrow, a State Department expert on Eastern Europe, was more concerned about unrealistic expectations for trade with Russia. An interdepartmental committee had been studying the problem, he noted in a memo, and had concluded that while the Soviets would have an overwhelming need for capital goods after the war, they produced little that Americans wanted.

Contrary to the general belief on this subject the United States and the Soviet Union are not complementary countries since there are very few products produced in the U.S.S.R. which we can take in exchange for American goods.[63]

For this reason Durbrow was doubtful that the Soviet Union could make timely payments on credits Washington might extend. Certainly these should total no more than $200 million. "It will be seen therefore that extreme caution must be taken in order to avoid false impressions being created regarding the possibilities of postwar trade with the Soviet Union."[64]

Harriman and Durbrow were talking about two different issues. The ambassador wanted control of economic negotiations in Moscow not out of concern for American markets but in order to shape reconstruction aid for political goals. Sometimes the issues overlapped. On the eve of the first Roosevelt-

Stalin meeting at Teheran, it still had not been decided where the discussions about postwar aid and credits would be conducted, and what priorities would be assigned to reaching an early agreement even for political purposes. Harriman had good reason to fret.

The Big Three began their discussions in Teheran on November 28, 1943. Stalin's agenda was, as before, headed by the all-important question of the second front. It had always been a political as well as a military question; now it was deeply imbedded in the politics of peace as well as the politics of war. Roosevelt brushed aside Churchill's talk about alternatives to OVERLORD, the invasion of France, and moved on to a private conversation with Stalin about "the future peace of the world."

Roosevelt had come to Teheran, Harry Hopkins told Churchill's aides, "to come to terms with Stalin, and he is not going to allow anything to interfere with that purpose."[65]

7

FROM TEHERAN TO TOLSTOY

This is really no time for ideological warfare. I am
determined to put down mutiny....I wish you all
success...in your Romanian negotiations in which
...we consider you are the predominant power.
Winston Churchill to V. M. Molotov,
April 16, 1944[1]

ON BOARD THE *USS Iowa* en route to the Cairo and
Teheran conferences, President Roosevelt and the Joint Chiefs
of Staff talked at length about British efforts to divert military
resources to the eastern Mediterranean and the Balkans. Roosevelt noted that Churchill was interested in working for a
"European economic federation." But the president did not
wish to get "roped into accepting any European sphere of
influence." He did not wish to be compelled, for example, to
maintain U.S. troops in Yugoslavia. Besides, the Russian attitude had to be considered.

When General Marshall complained that British plans would
prolong the war in Europe and delay the end of the war in the
Pacific—and grumbled that the United States was preparing for
OVERLORD all the way back to the Rocky Mountains while
London was thinking of "ditching" the planned invasion of
France for other operations—Roosevelt suggested telling the

British they ought to take their troops in the Middle East, "close to the Balkans," and send them to the Far East.

Russian troops, FDR observed, were within sixty miles of the Polish border and only forty from Bessarabia. Once they crossed the Bug River they would be on the point of entering Rumania. Under these conditions Stalin might take another look at Western strategy and ask for a change, an attack up from the Adriatic to the Danube. General Marshall urged the president not to float such an idea at the Big Three conference. Churchill would, he feared, pick up any hint of a shift in Roosevelt's thinking to argue for a Balkan strategy, which he could then put to Stalin as an Anglo-American plan.[2]

At Quebec some months earlier, Roosevelt and Churchill and their advisers had gone round the Russian "question" several times without ever moving toward the center. Now the center, Stalin, was present to hear what they had decided. At the outset of the war Roosevelt had taken a stand against any wartime efforts to settle territorial questions. Churchill had pushed him, on the other hand, not to allow the Atlantic Charter to stand in the way of reaching an agreement with the Russians. When the prime minister argued that position, of course, it was uncertain when or where Western power could make itself felt again. Now that decision time had arrived, Churchill hoped that Anglo-American military power could redeem some of what had been sacrificed at a low point in Western fortunes.

Neither Roosevelt nor Churchill enjoyed the prospect of seeing Russia replace Germany as the dominant power in Europe. But neither Roosevelt's "second front" strategy nor Churchill's "peripheral" strategy had prevented the necessity of difficult choices. However much he may have been disappointed by the course of events, Roosevelt did not intend to allow Churchill to embroil him in an Anglo-Russian contest to dominate Southeastern Europe. He could not see how such a challenge to the Soviets would improve the outlook. His own plans for dealing with the Russian question remained vague, and based loosely on preserving the Grand Alliance. Beyond some nebulous thoughts about using economic aid to encourage postwar Russian cooperation, never actually presented to Stalin at either Teheran or Yalta, the president had only his determination to avoid the appearance of an Anglo-American "bloc" as a settled policy for winning the peace.

Despite Marshall's warning, Roosevelt did suggest the possibility of an Adriatic operation, in cooperation with Tito's partisans, northeast into Rumania to effect a junction with the Red Army. Churchill leaped at the idea, as expected; and Stalin just as quickly rejected it, as expected. Although his military advisers and Harry Hopkins were nearly aghast at Roosevelt's sudden fascination with the "Adriatic business," it may have been the president's way of getting Churchill out on a limb and letting Stalin cut it off.[3]

However that may be, in private discussions with Stalin about the Baltic states Roosevelt was at last ready to state his "policy" toward that area. He prefaced his comments to Stalin with an extended explanation of his hopes for the future world organization. Somehow, sometime in the future, after the Big Three had gotten all "mixed up together," he wanted to believe they could reconcile their world leadership with a reasonably Wilsonian outcome.[4]

That was to be hoped for, at least, but the moment demanded that Stalin be reassured. As to the Baltic states, therefore, Roosevelt had to say there were political difficulties about recognizing their incorporation into the Soviet Union— the millions of Americans of Baltic extraction. But the president "did not intend to go to war with the Soviet Union on this point." All he wanted was a referendum or some expression of the people's will.

Stalin was not equally forthcoming, commenting only that the Soviet constitution allowed sufficient opportunities for the expression of public will. When the discussion turned to Poland's postwar boundaries, Roosevelt raised a similar caveat about American voters of Polish extraction. He had not been present when Churchill and Stalin talked about those frontiers— and used matchsticks to move them around on the dinner table—and he was just as happy to leave the lead to Churchill. Personally he agreed with Stalin's wish to move the borders of Poland westward, but there were six or seven million voters of Polish extraction he must consider, and thus he "could not participate in any decision here in Teheran or even next winter on this subject and . . . could not publicly take part in any such arrangement at the present time."[5]

Interestingly, Roosevelt did not even raise the question of Russia's western frontiers with British policymakers, preferring, as he had always insisted, to deal with Stalin alone.[6] One can only conclude this: although FDR believed he might be talking about exactly the same boundaries, exactly the same areas (e.g., the Baltic states), and exactly the same *immediate* results, he was convinced that the *long-term* implications of a Churchill-Stalin agreement or even a Big Three arrangement were somehow different from a Soviet-American understanding.

Roosevelt returned from Teheran to spread the word among his close advisers that "Uncle Joe" was get-at-able. During a lengthy monologue on the conference, the president enthused over the results and his new relationship with Stalin. "The President defended Stalin's attitude with regard to Esthonia [sic], Latvia, and Lithuania. He said Stalin did not want Finland but did want that part of Finland which was necessary to protect Leningrad and which Russia had obtained in the war against Finland in 1940." Nor did he disagree with Stalin's view that Poland should be satisfied to receive East Prussia, with its better lands, in exchange for losing territory up to the so-called Curzon line in the east.[7]

Roosevelt's report did not sit well with at least one cabinet member, Secretary of State Cordell Hull. Talking with Secretary of War Stimson, he asserted that the main point to establish was that there could be no acquisitions by force. That, of course, was the very principle Stimson had enunciated in his famous "Stimson Doctrine," opposing the Japanese movement into Manchuria. Throughout the 1930s Stimson had continued to chide the British for not supporting him fully during the Manchurian crisis. But now he argued the other side to Hull:

I thought we had to consider other things more realistic than that, such as the feelings which would actuate Russia: (a) that she had saved us from losing the war; (b) that she prior to 1914 had owned the whole of Poland including Warsaw and running as far as Germany and that she was not asking for restitution of that, etc. etc.[8]

Ambassador Harriman, meanwhile, had returned to Moscow believing he had been empowered by Roosevelt to carry out a fateful mission. During the conference the president had talked with Hopkins and Harriman about a plan for postwar economic aid to Russia. But he had said nothing to Stalin. Roosevelt "regretted" there had not been time during the crowded schedule to discuss the question of American reconstruction aid, Harriman explained to Molotov, but he had been authorized to begin negotiations.[9]

At their next meeting, on December 31, 1943, Molotov asked what the ambassador thought might be done. Harriman believed an American government agency might extend credits for the purchase of equipment and supplies for reconstruction. It would be necessary to get around Lend-Lease restrictions, of course, and to place these new orders on a different basis. Harriman thought that if U.S. specialists came to Moscow, a list might be compiled for planning purposes.

Harriman's major concern at this stage was to keep the aid question under his control in Moscow. He viewed his mission as a follow-up to the Teheran conference, and indeed as the culmination of his work on Soviet-American relations from the time of the decision to extend Lend-Lease aid. Roosevelt had largely bypassed the Washington bureaucracy in expediting that crucial decision, and this matter was no less important.

But having broached the question so confidently with Molotov, Harriman found himself unable to provide the specifics of a concrete plan. He had hoped to present a proposal that would appeal to the Russians—if they showed a willingness to cooperate with their Western partners in refraining from a policy of conquest and aggrandizement in Eastern Europe. Of a sudden

Harriman's direct line to Roosevelt failed. Whether it was because of concern over risking a confrontation with Congress in an election year, or for some other reason, the president chose not to intervene as the State Department moved in to take control of the negotiations with Moscow.[10]

When Harriman launched his plan, Harry Hopkins had been taken ill, a situation, some have argued, that made it impossible for the ambassador to restore his connection with the White House.[11] But it was Hopkins who suggested to Harriman a plan devised by Lend-Lease administrator Oscar Cox—to use Lend-Lease as a stopgap measure until a final policy could be worked out, under provisions that allowed goods to be delivered until 1947. Cox's idea was that goods not taken by war's end could be negotiated under a different credit arrangement which would still comply with the Lend-Lease law. In other words, the Russians would be obligated to take the items contracted for under Lend-Lease, but to pay for them under a newly negotiated agreement. Given the fact that the Soviets had never imported as much as $100 million from America in prewar years, the Lend-Lease supplies in the works could be used for reconstruction purposes and would be at least twice as great as they had received in any prewar year. "Using the method I have suggested," Cox told Hopkins, "would start them well on the road to reconstruction."[12]

This became the basis of the Washington plan that American officials tried to negotiate with the Russians over the next six months. Harriman regarded it as a stopgap measure that did not begin to meet Soviet requirements or those of his own plan for channeling the Russians along proper lines into the postwar world. Cox himself agreed with Harriman's estimate, and pushed for additional credits from the Export-Import Bank on terms that would be acceptable even to the "National Association of Manufacturers."

> At the present time, the Export-Import Bank has borrowing authority up to $700,000,000 and only about $200,000,000 of it has been used. I should think that, by supplementing what

private manufacturers and private banks can do, this margin of $500,000,000 could be used to finance at least a billion and a half of reconstruction work for the Soviets. Also, as a political and practical matter, I don't think it would be too tough to get the borrowing authority of the Export-Import Bank raised by the Congress.[13]

Cox was no match for Cordell Hull. The secretary of state might not be allowed into the war councils of the Big Three, but when it came to postwar planning his department's voice carried much more weight on Capitol Hill than that of presidential advisers. If he said the Export-Import Bank's lending authority was nearly exhausted, that was also a way of saying he was unenthusiastic about leaving such important matters in charge of Oscar Cox or Averell Harriman. What counted most, nevertheless, was Roosevelt's disinclination or inability to set the ground rules between the State Department and the Moscow embassy.[14]

When the issue had been Russian survival in the early stages of the war, the White House pushed all the buttons and pulled all the levers necessary to get Lend-Lease aid to Russia. Now Harriman's several appeals to Hopkins to support him in devising a "well forged instrument" produced no results. They are worth citing at length. On March 13, 1944, for example, the ambassador pleaded that Washington think about the larger issues at stake. "I am impressed with the consideration that economic assistance is one of the most effective weapons at our disposal to influence European political events in the direction we desire and to avoid the development of a sphere of influence of the Soviet Union over Eastern Europe and the Balkans."[15] And again:

> If aid for Russian reconstruction is to be of real value in our overall relations with the Soviet Government as a benefit which they can obtain from us if they play the international game with us in accordance with our standards we must have a well forged instrument to offer them. Vague promises excite Soviet suspicions whereas a precise program offered now to them but kept

always within our control to suspend would be of extreme value. Stalin must offer his people quick reconstruction to retain supreme leadership. We on the other hand want Russian business quickly during our period of conversion from war production. I therefore urge that this matter be not left to an interdepartmental committee for study alone but that the subject be energetically pursued in the hope of finding a solution permitting prompt action. I realize of course the political difficulties at home but I hope that the double barrelled advantage of prompt action may offer ammunition for dealing with this aspect.[16]

As Harriman dictated these words, Roosevelt had already approved the establishment of an interdepartmental committee to study "the best means by which we could be of assistance to them." State should chair the committee, said Hull, and it should have representatives from Commerce, Treasury, the Tariff Commission, the Foreign Economic Administration, "and perhaps the War and Navy Departments." Roosevelt wrote on the memo, "O.K. Who will be the personnel?"[17]

Again, contrasted to his urgent messages to get moving on Lend-Lease for Russia in 1941 and 1942, Roosevelt's attitude appears surprisingly "relaxed." As might be expected, the procedure turned into an endless series of negotiations into the summer over credit terms for implementing the original Cox proposal. These were carried on in a chilly atmosphere. "Even the heat of our room," Dean Acheson later recalled, "could not warm the chill between allies into cordiality."[18] The arguments over fractions of a percentage point of interest, total years of the amortization period, and prices of goods more than realized Harriman's worst fears.

When George Kennan returned to the embassy in Moscow in 1944 after a seven-year absence, he set out to disabuse Washington of the "quaint" notion that Russia could be channeled in the direction of postwar collaboration. Listing men who were little known in the West but whose voices in Soviet councils ranked highest save for one or two, Kennan wrote:

These prominent Soviet leaders know little of the outside world. They have no personal knowledge of foreign statesmen. To them, the vast pattern of international life, political and economic, can provide no associations, can hold no significance, except in what they conceive to be its bearing on the problems of Russian security and Russian internal life. . . . God knows what strange images and impressions are created in their minds by what they hear of life beyond Russia's borders. God knows what conclusions they draw from all this, and what recommendations they make on the basis of those conclusions.[19]

Kennan's forecast was therefore much gloomier than Harriman's guarded hopes for the future. Both distrusted the idea of working things out from the bottom up. Viewed from the American embassy in Moscow, Washington's policy seemed all too consciously aimed at keeping Russia "in its place" by such methods. Molotov had suspected, so he claimed later, that such was Roosevelt's game from the beginning. "Roosevelt believed in dollars. Not that he didn't believe in anything else, but he considered his people to be so rich, and we so poor and so worn out, that we would come begging. 'And then we'll kick their asses, but now we have to help them to keep going.' That's where they miscalculated," boasted Molotov in old age. "That's where they weren't Marxists, and we were. They woke up only when half of Europe was taken from them."[20]

Roosevelt's sharpest critics, Kennan among them, later blamed the president for believing that personal diplomacy could substitute for carefully prepared policies, and even more for believing that he could bridge vast ideological gaps by gathering Churchill and Stalin around him at a conference table. Yet in the case of postwar economic aid to Russia, Roosevelt's sense of limitations on his personal ability to influence decisions is the most striking element to be accounted for in reconstructing the situation. Obviously the White House could no longer simply discount congressional opposition, as it had in the early days of the war when the nation looked to the executive to preserve national security. Also, the vast bureaucracy that was built into the executive branch in order to expedite decisions for making war effectively now stood as a hindrance to quick decisions for peace. Perhaps Roosevelt's reticence was only a reflection of these situations, which created a "weak" president in the transition period from World War II to the onset of the cold war.

In any event, it was not only Harriman who felt himself stranded in the post-Teheran uncertainty. British policymakers also decided that Roosevelt was almost as much of an enigma as the Russian bear. And they fretted that America might turn out to be no help at all in the postwar period. As Eden told the war cabinet in late January 1944:

> We had to face the fact that, once we agreed to Russia having the Baltic States, and to the transfer to other areas of large masses of German population in East Prussia and East of the Oder to make room for dispossessed Poles, we should be challenged on the ground that such action was contrary to the Atlantic Charter. The ideal position would be to postpone any decision about frontiers until after the war, and then to consider all frontier questions together. But we were not free agents in the matter. The Russian armies were advancing into Poland.[21]

Eden's lament about the discussions at Teheran, and what they portended "once we agreed" to a shift in Polish frontiers, came as the first decisions had to be made about a postwar government for Italy. Determined not to allow Soviet influence to unsettle plans for a pro-Western regime in the defeated enemy state, and with no hope of a major military action in the Balkans, the British began to think about their own follow-up to the Teheran Conference. They could not offer important economic inducements to Moscow, but Churchill was anxious to try his hand at personal diplomacy.

At the Moscow Foreign Ministers' Conference it had been agreed to establish a Big Three European Advisory Commission which was, theoretically, to decide on the internal organization of provisional governments during the transition period after the war. But the EAC was scarcely consulted about Italian affairs as the British went about the process of setting up a new government.

In mid-March 1944 Moscow suddenly announced it was establishing relations with the rightist regime of Marshal Badoglio, which had maneuvered itself into power after the fall of Mussolini. Far from being pleased at Russian "eagerness" to cooperate, the British wished to keep Moscow away from direct contacts with Rome. Relations with the Italian government should be through the EAC, London insisted in diplomatic notes to Moscow. Moscow replied with a statement that there must be equal participation by East and West in all such questions. ". . . It is necessary to keep in mind that up to the present time the Soviet Government having no direct contact with the Italian Government was in an inequal position as compared to its Allies who had established from the very beginning a direct contact with the Government of Badoglio through their numerous institutions and numerous representatives on the territory of liberated Italy."[22]

Of course, Russian suggestions for the enlargement of the Badoglio government raised fears that Moscow had more than the equivalent of "numerous institutions and numerous representatives" in its control of the Italian Communist party.[23] To Churchill, the answer to such questions was to take up the Russians on an offer they had not made—in exchange for specific concessions on the Baltic states, the Polish boundaries, and the Balkans, Moscow would agree not to use its control of communist elements to undermine the British in Italy and Greece, or to deny the Poles a chance for an independent existence.

What would motivate Churchill at the TOLSTOY meetings in Moscow in mid-October 1944, then, was his desire not simply to limit the Red Army from spreading Russian rule but also to contain communism as a system. Eden, who had been the most eager to come to an agreement on the Polish frontiers, summed up the new fears about the Italian moves in a comment on a Foreign Office paper, April 3, 1944: "Why are they gatecrashing in Italy this way? Their conduct could be explained as

184 · *Spheres of Influence*

a calculated attempt to smash all left parties, and center parties, save the Communists. It is difficult to explain any other way."[24]

Churchill noted on this same document that despite his "effusive personal approaches" to the Soviets, he could feel not the "slightest trust or confidence in them. Force and facts are their only realities." Amidst much speculation in the war cabinet that the ultimate Russian aim might be the communization of Italy, Churchill declared that Moscow had no military forces in the area. "The decisive voice in issues such as the present ought . . . to rest with those who had carried the burden. He reminded the War Cabinet that we were not claiming to interfere with the Russian handling of the situation in conquered or liberated countries in Eastern Europe."[25]

During these weeks before D day and the invasion of France, Eden and Churchill went back and forth many times over Poland, Italy, Greece, and the rest of the Balkans. Churchill would talk about the time when the Soviets would need the Western powers, and Eden would meander around the question of postwar cooperation with Russia. At one point the prime minister growled to his colleagues, "I am anxious to save as many Poles as possible from being murdered." Yet some days later he advised a visiting American that the postwar world organization "should be firmly founded on a tripod consisting of the three Great Powers."[26]

The day after this last interview with the American planner Isaiah Bowman, Churchill initiated a correspondence that would culminate at TOLSTOY. Lest Molotov miss the meaning of his gesture, Churchill wrote to the foreign minister, "We regard you as leaders in Romanian affairs." The historian David Carlton argues that the Russians replied by protesting the presence of British Special Operations Executive (SOE) officers in Rumania, thereby opening the way for what Churchill desired, a spheres-of-influence bargain over Greece and Rumania.[27]

The Americans were being impossible about this. Before and after Teheran Roosevelt had made it plain he would not countenance any effort to establish a significant military presence in Southeastern Europe. On the other hand, while he had shown signs of accepting the alternative of a political settlement with Russia before the end of the war plunged Europe into chaos, his frequent protests that election-year politics prevented him from going further worried British policymakers that they might be too late to "save" anything for the West.[28] If, as Roosevelt insisted, final decisions on territorial questions must be put off until the end of the war, the British fretted, that would do nothing to restrain the Russians from seeking to gain political influence, as the Italian case suggested, *inside all the liberated areas.*

What made matters worse, Eden observed wryly, was that by supporting Tito in Yugoslavia and the leftist EAM in Greece, London had set the stage for the Russians to follow "in our footsteps." "For it is we ourselves who have built up Tito and his Partisan communist organization. And the same applies to Greece where it was S.O.E. who originally launched and supported E.A.M. In both cases we backed them for immediate operational reasons in spite of their being communist movements. It is an unfortunate fact that communists seem to make the best guerilla leaders."[29]

Although it was not useful to Churchill's immediate purposes, Roosevelt's studied aloofness had certain advantages for the prime minister as he pondered his next step. If what he worked out with Stalin came apart, either because so many questions hung in the balance, or because of a shift in the power situation, he could invoke American aid in defense of the Atlantic Charter. Probably the prime minister had not thought this out so neatly, but when the crunch came, this was precisely the course he followed.[30]

But the path that far ahead was not yet clear when Eden pressed the Russian ambassador, Feodor Gousev, who had replaced Maisky, to consider the "practical matter" of each nation accepting the other's lead, the Russians in Rumania and the British in Greece. Gousev liked the idea but asked if the Americans had been consulted. No, replied Eden, but he "could not imagine that they would in any way dissent. After all, the matter was really related to the military operations of our respective forces. . . ."

If the Americans consented, said Ambassador Gousev, the Soviet government would be prepared to give "a final affirmative answer."[31] Taken aback, Eden noted at the bottom of his minute for the attention of his aides, "Please consider how to handle this with Americans."[32] Ambassador Halifax at first held back the information that the idea had been discussed with the Russians—"I did not tell him [Secretary of State Hull] that you [Eden] had already spoken to Russians and I represented your suggestions as fruit of your own independent reflection." And he had stressed to Hull, Halifax went on, that the whole notion arose only out of military and geographical considerations. It would in no way prejudice the interest of the Big Three nations in the postwar settlement. Hull's fears were not allayed. Any action that might "appear to savor of creation or acceptance of [the] idea of spheres of influence," the secretary of state protested, "would come back at us later."[33]

In fact, it came back the next day. At a press conference Hull was asked to respond to a criticism of American policy by the Netherlands foreign minister, who charged that Washington favored dictation to the small nations by the Big Three. The secretary launched into an angry denial of the accusation, declaring, "We have for 150 years preached liberty to all the nations of the earth, to all the peoples of the earth and we have practiced it. We have encouraged all nations to aspire to liberty and to enjoy it. Our attitude towards the Philippines is a striking example. Nobody had to put us on the witness stand to know what we were doing for them."[34]

The Philippine "example," which Americans were wont to throw back at critics and to use as a "standard" for other nations' behavior, was hardly equivalent to the issues under consideration. A more accurate comparison was, from London's point of view, U.S. hegemony in Latin America. Churchill used it implicitly in his appeals to Roosevelt. But the Foreign Office was not happy when Churchill sent his first message to the president on the Greece/Rumania bargain. Not only did they prefer to keep the prime minister out of their efforts to "handle" the Americans, but Churchill now revealed what Halifax had withheld—that discussions with the Russians had taken place, and that the burden of these was the British proposal for an Anglo-Russian agreement. Churchill also revealed that Moscow wanted to know whether Washington agreed. "We do not of course wish to carve up the Balkans into spheres of influence . . . ," Churchill reiterated, and the "arrangement" would apply only to war conditions.[35]

Roosevelt passed the message on to the State Department, which immediately noted the differences between Halifax's statement to Hull and Churchill's telegram. Acting Secretary of State Edward R. Stettinius expressed great concern to Halifax about the apparent duplicity. Because it now appeared that the subject had been discussed beforehand with the Russians, Stettinius said, the U.S. government was "embarrassed how to reply." A message was being prepared for Roosevelt to send to the prime minister.[36]

When this conversation was reported to Churchill, the prime minister stepped deeper into the waters with another message to the Washington embassy. There was no question of spheres of influence, he insisted, but the Big Three had to act together, and someone must play the hand. The Greeks were old allies of the British who had sacrificed forty thousand men for them in 1941. He had reason, he went on, to believe that Roosevelt was "in entire agreement" with the line he was taking on Greece and Yugoslavia. The worst thing for any of these countries would be to subject them to decisions reached by triangular or quadrangular telegraphing. On the other hand, said the prime minister, London followed the U.S. lead in Latin America "as long as it is not a question of our beef and mutton. On this we naturally develop strong views on account of the little we get."[37]

Halifax was told he could show the telegram to Hull or anyone else. He may have thought the reference to Latin America would shame the Americans, who were demanding that their views on Peronist Argentina be honored regardless of the impact on British supplies of meat; or he may have thought the hint that Churchill and Roosevelt had an understanding on the Balkans would rein in the State Department. He was mistaken on both counts. Meanwhile, Stettinius had advised Roosevelt that "however adroitly" the British proposal was presented, it was an effort to obtain American approval for spheres of influence—and the State Department wanted nothing to do with it. More than that, the department's proposed reply to Churchill, which Roosevelt used, refused the British in words that suggested Washington had the final say:

> ... We acknowledge that the militarily responsible Government in any given territory will inevitably make decisions required by military developments but are convinced that the natural tendency for such decisions to extend to other than military fields would be strengthened by an agreement of the type suggested. In our opinion, this would certainly result in the persistence of differences between you and the Soviets and in the division of the Balkan region into spheres of influence. . . . [38]

Foreign Office officials feigned surprise over the American attitude, though they really had no reason ever to think that an approach to Cordell Hull's guardians of the Wilsonian vision would produce anything different. Permanent Under Secretary Alec Cadogan noted, "The Americans have an astonishing phobia about 'spheres of influence.'" The real problem, it seemed, was to minimize the embarrassment caused by Halifax's gaffe and Churchill's ill-timed cable to Roosevelt, and somehow to put the onus on the Russians for forcing the issue. Accordingly, a brief telegram explained that the "Soviet Government's proposal . . . arose out of [a] chance remark ['informal comment' was crossed out] by [the] Secretary of State [Eden]. . . ." There was thus no opportunity to discuss it with the Americans at its inception. But as soon as the Soviets took up this "chance remark and converted it into a formal proposal we consulted U.S. Government as indeed [the] Soviet Government suggested we should do."[39]

Eden was furious—with Churchill. "This is [the] outcome of P.M. 'butting in,'" he told his colleagues. "What do we do now?"[40] Whatever discussions ensued, Churchill decided he must press Roosevelt harder. His second telegram to the president, June 11, argued that the alternatives were chaos and paralysis. The prime minister did not shy from talking politics this time. He repeated what he had instructed Halifax about the sacrifices Britain had suffered on behalf of the Greeks, and put the question squarely: "The Russians are ready to let us take the lead in the Greek business, which means that E.A.M. and all its malice can be controlled by the national forces of Greece. Otherwise civil war and ruin to the land you care about so much."

He always reported to the president on such matters, he said, and Roosevelt would see every telegram he sent. "I think you might trust me in this." Russia was about to enter Rumania, a country that had gone to war against the Soviets "with glee" and had inflicted many casualties on the Red Army. Considering there were no British or American troops in the area, and that the Russians were likely to do as they pleased, "it would be a good thing to follow the Soviet leadership." Churchill's only concession to the idea that such an arrangement was temporary was to suggest that the president agree to a three-month trial.[41]

This plea brought results, though not quite what Churchill wanted. Without consulting the State Department, Roosevelt sent the briefest of replies, accepting the three-month trial period. "We must be careful to make it clear that we are not establishing any post war spheres of influence." The prime minister's reply once again clearly departed from the original British line with Washington—that the proposal dealt only with military matters. Thanking Roosevelt, Churchill said he was asking Eden to convey the American position to Molotov, "to make it clear that the reason for the three months limit is in order that we should not prejudge the question of establishing postwar spheres of influence."[42]

When Eden informed Molotov, through Ambassador Gousev, of Washington's agreement to the three-month trial, he put the arrangement in terms that even Hull could be expected to accept as the lesser of two evils, or so Eden hoped. Explaining

American concern about permanent spheres of influence, the foreign secretary declared that he had always intended the arrangement to apply only to the war period, "and should not affect the rights and responsibilities which each of our three governments will have to exercise at the peace settlement and afterwards in regard to the whole of Europe."[43]

With so many caveats in the air, Churchill trying to assuage Roosevelt, Eden trying to protect future options on the Russian side, and with the events surrounding D day, June 6, 1944, preoccupying policymakers, what had actually been agreed upon was confusing at best.[44] To the State Department that made matters worse. Hull's aides were appalled at "this dangerous proposal." Hull noted that the proposition was not confined to Greece and Rumania but by Churchill's description covered the entire Balkan region. He also regarded it as insulting that the prime minister advanced "our position in South America as an analogy."

Not stopping there, the secretary reverted to the discrepancy between the Halifax and Churchill versions of the origin of the proposal, and London's efforts to paper over the whole thing. Now it appeared that if the *Russians* had not raised the question of American approval, "this Government would have been faced with a concluded spheres-of-influence agreement...."[45] Hull gave FDR a draft cable to Churchill, which Roosevelt sent, expressing American concern about the handling of the matter and the hope that important questions not be allowed to develop "in such a manner in the future."[46]

Churchill insisted again that only the Russians could do anything in Rumania. Recognizing this reality was the only way he could persuade them to quit boosting the leftist EAM in Greece. "I cannot admit that I have done anything wrong in this matter." It was impossible to do business, he wrote, if no one of the Big Three could make a suggestion to either of the others without simultaneously "keeping the third informed." Apparently he had forgotten his alarm over separate Roosevelt-Stalin negotiations. The prime minister then cited FDR's talks with Polish leaders—about which "as yet, I have heard nothing from you"—as an example.[47]

For reasons of its own, Moscow now backed off from the British proposal, commenting that it might introduce something "new in the already formed actual situation," and required additional study. Perhaps delay suited Stalin's purpose perfectly: as the Red Army advanced into Rumania he continued to have absolute freedom of action and gain more and more leverage elsewhere.[48] More likely, the Soviets did not like Eden's explanation of American attitudes and suspected they were being asked to accept a bargain that could later be upset by an Anglo-American reversal. If Russia agreed to the Eden version, did that not mean the three-month trial was really a way of stalling political developments until the West was in a stronger position vis-à-vis Russia in Eastern Europe?

On July 1, 1944, the Soviet embassy in Washington sent an aide-mémoire to the State Department setting forth this concern, wrapped inside an inquiry about the American point of view.[49] The embassy's inquiry gave the department an opportunity to say in the strongest terms yet that the United States would never have countenanced the arrangement except for "present war strategy." Its reply repeated over and over again that Washington would agree to no arrangement that militated "against the establishment and effective functioning of a broader system of general security in which all countries will have their part."[50]

Stalin may have taken satisfaction with this answer and interpreted it to mean that the British proposal was in fact, and had always been, a ploy to keep the door open in Eastern Europe until the military situation allowed the rollback of Russian power. But the State Department was most certainly grateful to Stalin for the opportunity to diminish the importance of Roosevelt's consent to the prime minister's "dangerous proposal."

The British embassy in Washington forwarded to London a copy of the State Department's response to the Russian inquiry almost two weeks later. In all, nearly a month had elapsed since the Russian note of July 1. Churchill was beside himself. "Does this mean that the Americans have agreed to the three months' trial, or is it all thrown in the pool again?" "I don't know," noted Eden. "Should we return to [the] charge at Moscow[?]," he asked himself and his advisers.[51]

Eden soon concluded from the American memorandum that the State Department wished Moscow to turn down even the three-month trial. Meanwhile, the Russians had sent a mission to ELAS, the Greek partisan headquarters. He had taken this up with the Soviet ambassador, the foreign secretary informed Churchill. If the reply was conciliatory there might still be a chance "of getting them to recognize our predominant position in Greece, but otherwise I fear not."[52]

The next day Eden presented to the war cabinet his case for sending an additional two hundred officers to the secret British mission in Greece, and a much larger force immediately upon the German withdrawal. Despite what he had said to Churchill about securing British predominance, Eden insisted to the cabinet that there was, "of course, no question of our forcing any particular form of government on the Greeks or interfering with their absolute liberty to choose the system under which they would in future live." Easily submerging any misgivings he may have had as a leader of the Labor party, Deputy Prime Minister Clement Attlee agreed with Eden's arguments and gave his assent—based on the humanitarian need to oversee relief shipments to Greece.[53]

Within a week Churchill was busy planning strategy for a parachute landing in the Athens area to seize the capital before EAM could act. He was disturbed at the thought that the cabinet did not wish the Greek king to return before a plebiscite had been held, and professed not to have agreed with any such decision. "The Greek government [i.e., the royalist regime under British protection] would follow almost immediately as soon as the landing ground had been secured by the parachutists and within a very few hours should be functioning in Athens where the people would probably receive the British parachutists with rapture."

The key to the success of this operation was to make sure the Americans were kept advised and brought along. Foreign Secretary Eden did not see it as quite so simple. The cabinet had indeed questioned the immediate return of the king. In the public mind in Britain, Greece, and America, he told the prime minister, there was a confusion, especially with EAM's constant refrain that "we are trying to put the king back by British bayonets."[54]

This was a veiled warning that Churchill's planned appeal to Roosevelt about sending troops to Greece risked the same response from American policymakers as British proposals for the Balkan arrangement. But Eden's counsel did not dissuade the prime minister from cabling Roosevelt. "We have always marched together in complete agreement about Greek policy," it began, "and I refer to you on every important point." The remainder of the message repeated, at a higher rhetorical pitch, substantially the same arguments the prime minister had put forward for the arrangement with the Russians. He added that the British would need the help of American air forces to fill out the ten-thousand-man parachute force.[55]

One of Churchill's aims may have been to force the United States to confront the consequences of its unwillingness to endorse an arrangement in Rumania under which Russia would have given up supporting EAM. In this view, Washington could either provide a diplomatic blessing for Anglo-Russian agreement or military support for a preemptive move—or see chaos and communism triumph in the Mediterranean. It was unlikely that Churchill had formulated such alternatives on a conscious level, but the effect was the same in Washington: the State Department felt backed into a corner by Churchill's persistent attempts to involve the United States in a power play which, in these pre–cold war years, it did not believe would be successful.

Roosevelt did not answer for several days. Meanwhile, a perhaps inspired column by Drew Pearson denounced British policy in Greece, labeling it, among other things, a policy of cooperation with Nazi collaborationists in an effort to secure postwar economic advantages and a cession of the island of Crete. British officials in the Middle East speculated that the Pearson article had been inspired by SOE's American counterpart, the Office of Strategic Services (OSS). OSS was running its own show in Greece, favoring people who were decidedly not pro-British. "They are out of hand," complained a message to Churchill, "and nothing but direct action by the President would seem likely to put an end to the trouble. They are in a position to provoke an Anglo-American quarrel over Greece and possibly to frustrate HMG's policy."[56]

Churchill considered writing directly to Roosevelt, thought better of it, and tried to bring pressure on the head of OSS in the area and to enlist Harry Hopkins's sympathy. Ambassador Halifax tried to calm the prime minister. There was no conspiracy to thwart British policy, Halifax pointed out, only sharp disagreement in Washington with the notion that the best way to combat EAM was to support the exiled king.[57]

It came as a great relief to the prime minister, then, when Roosevelt responded to his appeal with assurances that he did not object to British preparations to send a force to insure order after the German withdrawal. And the president promised that if American airplanes were available, they could be used in such an operation.[58] Roosevelt's unqualified endorsement of British plans for Greece remains somewhat puzzling. Arguments with Stalin over efforts to send relief to the Warsaw uprising, election concerns, simple weariness (the message was drafted by Admiral Leahy)—all may have played a part. But as the editor of the Roosevelt-Churchill correspondence points out, "this telegram constituted a major step toward an endorsement of the British policy for liberated Greece."[59]

As his armies advanced, meanwhile, the Soviet leader entered into negotiations with a number of parties in Eastern Europe. He was not especially partial to the communists, whom he called "peasant politicians." He may have worried that delay would open the way, God forbid, to genuine "revolution" throughout Eastern Europe. Thus, writes John Erickson,

Building a formal "communist bloc" in eastern Europe at this time does not seem to have figured in his plans: on the contrary, partition suited him down to the ground, promising as it did the prospect of the uninhibited exploitation of this relatively unscarred region in the interests of Soviet economic recovery.... Those who impeded this bargaining, either out of communist principles or national self-respect, inevitably incurred his wrath.[60]

Churchill initiated the suggestion for a tête-à-tête with Stalin in late September, ostensibly to review all the questions before them, suggesting to Roosevelt that the main concerns he had in mind were Russian plans to come into the Far Eastern war and the Polish boundary. And, oh yes, there were "other points" about Yugoslavia and Greece that needed discussion. When the prime minister published his personal account of the TOLSTOY meetings in 1953, he nonetheless explained the journey to Moscow as a containment effort—necessitated in large part by American slowness in "realizing the upsurge of Communist influence, which slid on before, as well as followed, the onward march of the mighty armies directed from the Kremlin."[61]

As he prepared to leave for Moscow for the TOLSTOY Conference, Churchill leveled a sharp blast in private at the Americans for their opposition to an Anglo-American military move into Southeastern Europe. "Stalin," said the prime minister gloomily, "will get what he wants. The Americans have seen to that."[62] On the other hand, according to his personal physician, Lord Moran, Churchill now believed he could deal with Stalin as successfully as Roosevelt claimed he had and would. "The atmosphere there is quite different since we brought off the landings in Normandy. I shall take advantage of it to come to an amicable settlement with Stalin about Poland. That is why I am going."[63]

On the Russian side, TOLSTOY represented an opportunity to probe British intentions about the possible resurrection of the post–World War I *cordon sanitaire*. Moscow held deep suspicions about various British proposals for European "confederations," about the roles of the exile governments that led a sheltered life under the benevolent eye of the British lion, and about diplomatic maneuvering to bring Turkey into the war. As Foreign Minister Molotov put it at the 1943 Moscow Foreign Ministers' Conference, "some of the plans for federations remind the Soviet people of the policy of the 'cordon sanitaire' directed, as is known, against the Soviet Union."[64]

Churchill had requested that the American ambassador, Averell Harriman, attend the TOLSTOY Conference to assure Stalin that "you approve of our mission . . . [and to] be available to take part in discussions"—but he would not be invited to many of the key conversations.[65] When they learned of the prime minister's plan to go to Moscow, Roosevelt's aides had feared precisely this development.[66] FDR could not really deny Churchill the ambassador's counsel. Several issues besides the Balkans and spheres of influence were on the agenda, and Washington was eager to know whatever Harriman could glean from British and Russian officials about the private discussions between Churchill and Stalin. To a large degree then, Churchill succeeded in having it both ways: Harriman was present when wanted to provide a sort of Big Three sanction, and kept outside the door when not.

Churchill's message to Roosevelt of October 5, 1944, before he left for Moscow, pinpointed the American dilemma.

> I am very glad that Averell should sit in at all our principal conferences; but you would not, I am sure, wish this to preclude private tete-a-tetes between me and U.J. [Uncle Joe, i.e., Stalin] or Anthony and Molotov, as it is often under such conditions that the best progress is made. You can rely on me to keep you constantly informed of everything that affects *our joint interests* apart from the reports which Averell will send [italics added].[67]

The way Churchill used the phrase "our joint interests" in this message more than implied that some subjects were not joint interests with the United States. They were special interests between Great Britain and the Soviet Union. Although it was far more common throughout the war for Stalin to express concern about an Anglo-American "understanding," Churchill feared (especially as the power relationship between Britain and America shifted decisively) that Roosevelt might seize an opportunity to employ a Soviet-American "bloc" on certain issues that touched the interest of the British Empire outside Europe. Both men viewed the Americans as a bit too free with advice and plans about areas that touched British and Soviet security interests.

Meanwhile, a State Department Russian expert, Charles Bohlen, had sent a memorandum to Harry Hopkins arguing that the Churchill-Stalin meeting should not take place. Without high-level American representation at Moscow, the world would conclude that the United States had "washed its hands of European political problems" or authorized Churchill to speak for Washington. Stalin and Churchill, Bohlen continued, would either engage in a first-class row or end up by dividing Europe into spheres of influence. But if the conference were held, the president should make it clear to Stalin that none of the agreements between the two could be considered binding on the United States.[68]

Hopkins agreed with Bohlen, shortstopped the message Roosevelt had planned to send, and sought out the president in his bedroom where he was shaving. Roosevelt listened attentively to his aide's rendition of the Bohlen arguments, and the two drafted a long cable to Stalin in place of the simple greetings of the president's original message. The new version began with Roosevelt's regrets that the "next meeting" had not been a Big Three conference. Stalin would "naturally understand" that there was no question, political or military, in which the United States was not interested. "I am firmly convinced that the three of us, and *only* the three of us, can find the solution to the still unresolved questions." Although he wanted Ambassador Harriman to take part as an "observer," he could not commit the United States on any question, and, said Roosevelt, he would prefer to regard the Anglo-Soviet discussions as preliminary to a Big Three meeting, which could take place any time after the election.[69]

To Harriman personally, the president repeated that no subject Churchill and Stalin could discuss was unimportant to the United States. "It is important that I retain complete freedom of action after this conference is over."[70] Stalin expressed surprise at Roosevelt's message, remarking that he had understood Churchill was coming as a spokesman for both Western powers. But while he acknowledged Roosevelt's caveat, he was soon deeply engaged with the prime minister in efforts to arrive at permanent arrangements—and not only about the Balkans.

According to his memoirs, as Churchill looked around the table at the opening session of the TOLSTOY Conference in the Kremlin, at 10 p.m. on October 9, 1944, he decided the moment seemed "apt for business." "Let us settle our affairs in the Balkans," he began, in a phrase much quoted ever after. Then the prime minister wrote out his proposed arrangement on a sheet of plain paper. Russia should have 90 percent predominance in Rumania, Great Britain 90 percent in Greece. They would share fifty-fifty in Yugoslavia and Hungary, and Russia would have 75 percent predominance in Bulgaria. He pushed the paper across to Marshal Stalin, who took a blue pencil, made a large tick upon it, and pushed it back.

"After this there was a long silence," recalled Churchill. Finally, the prime minister spoke: "Might it not be thought rather cynical if it seemed we had disposed of these issues, so fateful to millions of people, in such an offhand manner? Let us burn the paper." "No, you keep it," replied Stalin.[71]

But that was not exactly the way it happened. At a preliminary session between Eden and Molotov at 7 p.m. that evening, the foreign secretary explained it was the prime minister's purpose to report on military progress in the West and to emphasize "our determination for the three to work together." "It was a year since their last meeting and this visit was intended to mark and to show that they agreed on every subject."[72]

When Churchill opened the actual discussions a few hours

later, he began not with the famous Balkan deal revealed for the first time in his memoirs, but with Poland and the question of the Curzon line. He suggested summoning a leader of the London Poles, Stanislaw Mikolajczyk, to Moscow so that the two parties, the London Poles and the Russian-sponsored Polish Committee for National Liberation, could be "forced to settle."

Having put the Polish issue as a matter for the two of them to decide, Churchill then turned to Greece and Rumania. Russian peace terms for Rumania, he began, were reasonable and showed much statecraft in terms of future peace. That was very much a Russian affair:

> But in Greece it was different. Britain must be the leading Mediterranean Power and he hoped Marshal Stalin would let him have the first say about Greece in the same way as Marshal Stalin about Rumania.

Stalin agreed that Britain "should have the first say in Greece." At this point Churchill suggested they express these matters in diplomatic language, because the Americans might be shocked. But as long as he and Stalin understood one another, he, Churchill, could "explain matters to the President."

Stalin remarked that he had received a message from Roosevelt about Harriman's status as an observer, and that the president regarded their discussions as only preliminary to a Big Three meeting. Churchill responded that he had no secrets from the president, but he did not wish Harriman's presence to prevent "intimate talks" between the two of them. The ambassador was not quite in the same position as they were. Stalin's reply to this opening is worth quoting in full.

> MARSHAL STALIN said that he had only sent a reply to the effect that he did not know what questions would be discussed, but as soon as he did know he would tell the President. He had noticed some signs of alarm in the President's message about their talks and on the whole did not like the message. *It seemed to demand too many rights for the United States leaving too little for the Soviet Union and Great Britain, who, after all, had a treaty of common assistance.*[73]

Churchill once again ranged far and wide before he returned to the Balkan situation. He had once been inclined to the American view about voting in the proposed United Nations— that the Great Powers should not be able to veto discussion of issues in which they were involved. But now he saw a great deal of force in the Russian position. Suppose China raised the question of Hong Kong, he said. Britain would have to leave the room while Russia and the United States settled the question.

This not so subtle comment spoke to a supposed need shared by Britain and Russia to protect themselves against American do-goodism or American imperialism. From that standpoint it mattered little whether U.S. postwar policy followed the line set forth by advocates of an "American Century" or the moral dictates of Vice President Henry Wallace's appeal for a "Century of the Common Man." But could Churchill, who so often referred to the Russians as completely untrustworthy (among other things), really imagine such a thing?

It appears that he could, at least on occasion. TOLSTOY represents the high point of Anglo-Soviet diplomacy during the war. Having laid out his new position on the great-power veto, the prime minister returned to the Balkan question, expanding the first discussion from Greece and Rumania to include Hungary and Yugoslavia. There he proposed Britain and Russia share influence equally. Stalin rejoined with a reference to Bulgaria— and, to test the waters at their deepest, Turkey. What about Russian rights in controlling the Black Sea straits? The 1936 Montreux Convention covering the entrances to the Black Sea gave Japan as many rights as Russia. If Britain was interested in the Mediterranean, Russia had an equal concern with the Black Sea regime still dominated by Turkey.

Suddenly on guard, Churchill asked what changes Stalin had in mind? For the moment, came the answer, agreement that the Montreux Convention must be altered was enough. "What would Britain do if Spain or Egypt were given this right to close the Suez Canal, or what would the United States Government say if some South American Republic had the right to close the Panama Canal? Russia was in a worse situation." Churchill accepted the principle, suggesting only that it had to be done in a friendly way so as not to frighten Istanbul. The prime minister then suggested that Stalin take up the Montreux Convention with the United States.[74]

Back on the Balkans, Churchill said he felt they should do something to prevent ideological civil wars in those countries. "They should be stopped by the authority of the three Great Powers." "Agreed," said Stalin. (Given the later history of the cold war, this was perhaps the most ironic moment in Big Three wartime diplomacy.) Saying that Britain would not try to force a king on Greece, Yugoslavia, or Italy, Churchill asked Stalin to "soft-pedal the Communists in Italy and not to stir them up."

Stalin said that would not be so easy, as the Italian Communists might tell him to go to the devil. In Bulgaria the Red Army had in fact stopped the Bulgarian Communists from forming Soviets. But on Bulgaria, Stalin continued, he could not agree that Britain should have a great share there. It was a Black Sea country. Was Churchill afraid that Russia intended to launch an attack on Turkey? He had no such intention. Before the wrangling continued, the prime minister suggested that they let Eden and Molotov work out the details.[75]

So it was not all done dramatically in a thrice, as Churchill would write in his memoirs. Harriman heard about the Balkan "agreement" the next day, October 10, at a "lunch" that went on for four hours. Sitting next to Stalin, he was told either by the Marshal himself or by an aide that the Russian leader had amended a joint telegram to the president about the Balkan talks, striking out the words "having regard to our varying duty towards them" which implied recognition of one another's sphere of influence. The ambassador's report of this extraordinary charade continued:

> After lunch talking across Churchill I told Stalin that you would
> be very glad that he had eliminated this phrase as you believed

that all questions should be dealt with by the three of us. Stalin said he was glad to hear this and reaching behind Churchill's back shook my hand.[76]

That evening the talks resumed on a less than comradely note. Molotov opened his conversation with Eden by stating that the fifty-fifty ratio proposed for Hungary was unacceptable. The Soviets wanted 75 percent. Eden countered with complaints that Yugoslav leader Tito had made a secret visit to Moscow without informing the British. The atmosphere was much chillier than it had been the night before, particularly after Eden declared that "His Majesty's Government were unhappy over the whole situation in the Balkans." An irritant for the British was the activity of Bulgarian officers in northern Greece, who in their treatment of British officers acted as if they had won the war, instead of the other way around.

Molotov was sympathetic, to a degree, and repeated that Bulgaria must be punished for its role in the war. But he argued that Russia must have 90 percent influence there, as in Rumania. There followed in rapid succession a series of proposals, with Molotov at times offering to trade various percentages in Yugoslavia for near absolute control in Bulgaria and almost the same in Hungary. At one point he attempted to define what these numbers would mean. In Yugoslavia, said the Russian foreign minister, 60/40 meant that Britain would control the coast and Russia the center. Eden eventually agreed to what he thought was a decent compromise—a 20 percent share for Britain in Bulgaria and Hungary, reflected in a two-stage arrangement whereby after the war ended, Russia would allow an allied control commission to function. For that, Molotov agreed to equal responsibilities in Yugoslavia. In all, the parceling out of the Balkans was at least reminiscent of the treatment of the Ottoman Empire after World War I, except that the stakes were people rather than oil.[77]

Churchill was impatient with the details. "I don't want you two to go after sticklebacks," he admonished Eden. "If you get on to a bad patch I'd move on to another. There are a lot of things which don't matter." "Bulgaria isn't one of them," Eden rejoined.[78] But Churchill was not much interested in quarreling with the Russians over abstract percentages. And he planned to send Stalin a letter explaining his position. It was not sent, apparently, because Harriman warned him against it—which suggests that in addition to a Churchill letter to Harry Hopkins, FDR was in a position to know all about the arrangement.[79] In the unsent draft Churchill expressed a hope that Britain, Russia, and the United States could work together in the Balkans to establish a solid foundation for an enduring world peace. The TOLSTOY decisions were only preliminary to a Big Three decision at the peace table, and the percentages were no more than a method to determine how close they were on specific issues—a guide, in other words, to how much adjustment was needed in their plans.

> As I said, they would be considered crude and even callous if they were exposed to the scrutiny of the Foreign Offices and diplomats all over the world. Therefore they could not be the basis of any public document, certainly not at the present time. They might however be a good guide for the conduct of our affairs. If we manage these affairs well, we shall perhaps prevent several civil wars and much bloodshed and strife in the small countries concerned. Our broad principles should be to let every country have the form of government which its people desire.[80]

Then Churchill talked about the ideological issue, mincing no words about the potential struggle between totalitarian forms of government and "those we call free enterprise controlled by universal suffrage." He was grateful, he said, that Stalin had declared himself against trying to change by force or communist propaganda the established systems in the Balkan countries. Excepting Nazism, which could not be tolerated, the Great Powers should feel easy about the internal situations of those countries "and not worry about them or interfere with them once the conditions of tranquility have been restored after this terrible blood-bath which they and indeed we have all been through."

It is from this point of view that I have sought to adumbrate the degrees of interest which each of us takes in these countries with the full assent of the other and subject to the approval of the United States, which may go far away for a long time and then come back again unexpectedly with gigantic strength.

Was Churchill issuing a warning that if Stalin failed to abide by the agreement, the United States would come back with gigantic strength? Or was he, as earlier communications with Stalin indicated, talking about the need for Britain and the Soviet Union to pursue the necessary arrangements, given the uncertainty of American postwar attitudes toward Europe?

It was impossible to mistake the next paragraph's meaning. Hitler had tried to exploit the fear of an "aggressive, proselytizing Communism which exists throughout Western Europe," and, though he was being beaten to the ground, Stalin well knew "this fear exists in every country because whatever the merits of our different systems, no country wishes to go through the bloody revolution which will certainly be necessary in nearly every case before so drastic a change could be made in the life, habits and outlook of their society."

The draft closed with a paragraph conveying the "feeling" that over the years the differences between the systems would grow smaller, as "the great common ground which we share of making life richer and happier for the mass of the people is growing every year." It was an altogether remarkable letter. While the prime minister kept repeating that the arrangement was, as Washington wanted it, only temporary, it was clear once again that Churchill had in mind establishing a lasting peace on the basis of a permanent understanding.

Given the prime minister's pre-TOLSTOY maneuvers to secure British freedom of action from American policy, which continued right up to the eve of the conference,[81] Churchill sent a remarkably candid report of his meetings with Stalin, and those of Eden and Molotov, to Harry Hopkins for transmission to Roosevelt. The message began with a statement about the friendly atmosphere in Moscow and the "sad tangle" of the

Balkans. Rehearsing British complaints about the secret Tito visit to Moscow and the behavior of the Bulgarians in Greece, Churchill explained that the Russians were taking "a great interest in Hungary" and claiming "fullest responsibility" in Rumania but were prepared to "disinterest themselves in Greece." "All these matters are being flogged out by Mr. Eden and Mr. Molotov."

He was seeing "a great deal of Averell," the prime minister went on, but "We have so many bones to pick about the Balkans at the present time that we would rather carry the matter a little further *a deux* in order to be able to talk more bluntly than at a larger gathering. I will cable fully to the President about this in a day or two."[82] Eden gave similar information to Harriman, including an explanation of why Churchill used the "unpopular" term "spheres of influence" to delineate a "practical agreement" on the Balkans, and the "relative responsibility" of Russia and Britain. Churchill and Eden hoped Roosevelt and Secretary Hull would be satisfied with these agreements, as they were convinced that unless something "along these lines is done there will be political turmoil in these countries if not civil war. . . ."[83]

Churchill's direct message to Roosevelt also stressed the danger of civil war, "when probably you and I would be in sympathy with one side and U.J. with the other." He would continue to keep the president informed and reassured him once again that any arrangements agreed upon at TOLSTOY were "subject to further discussion and melting-down with you."[84] In these three contacts with Hopkins, Harriman, and FDR, Churchill and Eden did not call their arrangements "temporary" —i.e., the ninety-day formula—but rather "preliminary," in the sense of something awaiting finalization.

Roosevelt's messages to Harriman during TOLSTOY were reminders that the ambassador was there only as an observer. He had read Harriman's account of the luncheon on October 10—where Stalin had supposedly blocked a phrase implying the creation of spheres of influence. FDR added, "My active interest at the present time in the Balkan area is that such steps as are practicable should be taken to insure against the Balkans getting us into a future international war."[85]

Throughout the war Roosevelt shifted back and forth, first refusing to countenance anything "provincial" negotiated by Churchill and Stalin behind closed doors, then deciding that if spheres of influence were to be arranged, they had better be "open" so that they might evolve into something better once the Big Three had got "all mixed up together," *and* if *he* negotiated them with Stalin. But now this vacillation had come down to a time for decision. Churchill and Stalin had reached their agreement.

Harriman had come to Russia as ambassador after the Teheran Conference convinced that he could facilitate a program for postwar political and economic cooperation along Wilsonian lines. He was already much disappointed. Roosevelt's interest in the Harriman mission—which the president personally designed—appeared to flag in the face of other problems, and the atmosphere in Moscow had not been conducive to completing solid agreements. Harriman now advised Harry Hopkins that he felt it was important for him to report personally to Roosevelt at the earliest possible moment. "Time has come when we must make clear what we expect of [the Russians] as the price of our good will. Unless we take issue with the present policy there is every indication the Soviet Union will become a world bully wherever their interests are involved. . . . I am disappointed but not discouraged. The job of getting the Soviet Government to play a decent role in international affairs is however going to be more difficult than we had hoped."[86]

Whatever else concerned the ambassador in the wake of the TOLSTOY Conference, and the failed attempt to use economic diplomacy to thwart spheres of influence, the job of getting the Soviets to play a "decent role" had become vastly more complicated by Churchill's initiation of the Balkan arrangement. It cast a shadow over resistance to Russian claims to dominate Poland, however much the prime minister or the president sought to maintain the illusion that Europe was not being divided among the Big Three.

8

DENOUEMENT: POLAND AND YALTA

Our friends still cling to their old preference for
dodging breathlessly round the field a few feet
ahead of the bull rather than make up their mind
to seize it boldly by at least one horn. In the end
I fear with you that they may find themselves
pinned in an uncomfortable corner.
Lord Halifax on the Americans,
December 1944[1]

AT TOLSTOY Churchill had begun signing his notes to
Stalin, "Your friend and war-time comrade." From the British
embassy in Moscow came suggestions that with the Americans
determined to withdraw their troops as soon as possible after
the war, the Russians would naturally look to London for their
primary consultants on managing affairs in Europe. They were
somewhat suspicious, in fact, of the power of American capitalism. While it could supply certain needs the British could not,
it might also overwhelm them. "They think of us as fellow
Europeans; they see in the British a people who, like themselves, have directly experienced enemy action, which has left
America untouched. To this extent therefore we have a good
start towards developing an atmosphere of greater confidence
with our difficult ally."[2]

Churchill seemed downright optimistic about prospects for the Grand Alliance. "We can settle everything," he told Lord Moran, "we three, if we come together." 'I'here were some small things to worry about, yes, but the future looked very bright. "But, Winston," Eden protested, "Poland is a big, not a small thing."[3] And it was growing bigger all the time. Churchill's sudden optimism about getting on with both Stalin and Roosevelt as "brothers," on a different level from all the rest, would be severely tested by the Polish issue. It upset all the plans for a political "truce" in the Balkans and became the first cold war conflict.

Great Britain had accepted war with Germany over Poland; Russia had been invaded twice through Poland; and the United States believed Poland to be the issue on which the success of the United Nations and all its plans for the postwar world might stand or fall. Yet Roosevelt had been ducking Polish issues throughout the war, almost, it seems, in a Micawber-like belief that "something would turn up" to save him from having to confront the Russians over that country's future. He had gone off to bed at the Teheran Conference when Churchill and Stalin discussed Poland's eastern frontiers, but he had carefully explained his political predicament in a private conversation with the Russian leader, citing the millions of Americans of Polish extraction whose feelings and votes he must respect. Stalin understood, but added that Roosevelt must do some "propaganda work" with those people.[4]

Back home Roosevelt was cautious, except in private, whenever he spoke about the coalition Polish Government in Exile in London, headed for a time by Stanislaw Mikolajczyk. Mikolajczyk led the Peasant party and was considered a moderate on questions of Russo-Polish relations. Roosevelt, by general account, respected Mikolajczyk and appreciated his problems. But he thought the London Poles had an exaggerated notion of what politics could provide that geography denied. Recalling what he had said to the Polish ambassador about the Russian advance, FDR made his point forcefully: "Do you think they will just stop to please you, or us for that matter? Do you expect us and Great Britain to declare war on Joe Stalin if they cross your previous frontier? Even if we wanted to, Russia can still field an army twice our combined strength, and we would just have no say in the matter at all."[5]

Furthermore, the president went on, a "fair plebiscite, if there ever was such a thing," might show that the eastern provinces would "prefer" to go back to Russia. The London Poles, he added, had been foolish about the "graves question." "Wow, what fools they were; I've no patience with them." This slighting reference to the 1940 Katyn Forest massacre of Polish officers, which had provoked a final break between Moscow and the London Poles, and was finally admitted by Russia only at the end of the cold war, did Roosevelt little credit. But it showed how determined the president was to avoid thinking about the German charges in the midst of war. For the longer run, he would employ much the same tolerance he had imposed upon himself with regard to British rule in India.[6]

Yet when Mikolajczyk visited Washington in June 1944, Roosevelt, while talking bluntly to the Polish leader about the rightist bent of the London government and the need for boundary concessions, assured him that he had not accepted the Curzon line. And he dissociated himself from any attempt by Stalin and Churchill to settle Polish frontiers by themselves.[7]

Nevertheless, at the TOLSTOY Conference in October 1944, after Stalin and Churchill had "settled" the questions at issue in the Balkans, they turned their attention to Poland. The TOLSTOY discussions were set against the background of Hitler's orders to raze Warsaw to the ground to punish its citizens for daring to attack the German army. The Warsaw Uprising of August–September had strained Anglo-Russian relations. Charges flew about Soviet unwillingness to aid the besieged Polish patriots, and, contrariwise, about the invidious behavior of the London Poles in staging the uprising in a foredoomed attempt to "liberate" Poland before the Red Army reached their capital city. As a recent study of the uprising puts it:

> The authors of the insurrection decided to act because they were convinced that, if the claims of the London Government to

govern and represent Poland were to be established in the eyes of the world, Warsaw must be liberated by forces loyal to that Government. By taking Warsaw the Home Army was to clear the ground for the final, decisive confrontation with Stalin, the outcome of which was to determine who would govern Poland—the London Poles or the Polish Communists and their sympathizers.[8]

Policymakers in Washington and London were chagrined by Stalin's refusal to permit British or American planes to land behind Red Army lines, thereby making air drops to the Warsaw "freedom-fighters" impossible. When things went badly for the Poles, some observers accused Stalin of deliberately encouraging the uprising in order to have the Germans eliminate a problem for him. The charge has been refuted.[9]

Whatever ideological and political strategy was behind the events of August and September 1944, the real losers were the London Poles. Three hundred thousand Poles lost their lives. And while their bravery may have strengthened the moral claims of the exile government, the uprising convinced Stalin and Churchill of the need to hasten yet another big-power "relocation" of Poland to suit their own needs. Hence they summoned Mikolajczyk to Moscow to hear their will.

Mikolajczyk was not awed in the presence of Churchill and Stalin. Much to the prime minister's annoyance, the Polish leader submitted a memorandum for the construction of a postwar regime that did not even mention the Russian-sponsored Polish National Committee of Liberation (known as Lublin) but talked about shares for political parties. And he refused to accept the Curzon line.

Stalin was just as adamant in pressing the claims of the Ukraine and Byelorussia to the disputed territory. After the discussion went on for sometime between Mikolajczyk and Stalin, with each man growing increasingly bitter, Churchill attempted several interventions, warning the Polish leader that it would be unwise for him to separate himself from Britain. "At the time when Britain declared war she stood alone and was nearly destroyed. It all hung upon a hair. He therefore had a claim to ask the Polish Government to make a beau gesture to enable them to find a road to the peace of Europe."

Molotov then intervened to inform Mikolajczyk that at Teheran President Roosevelt had also agreed to the Curzon line, "but he did not wish it published for the moment." They could conclude, said the Soviet foreign minister, that the points of view of the Soviet Union, Britain, and the United States were the same. "He had thought it necessary to refer to this point because M. Mikolajczyk had appealed to the good will of the Three Powers."

Ambassador Harriman, who was present at this meeting, was not pleased by Molotov's invocation of Roosevelt's views. Rather than dissent in the presence of the Poles, he spoke to Churchill after the meeting. The prime minister agreed that the president at Teheran had specifically taken no position on the Polish territorial arrangements, and said he would speak privately to Molotov about the error.[10]

Meanwhile, Mikolajczyk asked if the Polish western frontier had also been mentioned at Teheran. After some desultory conversation about the specifics of the western frontier, Churchill asked if the Curzon line could not be accepted "as a working arrangement subject to discussion at the Peace Conference. . . ." Stalin would not allow that to pass. There could not be one frontier today and another tomorrow. As Russian troops advanced they were restoring Soviet authority and collective farms. For that reason there had to be a definite frontier, as with Rumania and Finland. "This might surprise their allies, but there was no other way out owing to the difference in the system of government."[11]

Churchill and Eden were thus left with the task of persuading Mikolajczyk to accept compensations in the west. They also wanted him to stay in Poland and take the leadership of an enlarged Lublin government. Could he get a guarantee of the proposed territories and assurances of the sovereign independence of the new Polish government from Stalin? Mikolajczyk asked Churchill. The prime minister agreed to try, and brought

212 · *Spheres of Influence*

back a statement from Stalin agreeing "in principle to a solution on the lines proposed." But that was not enough. Mikolajczyk said that Poland must have the city of Lvov in the east. At that Churchill and Eden both threw up their hands. Stalin would never agree, and responsibility would fall upon the London Poles for the failure.[12]

Mikolajczyk then countered that he would accept the Curzon line as a demarcation line—except for Lvov—and try to persuade his colleagues in London of the inevitability of final acceptance of the boundary. And he would agree to stay in Poland as head of the Lublin government—if he were promised 75 percent control of the "expanded" government. When Eden and Churchill next saw Stalin, the Soviet leader commented that Mikolajczyk was so stubborn he might be a Finn. The British assured him that Mikolajczyk was of pure Polish peasant stock.

Clever words were followed by dark hints. At one point Stalin confided privately to Churchill that he and Molotov were the only two in the Kremlin who favored dealing "softly" with Mikolajczyk. He was sure there were strong pressures in the background, Churchill advised Deputy Prime Minister Clement Attlee, both party and military. On the other hand, the Russian leader had said that if Mikolajczyk agreed to the frontier he would have no difficulty allowing him to head the new government. Churchill, who had once thought the frontier to be the key issue, now believed that equally great difficulties resided in the choice of government. The Lublin Poles had made the worst possible impression on him, and he had told Stalin he considered them only an expression of the Soviet will. "They have no doubt also the ambition of ruling Poland and are thus a kind of inverted Quislings."[13]

Alone with Mikolajczyk, however, Churchill shouted at him in frustration. "If you think you can conquer Russia, well, you are crazy, you ought to be in a lunatic asylum. You would involve us in a war in which twenty-five million lives might be lost." Britain now had Russia's friendship, he went on, and he meant to keep it that way. "I tell you, we'll become sick and tired if you continue arguing. We shall tell the world how unreasonable you are. We shall not part friends."[14]

Mikolajczyk saw Stalin alone on October 18, 1944, and received the impression that the Russian leader would accept him as leader of the postwar government but would only agree to a fifty-fifty arrangement between Lublin and the London Poles. Churchill and Eden took heart from Mikolajczyk's account of the interview and were prepared to extend him all the help they could in his efforts to persuade his London colleagues of the need to accept the Curzon line—including, if necessary, measures against certain of the more nationalistic Polish exile newspapers.[15]

When Churchill sent one of his "reports" to Roosevelt on TOLSTOY, he stressed the disagreement between Mikolajczyk and Stalin on the Curzon line. Then he took up the differences in the British and American positions. He had made it clear that while he was committed to the Curzon line, the United States was not committed in any way by what he had told Stalin. He also defined, however, a somewhat different position for himself with Stalin—"our 20 Years Treaty with Russia makes it desirable for us to define our position to a degree not called for from the United States at the present time."[16]

Such a caveat could cover not only Poland, of course, but the Balkans as well. However that may be, the prime minister also took note of Harriman's caution that the president had not committed himself to the Curzon line at Teheran. When he mentioned the ambassador's demurrer to Stalin, said Churchill, he was told this had taken place in a "private conversation with you." "I could not of course deal with this assertion." The message to FDR closed with some words about Stalin's renewed pledge to enter the Far Eastern war, and the briefest of comments about the Balkans. The arrangement was the best that could be obtained: Greece had been saved for the West, Yugoslavia divided fairly, and Russian "ascendancy" in Rumania and Bulgaria unavoidably conceded.[17]

If the president was embarrassed by Churchill's apparently casual reference to private Roosevelt-Stalin exchanges, or chagrined by the prime minister's somewhat more pointed reference to the 1942 Anglo-Russian treaty, he did not respond. At the next Big Three meeting, at Yalta, Roosevelt confirmed that he had generally supported the Curzon line at Teheran.

One Churchill observer, his physician Lord Moran, suggests that on the prime minister's return from Moscow he realized that he had in fact gained nothing by seeking friendship with Stalin. But, argues Moran, it was failure to enlist Roosevelt's support for a firmer stand toward Russia (meaning, one supposes, military action as well in Southeastern Europe) that led him to undertake TOLSTOY. "At one moment," according to Moran's diary for October 30, 1944, "he will plead with the President for a common front against Communism and the next he will make a bid for Stalin's friendship. Sometimes the two policies alternate with bewildering rapidity."[18]

Roosevelt was ambiguous too, if on a somewhat different level. Yet he could be blunt when confronted by State Department principles. When Arthur Bliss Lane was told not to go to London as ambassador to the exile Polish government until it accepted the Curzon line, he protested to the president that he should be tougher with the Russians. Roosevelt shot back, "Do you want me to go to war with Russia?"[19]

Mikolajczyk, meanwhile, found himself unable to persuade his comrades in London of the need for compromise, and resigned. For the Soviets this was confirmation not simply of Mikolajczyk's unreliability but of his weakness. Later, whenever British or American negotiators brought up his name as their lead candidate for the provisional government pending "free elections," Molotov was sure to cite Mikolajczyk's supposed spinelessness in the aftermath of TOLSTOY. Protests that he could have done nothing else to retain a semblance of independence from hardline anti-Russians in the London government only made the situation worse, for it was virtually a confession that the body of the exile government, head to toe, was anti-Russian.

Just as he had said he would do, Churchill launched a free-wheeling attack on the exile government during a debate in

Commons. Mikolajczyk had resigned, he said, because of the obstinate and inflexible resistance of his former colleagues. There was nothing but trouble ahead. The prime minister predicted clashes between the Polish underground and the Red Army. And he not only defended British support for the Curzon line as the boundary between Russia and Poland but included in the new Russian territory the city of Lvov, which had been the subject of negotiations at TOLSTOY. Concluding his remarks, Churchill expressed regrets that "various factors" in the domestic situation in America had made it impossible for Washington's position to be stated with precision.[20]

In the late fall of 1944, then, the main argument over Poland was between London, and to a lesser degree Washington, and the London exile government—not between the West and Russia. Roosevelt had barely succeeded in keeping a low profile on the issue before the November elections. After his reelection he told Mikolajczyk, who was the only London Pole in or out of government whom Roosevelt would talk with seriously, that, "In regard to the future frontiers of Poland, if mutual agreement on this subject, including the proposed compensation for Poland from Germany, is reached between the Polish, Soviet and British Governments, this Government would offer no objection."[21]

Did that signal the end of those domestic complications Churchill had complained about in Parliament? Quite the opposite. In the weeks before the Yalta Conference, domestic factors in both Britain and the United States made it difficult for Churchill and Roosevelt to keep foreign affairs to themselves. Wartime political coalitions were splintering in both countries. While this would *not* account for the final breakdown over Poland, it complicated matters enormously and left the two Western leaders less maneuvering room. Stalin never had such worries, but even he had to scramble a bit, if only not to force a final breakup of the wartime alliance too soon.

In the United States the shift to the right began at the 1944 Democratic convention when Vice President Henry A. Wallace was replaced on the ticket by Senator Harry S Truman.

Roosevelt had informed Democratic leaders that if he were a delegate he would vote for Wallace—but he shied from a fight with party leaders to secure Wallace's renomination. As early as 1943 Roosevelt had decided, according to one account by Averell Harriman, that he could not run again on a New Deal platform; the domestic trends all pointed toward conservatism. He had to be prepared to run on "pleasing post-war plans."[22] Yet FDR's concern about a reactionary "coup" within the Democratic party led him to make a confidential proposal to the man whom he had beaten in 1940, Wendell Willkie.

Nothing could be done before the election, but Roosevelt's idea was that by joining forces, "Willkie and I together can form a new, really liberal party in America." Using speech-writer Sam Rosenman as his go-between, the president contacted the Republican leader. Willkie displayed a keen interest in the idea. He did not think anything could be done before the election, either, but he was most concerned about foreign affairs. "A sound, liberal government," he told Rosenman, "is absolutely essential to continued co-operation with the other nations of the world. I know some of these reactionaries— especially those in my own party."[23]

By Election Day 1944 Willkie was dead. Even had Roosevelt the strength, without someone like Willkie the idea could not be carried further—then or later. The men around the president, especially Harry Hopkins, were certainly aware of the shifting ground under the New Deal coalition. Hopkins had been alerted, for example, to the dangers of the Polish question as a conservative wedge against the administration's policy of coop-eration with the Soviet Union. "I have always felt," he wrote Ambassador John Gilbert Winant, "that both immediately be-fore and during the war the Vatican was more interested in the defeat of Russia than of Germany." But he was hopeful that "public opinion here in the last few months" was becoming "quite reconciled to the type of settlement that seems to be impending."[24]

This strange phraseology suggested that a policy that con-doned a new partition of Poland was in fact a liberal policy! An awkward position, to say the least. And one that Republican candidate Thomas Dewey exploited in a bid for ethnic votes, criticizing the president's "secret" diplomacy and his failure to secure Russian recognition of the London Poles.[25] Hopkins and others had imagined that a Republican triumph—or better put, a conservative resurgence that dominated both parties—would mean an "isolationist" foreign policy.[26]

While Hopkins hoped that the "impending" settlement would not end up as the old balance of power—a sure formula for failure at home as well as abroad—the realities of the situation in Eastern Europe suggested no other solution, at least as a beginning point for the postwar world. Like Roosevelt, therefore, Hopkins could reconcile old-style power politics as the means to a liberal end, as long as the United States kept the final decisions for itself. Hence his intervention at the time of the TOLSTOY Conference to forestall Roosevelt's approval of a "European" initiative and to maintain the power of choice in American hands. Roosevelt's course thus wound along a narrowly treacherous path. To the right, conservatives saw the advancing Red Army as socialism on the march, in much the same way as European monarchists had once feared the advance of the French Revolution on the bayonets of Napoleon's army. To the left, liberals disdained the bargaining for position among the Big Three as a betrayal of war aims originally set forth by Woodrow Wilson and now enshrined in the Atlantic Charter.

John Maynard Keynes witnessed the reemerging debate when he visited Washington in late 1944. "Responsible" people, he said, were friendlier than before, and more than ever convinced a strong Britain was essential to American well-being. "Further acquaintance with Russia does not increase intimacy or confidence." Yet Central Europe was seen as "a dreaded cavern of misery and chaos."[27] As events developed in late 1944, public attention shifted from that forbidding scene to Greece, where British troops sought to suppress leftist guerrillas in the wake of the German withdrawal. A soon-to-be famous cable from Prime Minister Churchill to his commander in Greece, advising him to treat Athens as a military objective, was leaked to columnist Drew Pearson, and suddenly newspapers around the country came alive to this new threat to the peace. The prime minister was "incensed" by this leak, no doubt because of the political uproar in Parliament. He could vent his anger at the American diplomatic representative in Greece, but he could not silence the outcry in Commons.[28] Neither could he persuade Roosevelt to make a public statement supporting British policy, an appeal he sent through Ambassador Winant to Harry Hopkins.[29]

While the British asked for American backing in the Balkans, Stalin announced his intention to recognize the Lublin Poles as the provisional government of Poland. Lend-Lease administrator Oscar Cox warned Harry Hopkins that if "some bold and dramatic action" were not taken soon, popular reactions to the Greek and Polish situations, and events elsewhere, would cause irreparable injuries to the Allied cause. "Already, for example, as you are well aware, some of the people on the Hill are asking why Lend-Lease supplies should be used to kill some of our Greek friends."[30]

Roosevelt often compared his situation with Wilson's plight at Versailles—with good reason, for he had been warned many times against "secret treaties" even before the Japanese attack at Pearl Harbor. He had refused to commit himself to any arrangements made at TOLSTOY, but now he was being pressed by both Churchill and Stalin not simply to accept responsibility for underwriting TOLSTOY but to join in suppressing nationalist movements against great-power domination. Within a few weeks Churchill would respond to attacks on his Greek policy by taking up the Polish issue himself, but now he continued to be distressed by ambiguous American statements about Poland's future, especially its borders, and the prickly question of forced transfers of populations.

In a speech to the House of Commons on December 15, 1944, Churchill went as far as he would ever go to suggest that Britain and Russia—"bound together as they are by the 20 years' alliance"—would support the redrawing of Polish boundaries, in the east in favor of Russia, and in the west in favor of Poland at Germany's expense. He reminded his colleagues that Russia bore the main responsibility for Poland's "liberation." And he was not worried about population transfers of several millions. "A clean sweep will be made. I am not alarmed by the prospect of the disentanglement of populations, nor even by these large transfers, which are more possible in modern conditions than they ever were before."[31]

The speech made a distinctly bad impression in Washington. Secretary of State Edward R. Stettinius, having already been assaulted by Francis Cardinal Spellman over Poland, now faced the wrath of Senator Arthur Vandenberg, who told him that across the country the feeling was that Roosevelt had turned Poland over to Stalin. Vandenberg warned that a full-scale debate in Congress on postwar policy was in the offing. The State Department then released a statement that did little to satisfy anyone. It set forth American policy as "unequivocally" for a strong, free Poland with the "untrammeled" right of determining its internal "existence." Territorial questions should be left for the peace conference, but if Russia and Poland reached a mutual agreement on frontiers, the United States would have no objection.[32]

He had never seen such a "timid" document, snorted Churchill. It would not do anything to get the Americans out of their difficulties, the prime minister cabled the British ambassador in Washington, nor him out of his. Ambassador Halifax agreed it was "Delphic," but both the right and the left wings of the press had bought it.

> As in other matters, our friends still cling to their old preference for dodging breathlessly round the field a few feet ahead of the bull rather than make up their mind to seize it boldly by at least one horn. In the end I fear with you that they may find themselves pinned in an uncomfortable corner.[33]

Michael Wright of the British embassy, in a discussion with a group of American broadcasters and commentators at the end of 1944, indicated that TOLSTOY still held sway in London's policy. Wright put two points to the Americans:

> We did not understand why the United States should refuse to accept political or military responsibility in an area such as the Balkans, and then accuse others of an exclusive sphere of influence there.
>
> We did not understand how it could be considered right to encourage, for instance, the Poles to expect American sympathy and support when it was perfectly evident that American boys would never be sent to fight for Poland against Russia.[34]

A measure of support for Roosevelt's predicament came from selected members of the old policymaking elite. Secretary of War Henry L. Stimson, the original opponent of Japan's move into Manchuria and formulator of the fateful nonrecognition doctrine designed against it, now advised a quite different policy in response to the Russian advance. The president ought not to object to changes in the Polish boundaries, he told Roosevelt. Rather, the United States should simply take no part.[35] Banker Thomas Lamont, another longtime "Asian" hand who had worked both with and against Japan, now wrote some words of caution to the famous liberal journalist Oswald Garrison Villard, on December 7, 1944—a significant anniversary:

> I don't like the way that Stalin has behaved about Poland any more than you do. But suppose, for example, you and I together had been constituted with complete authority as Russia's advisers on frontiers. Knowing that at best the peace that we shall have may be imperfect and that every man may have to be called upon to defend his own: what in that event should we advise Russia to do? In the light of history I should certainly advise a frontier as far west as the so-called Curzon Line; and Poland, having been partitioned three times within a century and a half and up to 1919 having had no independent existence of its own, ought not to be too sticky at achieving her full aims.[36]

Of course, Roosevelt's problem was much more complicated. Stalin had put the point directly to him: Would he recognize

Lublin? Roosevelt's reply was in line with the State Department's public pronouncements on Poland, but he emphasized that he was not asking the Soviets to "curtail your practical relations with the Lublin Committee" nor to "deal with or accept the London Government in its present composition." Only a part of Poland beyond the Curzon line had been liberated, and so there had been no opportunity for an expression of Polish opinion. Poland was a "difficult and dangerous" question. Why must Stalin hurry his Allies in this fashion? When the three met again, the president was convinced, there would emerge a solution. "I cannot, from a military angle, see any great objection to a delay of a month."[37]

Stalin replied that he was "powerless" to grant the president's wish, for the Presidium of the Supreme Soviet had already decided not to delay for even one day. This was not unlike some of Hitler's responses to Chamberlain during the Munich crisis.[38] Moscow accorded the Lublin regime diplomatic recognition on January 1, 1945. In so doing, Stalin helped Churchill out of a predicament. The prime minister could now abandon his strained efforts to defend the TOLSTOY line in Parliament and focus on Russian behavior in general. He had refrained from attacking Soviet actions in Rumania out of fear of upsetting the Anglo-Russian understanding over Greece; and he had felt uncomfortable with the demands of the London Poles and their supporters. By diverting attention from the Balkans, Stalin's action released Churchill from a self-imposed ban on criticism of Soviet policy in Eastern Europe.

British determination to crush leftist forces in Greece had brought the prime minister grief from the left, his Polish policy a combined assault from both left and right. Churchill had made it plain to Stalin, however, that his "concessions" on Poland's boundaries did not extend to complaisance about the composition of the future Polish government. So he was now in a position to invoke a general disapproval of the Kremlin's behavior without actually breaking with TOLSTOY.

In the United States a State Department sampling of public opinion sent to the president indicated dissatisfaction with Big

Three cooperation. But it also suggested that Americans were unsure what policy they wished their government to pursue. Sentiment seemed to prefer a more active role "to assure a fair deal for the smaller countries," but the weight of opinion did not oppose a cession of Polish territory to Russia in the east if Poland were compensated in the west. Interestingly, the poll revealed that the British were "chiefly blamed" for the lack of cooperation among the great powers.[39]

State Department briefing papers, prepared for the proposed meeting of the Big Three to be held at Yalta at the end of January 1945, stressed that, as matters stood, mutual suspicions of British behavior in Greece and Russian support for Lublin would push London to support rightist elements and Moscow to back leftist factions—as far east and west across Europe as they could. It was up to the United States, therefore, to find groups and individuals in the liberated areas who could allay such suspicions.

> These governments must be sufficiently to the left to satisfy the prevailing mood in Europe and to allay Soviet suspicions. Conversely, they should be sufficiently representative of the center and *petit bourgeois* elements of the population so that they would not be regarded as mere preludes to a Communist dictatorship.[40]

How these moderates were to be found in areas occupied first by German forces and then liberated by the Red Army or by forces in support of exile governments, the paper did not say. It was essential to American interests, read a second paper, that trade in Poland and the Balkans be returned as soon as possible to a multilateral basis "under the freest possible conditions." At stake was whether the pattern in Europe's commercial policy would look forward to progressive growth and liberalization or backward to bilateralism, restriction, and autarky, with all that implied. "The pattern of Europe's future commercial policy will be strongly influenced, if not largely determined, by policies and procedures established during the period of reconstruction." Russia would exert predominant political influence in the areas. The United States would not oppose that development, but it would not wish to see its influence "completely nullified." That influence could be felt only if the U.S. had "some degree of equal opportunity in trade, investment, and access to sources of information."[41]

Where the State Department sought to pursue these goals through declarations of mutual restraint and investigative commissions, Hopkins and Roosevelt counted on personal diplomacy. They feared forcing the issue too soon.[42] The president still had no clear idea when to play what policymakers thought were Washington's best cards. On January 5, 1945, Roosevelt instructed the foreign economic administrator to get Russia the "maximum amount of supplies" under old Lend-Lease arrangements. Pending completion of a new protocol, "it is my desire that every effort be made to continue a full and uninterrupted flow of supplies to the U.S.S.R."[43]

But Ambassador Harriman, meanwhile, had passed to the State Department Foreign Minister Molotov's somewhat startling request for $6 billion in long-term credits for purchases of American industrial goods. Harriman had long believed that Russia's desire for economic aid would be the key to opening the Kremlin to American influences. He had begun his mission as ambassador in late 1943 with a public announcement that negotiating such an arrangement was his priority. And he had been disappointed that FDR would not interfere in the State Department's painfully slow and unimaginatively precise efforts to come to an agreement on the fraction of interest that the Russians should have to pay on postwar credits.

Negotiations on an aid plan had broken down in September 1944. Now Molotov was proposing a new start.[44] Harriman expressed surprise at the foreign minister's "strange procedure" in reopening the subject, but he repeated what he had been saying all along: "The Soviet Government placed high importance on a large postwar credit as a basis for the development of 'Soviet-American relations.'" Molotov had, however, put the proposal as a Russian offer to save American capitalism from postwar depression. Clearly the Kremlin must be disabused of that notion and given to understand that the granting of credits or other forms of economic aid was closely linked to Russian political cooperation. Poland would be a good test, thought Harriman, of whether economic aid to Russia would loosen Stalin's grip on Eastern Europe.[45]

Secretary of the Treasury Henry Morgenthau, Jr., disagreed with that approach. The Treasury had proposed an even larger credit, $10 billion, as a contribution to "ironing out many of the difficulties we have been having with respect to their problems and policies." This carrot should be placed before their nose when Roosevelt and Stettinius first arrived in Yalta, Morgenthau believed, and kept well in sight throughout the negotiations. The president came down on Harriman's side. He was not taking any financial people to the conference. "I will just tell them we can't do anything until we get back to Washington.... I think it's very important that we hold this back and don't give them any promises of finance until we get what we want."[46]

"During the interim period we and our Allies have a duty," Roosevelt told Congress in his State of the Union Message on January 7, 1945, "to use our influence to the end that no temporary or provisional authorities in the liberated countries block the eventual exercise of the peoples' right freely to choose the government and institutions under which, as free men, they are to live."[47] The key word here for Roosevelt was "eventual." Did that mean months—or years? How was he to build up trust so that Stalin need not use such things as the sham proceedings of the Supreme Presidium to mask unilateral actions in Poland and elsewhere?

What Morgenthau wanted Roosevelt to do would require congressional action. An appeal for legislative approval of large-scale aid to the Soviets, while questions about Poland and Anglo-Russian "deals" to divide Europe circulated on Capitol Hill, risked a turndown and a much worse environment for FDR's personal diplomacy. Perhaps his caution was unwarranted; probably now it was not. The time had passed for maximum presidential influence on this question. Roosevelt had left Harriman stranded. He could not recoup that lost ground, but he could show his sympathy for Russian needs in other ways, as for example on the question of reparations from Germany.

A parallel proposal to Morgenthau's argument emerged in a speech to Congress delivered about the same time by Senator Vandenberg. The Republican leader, a convert to internationalism, suggested that the United States and Britain offer the Soviets a security treaty over Germany. The speech was an immediate sensation. *Life* magazine declared that "Senator Vandenberg's forthright proposal swept away months of accumulated confusion and doubt."

> Having made such a treaty—and only after having made it— America would then have the "duty and the right" to demand that political and boundary questions in Europe be kept open. . . . This might stop the present series of unilateral acts. If we do not stop it we are heading for trouble.[48]

The president took a copy of Vandenberg's speech with him to Yalta, but he never referred to such a treaty during any of the discussions there. His objections to the Morgenthau approach also applied here. And if he adopted Vandenberg's proposal, which was really couched as a way of blocking Soviet actions, and a full debate ensued, that could make matters much worse.

Those who traveled with Roosevelt to Yalta came prepared to plug in the final connectors on some of that machinery the State Department had been working on since the war began, so that the engines could start even before an Axis surrender. FDR had always been reluctant to rely too heavily on engineers or mechanics. He still believed, as he had throughout his presidency, that there was no such thing as a machine that would run of itself—safely. Apart from the plenary sessions at Yalta, for example, in discussions within the American delegation Roosevelt opposed State Department proposals for an emergency high commission to bridge the transition period from the Axis surrender to the functioning of the proposed United Nations Organization. From cryptic notes taken by one of those present, it appears that the president was most concerned about confusing a statement of principles for the peace with Big Three interference in the internal politics of liberated areas. He did not wish to burden Allied unity with more than it could bear at the most vulnerable moment in the peace process.[49]

He preferred keeping the proposed Big Three Declaration on Liberated Europe, with its allusions to the Atlantic Charter and democratic processes, separate from an enforcement agency. Where necessary, there could be ad hoc commissions to look into conditions in any liberated country, a less minatory way of dealing with the inevitable differences that would arise.[50] He knew full well he might not be able to hold that position if overall relations deteriorated, but he was not yet willing to start down a path that, he believed, almost insured the kind of confrontation that would bring about such a collapse.

All around the Big Three at Yalta was evidence of earlier failures—a world torn asunder by Axis arms, facing even in victory the renewed peril of old arguments and suspicions, and the resumption of bitter ideological disputes on both an international and (especially) an *intra*national scale. Of the three leaders at Yalta, Roosevelt was perforce the most optimistic. The role the United States expected to play in the postwar world, if no other reason, demanded that of him. He was asked, as he had been at Teheran, to chair the plenary sessions at Yalta, a symbolic honor which reflected even more than America's growing military might the initiatives of American planners in creating the framework and machinery designed to provide solutions to the political and economic chaos of the prewar era.

Economic aid for Russian reconstruction came up once or twice directly, and indirectly during discussions of German reparations. Molotov initiated the question of long-term credits at the close of the first session of the Big Three foreign ministers on February 5, 1945. Stettinius responded that "personally" he was ready to discuss it at any time, at Yalta or later in Moscow or Washington. "Now that the end of the war was in sight," added the Russian, "it was most important that agreement be reached on these economic questions."[51]

Stettinius had made the case against the Morgenthau loan proposal in Washington before the Yalta Conference began. Looking back some years later, however, he would write, "Whether such a loan would have made the Soviet Union a more reasonable and co-operative nation in the postwar world will be one of the great 'if' questions of history."[52]

There are many reasons to conclude that the differences between the Big Three were so great that a more forthcoming policy would not have made cooperation easier. Be that as it may, the Soviets at Yalta had tested the ground and found it soft. There was no firmer foundation under the political discussions about German dismemberment. FDR did not mention the Vandenberg proposal to either the British or the Russians. And, to finish off this point, the president left both his wartime partners in the Grand Alliance to puzzle out future American policy from sometimes casual statements about his unwillingness or inability, for example, to keep American troops in postwar Germany for more than two years.

It was against such a background of vagueness that the Yalta discussions over Poland's boundaries and government began. Stalin's recognition of the Lublin Committee as the provisional government of Poland let the British off the hook, not only because Churchill gained political maneuverability but also because the British no longer felt the need to support Polish claims beyond the Curzon line. Foreign Secretary Anthony Eden reminded his colleagues that when it was thought to be a matter of inducing the London Poles to accept amputations of Polish territory in the east, they had favored a generous settlement in the west. In addition, while Churchill had said that population transfers would not pose any great difficulty, the cabinet was concerned that a Germany crowded with refugees would become a serious economic and political burden.[53]

In no previous undertaking, Eden explained to Stettinius when the two met on February 1 at a pre–Big Three interlude at Malta, had His Majesty's Government agreed to recognize Stalin's generosity in offering Lublin the Western Neisse River as the western boundary for Poland. To do so would mean adding more than three million refugees to the five million that would have to be relocated in an already shrunken postwar Germany. Eden did not mention what was obvious: such transfers of land and people would make the new Poland permanently dependent upon Russia for defense of its territorial integrity.[54]

Britain's position at Yalta, Eden concluded, would be that all previous understandings were subject to reexamination, including any willingness to see Poland extended west to the Oder River, "since we need not make the same concessions to the Lublin Poles which we were prepared to make to M. Mikolajczyk in order to obtain a solution of the Polish problem."[55] In its own discussions the American delegation reaffirmed an earlier paper and decision that it should "resist vigorously efforts to extend the Polish frontier to the Oder Line or the Oder-Neisse Line."[56]

The first plenary session at Yalta on February 4 was completely given over to military affairs. Amidst the banter of the Big Three dinner that evening in the Livadia Palace, Stalin suddenly became serious. Some of the liberated countries, he said, seemed to forget "that the Great Powers had been forced to shed their blood in order to liberate them and . . . were now scolding these Great Powers for failure to take into consideration the rights of these small powers." The Soviet Union was ready to do its part to preserve the peace, but it was ridiculous to believe that a country the size of Albania could have an equal voice with the powers that had won the war and were present at this dinner.[57]

Roosevelt agreed. The great powers bore the greater responsibility; the peace should be written by them. Churchill, perhaps grasping Stalin's point more firmly, and worried about Roosevelt's somewhat inattentive behavior at the plenary session, demurred slightly.[58] The great powers should write the peace, but they must also discharge their moral responsibilities and exercise their power with moderation and with great respect for the smaller nations. "The eagle should permit the small birds to sing and care not wherefor they sang," he quoted. Deputy Foreign Secretary Andrei Vyshinsky leaned over to the American next to him during this exchange and observed that Russia would never permit the small powers to judge the acts of the great powers. Charles Bohlen mentioned something about American public opinion, to which Vyshinksy replied, "The American people should learn to obey their leaders."[59]

The dismemberment of Germany, reparations, voting procedures in the proposed world organization, and various issues related to those questions had already been discussed—often in opaquely coded terms—when Franklin Roosevelt opened the floor to the Polish "question" near the close of the third plenary session. Stalin had questioned Roosevelt closely about his old proposal that Germany be divided into five parts, and he watched as Churchill successfully diverted discussion of that idea into a "study" plan for the future. How much the German question weighed on Stalin's mind as the discussion moved onto Poland's future cannot be determined, but it certainly did not lessen his insistence on shaping Poland's frontiers against the eventuality of a German "resurrection."

The president proposed that Poland's eastern frontier should be the Curzon line, with, if possible, a cession of Lvov and certain oil lands to the Poles. "Coming from America," he said, "he took a distant point of view of the Polish question." Most of the five to six million Poles in America were second-generation, and they did not oppose the Curzon line. But it would make it easier for him if the Russians made a gesture over Lvov.[60] He also suggested the creation of a Polish presidential council, composed of the heads of the five main political parties, who would create a "representative government." He did not mention the western frontier issue in this opening statement.

Churchill spoke next. He waved aside the Lvov issue to concentrate on the internal situation. Britain, he said, had no material interest in Poland; but it had gone to war to protect Poland against German aggression "at a time when that decision was most risky, and it had almost cost them their life in the world." It was a question of honor; he could never be content with a solution that did not leave Poland free and independent.

He then offered three of the London Poles, Mikolajczyk (also mentioned by Roosevelt), Grabski, and Romer, as members of a new government that the Big Three might form now, during the conference. They could all agree to recognize it as an interim government pending free elections. Political freedom for Poland, he concluded, could not be a cover for hostile designs, possibly in intrigue with Germany, against Russia. Subject to this one reservation, it was Britain's desire that Poland "should be mistress in her own house and captain of her own soul."[61]

Stalin requested a ten-minute recess. Perhaps he needed the time to calm down. When he returned he launched into a history lesson: what a "weak" Poland had meant to the Soviet Union in terms of German aggression. For his country it was not only a question of honor but literally life and death. As for adjustments in the Curzon line, he would remind his colleagues that it had been drawn by Curzon and Clemenceau against Russia's will. The Russians had not even been invited to the peace conference after World War I when the line was fixed. Could he return to Moscow and face people who would say he had been less of a defender of Russian interests than Curzon and Clemenceau? He then used Mikolajczyk's arguments during TOLSTOY to support the claim to the Oder-Neisse line in the west.

As to the form of the Polish government, Stalin continued, he was accused of being a dictator. But what of Churchill's plan? How could a government be created without consulting the Poles? He meant, of course, the Lublin (now also called the Warsaw) government. Surely the prime minister remembered that there had seemed to be a good chance of "fusion" when Mikolajczyk left Moscow after the TOLSTOY Conference, but he had been "expelled" because the London Poles wanted no agreement. In these circumstances it would be difficult to bring the two sides together. But Stalin was ready to "support any attempt" at a workable solution. Should they, then, ask the Warsaw Poles to come to Yalta or to Moscow? "I must say that the Warsaw government has a democratic base equal at least to that of de Gaulle."

Churchill did not intend to leave it there. His information was that the Lublin Poles represented no more than a third of the population and would not survive if the people were free to express their opinion. Then, in response to Stalin's claim that the Polish underground army, backed by the London Poles, had killed more than two hundred Red Army soldiers, the prime minister raised the possibility of a full-scale civil war in Poland if a solution could not be found.[62]

> "We had greatly feared that these collisions would lead to bitterness and bloodshed . . . and it was for this reason that we had been so anxious for a joint arrangement. We greatly feared the effect which all this would have on the Polish question which was already difficult enough."[63]

The American minutes of this session end at this point, with Roosevelt declaring it was time to adjourn. The British and Russian minutes include FDR's parting words, which hint at the final denouement of the Polish issue at Yalta. The British version reads:

> THE PRESIDENT said that Poland had been a source of trouble for over 500 years.

> THE PRIME MINISTER said that we must do what we could to put an end to these troubles.

> The conference then adjourned.[64]

The Russian minutes provide still another reading in a similar yet slightly different vein:

> ROOSEVELT pointed out that the Polish question had been giving the world a headache over a period of five centuries.

> CHURCHILL stated that an effort should be made to stop the Polish question from giving mankind a headache.

> STALIN replied that that must certainly be done.[65]

The opening positions stood this way: Roosevelt and Churchill had proposed creating a coalition government, perhaps even before the conference ended, while Stalin was willing only to consider taking some London Poles into the existing government in Poland. Roosevelt sent Stalin a letter after this session, with British stiffening amendments, which stated that the United States could not recognize the Lublin government "as now composed," and warning that the world would regard it a "lamentable outcome" if they parted in open and obvious disagreement on the Polish issue. Then he repeated his proposal for summoning to Yalta representatives of three groups: London, Lublin, and democratic leaders inside Poland.[66]

The next day Foreign Minister Molotov offered a six-point Russian counterproposal. The boundary question, points one and two, would be settled in the east as the Curzon line and in the west as the Oder-Neisse. Point three, the key point, read: "It was deemed desirable to add to the Provisional Polish Government some democratic leaders from Polish *émigré* circles." The last three points described briefly how this might happen, and what would come next: American and British representatives would meet with Molotov in Moscow to consider how to carry out this mandate, then the "enlarged" Polish government would be granted diplomatic recognition. "As soon as possible" it would organize a general election for the "permanent organs of the Polish Government."

After he read out this proposal, Molotov added that attempts to reach the Lublin Poles by telephone had not succeeded, so it was apparent that time would not permit carrying out the president's suggestion for calling them to the Crimea. But he felt the Russian proposal "went far toward meeting the President's wishes." In fact it merely restated Stalin's position in formal terms—adding to it a unilateral declaration on the western frontier.

Roosevelt nevertheless saw room for maneuver. Molotov's proposals represented, he said, some progress ("definite" progress in one set of minutes) in the discussion. He did not like the word *émigré*, however, and did not even see the need to go to émigrés, "since you could find enough Poles in Poland for the purpose."[67] The only London Pole he knew personally was Mr. Mikolajczyk. This was, of course, a restatement of his original position. When Churchill suggested that before they study the proposal in detail it should contain a reference to other democratic leaders from within Poland, Stalin agreed at once.

And why not? He had gained, or appeared to gain, acceptance of an "enlarged" Lublin-dominated Polish provisional government. Roosevelt and Churchill, on the other hand, had managed only to save an opening for later diplomacy. But to move the Russians through that opening depended upon a solid framework within which Polish questions could be resolved, and the Yalta conferees did not appear to be moving close to final decisions on any of the key issues of such a framework.[68]

In a brief private meeting with Stalin before the next plenary session, Roosevelt talked about providing surplus shipping to the Russians on a noncommercial, long-term credit basis. Then he turned to Far Eastern questions and the political requirements for Soviet entry into the war against Japan. Talk about internal affairs in China may have contained coded references to earlier exchanges over Poland. Roosevelt said, for example, that the failure to agree on a coalition of communists and Kuomintang to fight the Japanese rested more with the latter; and Stalin argued that leadership should belong to Chiang Kai-shek. "He recalled in this connection that some years ago there had been a united front and he did not understand why it had not been maintained."[69]

When the Big Three reconvened, Molotov moved quickly to respond to Roosevelt's hint that they did not need to search for émigrés by suggesting that three Poles from Lublin and two from the president's list of democratic leaders inside Poland be invited to Moscow for initial discussions. Here was a wedge against Churchill, who responded, as might be expected, with a long statement that he would be subject to the most severe criticism if, having given in on boundary questions, he broke with the body recognized all through the war as "the lawful government of Poland."

When Molotov pressed harder, Churchill replied that if a Polish government of national unity could be formed, "it would follow that we should withdraw recognition from the London Government of Poland and accredit an Ambassador to the new Government."[70] Roosevelt had originally suggested that a tripartite "presidential" committee of Poles form a new provisional government from representatives of democratic elements inside Poland and "from Polish leaders abroad." In response to Molotov's counterproposal, he had downplayed the London Poles, mentioning only Mikolajczyk as a potential candidate. So when Churchill recast the question as London versus Lublin, FDR tried to finesse the situation, saying that since they were all agreed on the need for free elections, "the only problem was how Poland was to be governed in the interval."[71]

Stalin had good reason to play along with Roosevelt's attempts to avoid a decision between London and Lublin. "It would," he began, "of course, be better if free elections could be held right off, but up to now the war has prevented this, but the day is drawing near, however, when such elections could take place and the people could express their view in regard to the Provisional Government."

Having fended off Churchill's attempt to front the issue directly, Roosevelt now pressed Stalin to give his allies some assurances about the scheduling of the elections, which they could take home for public consumption. The Russian leader suggested that it might be as early as one month. The meeting ended soon after, but not before Stalin had occasion to remind Churchill of their TOLSTOY obligations to each other in the nicest of diplomatic circumlocutions. He wondered what was holding up affairs in Yugoslavia, and, with no intent to criticize, he wished to know what was going on in Greece. They had had a rather rough time in Greece, replied the prime minister, "and they were very much obliged to Marshal Stalin for not having taken too great an interest in Greek affairs." On this exquisitely delicate note, the Big Three adjourned.[72]

Dinner that evening was a chummy affair. Roosevelt referred to the Big Three as a "family." Churchill enthused about Stalin as a "great man, whose fame has gone out not only over all Russia but the world." He walked with greater courage, said the prime minister, because of their relationship of "friendship and intimacy." "My hope is in the illustrious President of the United States and in Marshal Stalin, in whom we shall find the champions of peace, who after smiting the foe will lead us to carry on the task against poverty, confusion, chaos, and oppression."[73]

What accounted for this paean to Big Three unity? Stalin's promise of early elections in Poland, or Churchill's hope that somehow they had recaptured the spirit of TOLSTOY and extended it to cover the situation in Poland? The next day reality set in again when their surrogates, the foreign ministers, returned to the Polish question. Stettinius led off with a proposal that dropped the plan for a Yalta convocation of Polish leaders and accepted the idea of consultations "in the first instance in Moscow with members of present Provisional Government and other democratic leaders from within Poland and from abroad with a view to the reorganization of the present government. . . ." Molotov asked for a translation before he responded, and it was done as the discussions continued—a seemingly routine procedure that would lead to a major dispute over the placement of the phrase "in the first instance in Moscow. . . ." The Russians had it "in Moscow in the first instance . . . ," which in their minds somehow gave added emphasis to the existing Polish government, as that meant in the "first instance" with the Lublin group, not merely that the consultations should be in the first instance in Moscow.

That tortured reading would later become a serious issue. At this meeting Molotov echoed Roosevelt's statement at the preceding plenary session: "In the Russian opinion the most important question was the holding as soon as practical of general elections in Poland." For both Eden and Stettinius, however, the Mikolajczyk question had become almost a sine qua non of a Big Three agreement. And here, for the first time, Molotov gave ground. It might be a "mistake" to say that Mikolajczyk was unacceptable. "Perhaps the Mikolajczyk question was not as acute as it appeared. But it could not be cleared up in the Crimea."

Eden decided that he simply could not let this diplomatic flummery continue to go unchallenged. Yes, early elections were important, he said, but "British opinion" would not see them as free or expressing the will of the people if Lublin controlled them. Stettinius joined in, saying they had to get away from the words "existing Polish Government" if agreement were to be reached. It would be better to start with an entirely new name. He wished to know what reaction Molotov had to his proposed name, "Polish Provisional Government of National Unity," for what came out of the forthcoming discussions in Moscow. Was Stettinius insisting on a genuine coalition or a fig leaf? Or did the Americans simply want to get away from the claustrophobic Yalta atmosphere in order to reorganize their diplomatic front for what they anticipated would be some hard bargaining?[74]

Either way, it was clear that Roosevelt wanted the Big Three Polish discussions brought to an end. It was at the sixth plenary session, on February 9, 1945, that Poland's fate was largely determined—but not in the sense of being settled. Rather, Poland was sure to continue to be an issue that threatened the transition from war to peace. Despite Prime Minister Churchill's pleas that they not rush the Polish question to a cobbled "solution" sure to come undone, Roosevelt insisted that he now found it "largely a question of etymology—of finding the right words." The election was the key; it must reassure the six million Poles in America that it permitted a genuine expression of national opinion. Then this exchange:

PRESIDENT: I want this election in Poland to be the first one beyond question. It should be like Caesar's wife. I did not know her but they said she was pure.

STALIN: They said that about her but in fact she had her sins.

PRESIDENT: I don't want the Poles to be able to question the Polish elections. The matter is not only one of principle but of practical politics.[75]

The Big Three's final declaration on Poland set the Curzon line in the east, postponed a decision on the western frontier until the peace conference, and called for the "reorganization of the present Government" to include democratic leaders from inside Poland and "from Poles abroad." The London government was nowhere named in the document. By Big Three fiat it was, in effect, dissolved, no matter what fictions might later be devised.

It is impossible to say even today whether there was ever any basis before or after Yalta for a true "agreement" on Poland among the Big Three. At Yalta Roosevelt's aides had warned him that the wording of the final protocol on Poland was "elastic." Admiral William D. Leahy had passed the president a note to that effect, and Roosevelt had responded, "I know, Bill—I know it. But it's the best I can do for Poland at this time."[76]

It was the best the Big Three could do to hold their alliance together, and it was not enough. The partition of Europe had been largely accomplished *before* the cold war began. Had it not happened that way, there might not have been a cold war, or, as seems more likely, it could have been worse, certainly for Europe.

9 | LET'S PRETEND IT NEVER HAPPENED

> I recall we once talked about the Islamite approach
> to the conquest of Europe, and how Charles Martel
> turned them back at Tours. We discussed such
> episodes in history as the turning back of the Turks
> at Vienna, and how Genghis Khan was stopped
> before he could reach Austria. . . . Roosevelt was
> just as interested as I was in history, and knew more
> about certain phases of it than I did.
>
> *Harry Truman, 1960,*
> *remembering conversations*
> *with Franklin Roosevelt*[1]

IF TRUMAN REMEMBERED correctly, in the last months of his presidency Roosevelt was largely absorbed with historic parallels to the impending confrontation with the Soviet Union in Central Europe. Even in the last two weeks of his life, however, when some observers saw Roosevelt "toughening up" his attitude toward the Russians, he wrote banker Thomas Lamont to thank him for a note praising the Yalta compromises on Poland's frontiers. "It is unfortunate, as you so wisely observe, that in the field of international politics so many Americans are still living in the age of innocence."[2]

Roosevelt himself contributed to the prolonging of America's age of innocence. He did not wish to disillusion "so many

Americans" who lacked understanding of what it would take to set the American Century, the Century of the Common Man, into operation—what short-term compromises with Stalin, what short-term accommodations with European colonialism, what adjustments at home. FDR was, of course, by nature a devious man, and, as the historian Warren Kimball emphasizes, a "juggler." "You know I am a juggler," Roosevelt joked in 1942, "and I never let my right hand know what my left hand does. . . ."[3]

Truman believed himself to be a pretty good student of history. Roosevelt only knew more about "certain phases" of history than he did. He was certainly impatient to *make* history at the July 1945 Potsdam Conference with Stalin and Churchill after Germany's defeat. "Jimmy," he said to his chief adviser, James F. Byrnes, "Jimmy, do you realize that we have been here seventeen whole days? Why, in seventeen days you can decide anything."[4]

At Yalta what had impressed Roosevelt, on the other hand, and as much as anything Stalin or Churchill said, was what he saw around him. Hitler's Wehrmacht had wrought terrible destruction. The marauders had been driven out of the Crimea, but at what stupendous cost, not only in Russian lives and property but to future prospects for peace as well. Even as victory over the Axis became inevitable, the last convulsions of the war threatened chaos and, at the very least, a long and uncertain recovery. Could civilization recover from the pummeling that began not in 1939 but much earlier, as far back as 1914? If the victors could not maintain their wartime alliance until new foundations were in place, what, then, was in store for the world?

Little wonder that in his report to the nation Roosevelt celebrated Yalta as an end to "the system of unilateral action and exclusive alliances." He went on to declare what was so clearly not the case, that Yalta also meant an end to "spheres of influence and balances of power and all the other expedients which have been tried for centuries—and have failed." He wanted to believe *he* had not failed, that the *Big Three* had not failed, so that the fragile wartime alliance might transform itself—by stages—into a firmer grand alliance for peace. Churchill had also celebrated their accomplishments as they made ready to leave Yalta, speaking words he did not fully believe. Stalin was the most guarded, constantly looking for signs that the other two would not admit Russia's claims—to reparations, to old rights in the Far East, to a dominant position in the Black Sea as well as in the Baltic.

When the post-Yalta euphoria dissipated, Roosevelt tried to find a historical parallel. He was not, as Truman later suggested, a president haunted by barbarian invasions. He looked rather to American experience in the postrevolutionary Confederation period, with all its harsh bickering and political struggles between big states and small, between states with great territorial claims in the West and seaboard states concerned for fisheries and the maritime trade.

Churchill and Stalin broke with TOLSTOY, or, better put, came to realize they needed stronger fences. Roosevelt's successors had to pretend that spheres of influence had never happened, to assert that the Yalta agreements were perfect, and consequently that all that had gone wrong was Stalin's doing. In part they were so obliged because Roosevelt had gone on denying the contradictions until his death. Churchill returned home to make the fantastic statement to the war cabinet that "Premier Stalin was a person of great power, in whom he had every confidence." Much depended upon his continuing to be in charge, said the prime minister.[5] Whatever Stalin's abilities to shape the future—and they were not small, of course—it was Roosevelt's ability to prolong the suspension of disbelief that gave him such leverage both within the alliance and at home.

When he died, American policymakers had to choose among "realities." Truman dared not talk about the deliberate ambiguities in the Yalta accords, but what he later wrote of the situation in China captured the dilemma.

President Roosevelt had built up the idea that China was a great power because he looked to the future and wanted to encourage the Chinese people. In reality it would be only with the greatest difficulty that Chiang Kai-shek could even reoccupy South China.[6]

Anthony Eden left the Crimea feeling disgusted with the whole process. Roosevelt, he wrote in his diary, had been "vague and loose and ineffective." Churchill had made too many long speeches trying to rally the West. "Stalin's attitude to small countries struck me as grim, not to say sinister."[7] There were doubts within the American delegation as well, but the general feeling was that Roosevelt had pulled off what had escaped Wilson. "All our hats are off to you...a world of orchids to you," cabled Roosevelt's son-in-law, John Boettiger, from the White House. "Never have I seen such overwhelming praise for anything as for your achievements at Yalta. It has even swept the enemies off their feet, and I mean American enemies as well as the Nazis and Japs."[8]

Press response to Yalta was "magnificent," added a White House aide in another cable. The conference was widely heralded as producing the best results of any Big Three meeting of the war. Political leaders in both parties were enthusiastic—even Herbert Hoover, who, the aide reported, had said, "It will open a great hope to the world."[9]

On board ship coming home from Yalta, Roosevelt was asked to comment on Churchill's latest statement that the Atlantic Charter was not a rule, just a guide. "He seems to undercut the Atlantic Charter," said a reporter. "The Atlantic Charter is a beautiful idea," the president replied. "When it was drawn up, the situation was that England was about to lose the war. They needed hope, and it gave it to them. We have improved the military situation since then at every chance, so that really you might say we have a much better chance of winning the war now than ever before."[10]

Roosevelt's sense that the orchids from Boettiger would soon wilt led him to temper, rather heavily, his comments on what could now be expected from the peace. Wilt they did. Within weeks—days even—the euphoria evaporated as the Polish agreement began to unravel, to be followed by general accusations of bad faith. Properly speaking, it was not the *Polish* question but the Polish *questions* that undid the fragile Yalta agreements, for Poland was both Scylla and Charybdis. On one side it was a swirling tangle of ideological and emotional claims that spun round the Big Three, first angering them, then setting them against one another in frustration; on the other it was a geopolitical obstacle that loomed over their deliberations as they struggled to end the war successfully so that a healing peace could begin.

Americans who had been present at the Polish discussions in Yalta came away with an accurate picture of what the final declaration meant and what needed to be explained, however carefully, to the American people. The State Department's Russian expert, Charles Bohlen, ordinarily no great believer in the prospects for Russo-American relations, told the president's speech writer that he could use the Polish agreement as a centerpiece to talk about the success of the conference. The disturbing British actions in Greece and Russian unilateralism in Poland would not have grown so acute, Bohlen said, if basic arrangements of the sort arrived at in the Crimea had been in effect earlier.

The alternative in the case of Poland, Bohlen continued, would have been civil war or a Russian-backed government which rapidly eliminated all elements that looked outside the country for support. Stalin had hinted at that with his stated unwillingness to tolerate anything in the rear of the Red Army that would "interfere" with its operations.[11]

Yalta meant, in other words, not that Russia would step back but that it was willing to listen to other points of view if its security was not threatened. James F. Byrnes, who would succeed Stettinius as secretary of state and advise Harry Truman on Poland, was more blunt. Confiding to newspaper reporters that agreement had come only after lengthy debate, he told them Stalin eventually yielded, but only to the extent that

Lublin would "take in" some of the London Poles. The Russians wanted to be sure the exiles knew "that they were being incorporated, not that they were doing the incorporating."[12]

Churchill would not have disputed Bohlen or Byrnes. Despite his encomium to Stalin and his celebration of the Big Three in cabinet discussions and parliamentary debate, he was highly uncomfortable with the Polish decision. The more controversy, the more uneasy he felt. He sounded like a man trying to convince himself all would be well. His concern was not whether Stalin would live up to his promises but whether he could hold together his Conservative coalition for the upcoming election with the added burden of the Yalta decisions.

He had expected difficulty, and decided how he would handle it. At the final dinner of the Yalta conference, Churchill leaned over to Stalin and said, "We are going to have an Election quite soon in England and I shall have to speak very harshly about the Communists." His listener appeared to be in a jovial mood. "The Communists are good boys," he said. "We are against them," Churchill continued, "and we shall have to make our case. You know we have two parties in England." "One party is much better," quipped Stalin.[13]

Throughout the war Churchill had enjoyed the luxury of one party. But the coalition was fast coming apart. From late 1944 reconstruction questions pushed their way into the cabinet rooms. Churchill tried to ward off these disagreeable intrusions by insisting that all bills on "controversial subjects," such as housing and health services, had first to be approved by the inner war cabinet before they went forward to Commons. Sitting across from him at the cabinet table these days, noted Hugh Dalton in his diary, were two Conservatives, "looking like a pair of very sinister capitalists, whispering to one another and suspecting socialism everywhere."[14]

Outside the cabinet room, where the wartime political truce no longer held, the prime minister attacked what he called Labor's easy promises of a "cheap-jack Utopia." Nationalization of industries was a system "borrowed from foreign lands and alien minds," he growled, rehearsing a theme he returned to often in the election campaign.[15]

How did Yalta and Poland fit in here? Defending the Yalta decisions on Poland cost Churchill scarcely more than twenty Tory votes in a showdown debate in Parliament, but these small losses did not reflect the anger within the party. "I must let you know," he wrote Halifax, "that the government majorities here bear no relation to the strong undercurrent of opinion among all parties and classes in our own hearts against a Soviet domination of Poland." He could not appear to have "underwritten a fraudulent prospectus" at Yalta.[16]

Yet Churchill could not square off against Stalin, at least for the moment. With Labor attacks continuing on his policy in Greece, Stalin's restraint in the Balkans had been important to him. Stalin was his reliable ally in Greece, certainly more so than the loyal opposition in Parliament. "As regards Greece," he told the cabinet,

> the Russian attitude [at Yalta] could not have been more satisfactory. There was no suggestion on Premier Stalin's part of criticism of our policy. He had been friendly and even jocular in discussions of it. . . . The Prime Minister added that Premier Stalin had most scrupulously respected his acceptance of our position in Greece. He understood that the emissary sent to the USSR by the Greek Communists had first been put under house arrest, and then sent back. . . . The conduct of the Russians in this matter had strengthened his view that when they made a bargain, they desired to keep it.[17]

Churchill would eventually seize upon the Yalta Declaration on Liberated Europe as superseding the TOLSTOY understandings; but he was not ready for that bold move which required, among other things, a stronger sense of an Anglo-American understanding about postwar Europe. Discussing the situation in Rumania with the cabinet, the prime minister mused that his hands were tied because of his "bargain" with Stalin. But it was for consideration, he went on, "whether the Yalta declaration on liberated Europe could be construed as superseding previous independent arrangements such as that in respect of Rumania and Greece which had been made at a time when we could not rely on United States assistance."[18]

He certainly needed assistance now from some quarter. When the London Poles read the final declarations of the Yalta Conference, they immediately convened to issue a statement:

> The method adopted in the case of Poland is a contradiction to the elementary principles binding the Allies, and constitute a violation of the letter and spirit of the Atlantic Charter and of the right of every nation to defend its own interests.[19]

On the eve of the first Moscow meeting of the Big Three's commission on Poland, Eden promised them that if the Russians refused to accept Mikolajczyk in the provisional government, there would be no agreement.[20] In Moscow Stalin anticipated precisely such a move. "Churchill wants the Soviet Union to share a border with a bourgeois Poland, alien to us," he told Marshal Zhukov, "but we cannot allow this to happen. We want to have, once and for all, a friendly Poland with us, and that's what the Polish people want too." After a pause, he added, "Churchill is out to groom Mikolajczyk who has spent four years sitting it out in Britain. The Poles will not accept Mikolajczyk. They have made their choice...."[21]

Or had it made for them. The initial meeting of the Polish commission took place on February 23, 1945. The atmosphere was quite cordial. Harriman and Sir Archibald Clark-Kerr presented their lists of candidates to Molotov, who promised to send them on to Warsaw so that they might be considered when representatives of that body came to Moscow. Seeing that Mikolajczyk was at the top of both the American and British lists, Molotov warned that he might not be acceptable to Warsaw. But the meeting ended with all three men apparently satisfied with the working framework for future discussions.[22]

Four days later the Russian foreign minister presented the Warsaw government's response. The head of that government, Boleslaw Beirut, had turned down many of the names on the list and suggested others in their place. As much as anything, the Western ambassadors resented Beirut's haughty language.

He spoke like the head of a sovereign government, not what one would expect of a body waiting for dispensation from the great powers. Harriman was clearly angry. They should invite Mr. Beirut and his colleagues to Moscow at once, he said, so as to "bring them into the atmosphere of the Crimea conference."

The cordial atmosphere disappeared. It was Harriman and Clark-Kerr who needed to be brought up to date on the atmosphere, and the wording, of the Crimea agreement, said Molotov. In the Russian text it was clearly stated that consultations with the Warsaw Poles were to take place "in Moscow in the first instance," which meant that that government had been given precedence. Harriman and Clark-Kerr rejoined that nothing in the wording allowed Beirut to pass on which Poles should be consulted or who should be left out.[23]

Mikolajczyk now made matters worse for the Western ambassadors by denying to the London *Daily Herald* that the Yalta accords had taken account of his suggestions, and proposing that Poland's government be created by means of a "round-table conference" of underground leaders in Warsaw.[24] Clark-Kerr advised the Foreign Office of Molotov's insistence that only those who accepted the Yalta agreement in toto were eligible to participate in the consultations. Could Mikolajczyk be persuaded to give a new interview in which he said the Crimea decisions were the only possible basis for a solution—and that he was ready to proceed to Moscow at once to take part?[25]

Harriman and the State Department joined in the request, but the Foreign Office was reluctant to pursue this path, at least for the moment, for fear of making Mikolajczyk's position untenable.[26] Even as Roosevelt delivered his report to Congress on the Yalta Conference, March 1, 1945, assuring the nation that the Big Three's decisions made Europe more stable than ever before, and that Poland, specifically, had been guaranteed an opportunity to develop a strong and prosperous nation with a government of the people, the Moscow negotiations had reached an impasse.

Churchill wanted the president to break the impasse with a formal demarche to Stalin demanding that he abide by Western interpretations of the decisions at Yalta.[27] Roosevelt was perfectly aware that Churchill's selective invocations of the Atlantic Charter, while raised out of genuine concern over the fate of the Poles, had much to do with domestic politics. Perhaps that is why FDR foolishly said during one press conference that there was no such actual "document" as the Atlantic Charter. Asked what had become of it, the president at first protested the question as "banal," then gave speculations another unneeded shove. "There isn't any copy of the Atlantic Charter, so far as I know." He went on to explain that it had been put together by bits and pieces, some on "scraps of paper," in various handwritings, then agreed to by himself and Churchill, and finally released to the press. "That is the Atlantic Charter."

A bewildered reporter then asked, "The spirit still is there, sir?" Roosevelt seemed deliberately evasive: "Well, we all agreed on it, that's all I know. I have got some memoranda that were signed by the British Prime Minister, but it wasn't the complete document. It isn't considered signed by us both."[28]

Three days later, amidst a swirl of public comment, reporters returned to the question of the whereabouts and actual existence of the Atlantic Charter.

Q. It seems that recently a number of people have felt that we are losing the purposes, or that they are slipping away from us...

THE PRESIDENT: (interposing) [I]t depends on which paper you read.

Q. Well, I would like to hear from the President and not merely from others. I would like to know what the President thinks about it?

He really ought to "prepare something a little formal, and think it over," the president said, then launched into a muddled discussion of famous "pronouncements" in history. "Some of them are of a good deal of importance," he said, "some of them do have an effect on—on the thinking of a public towards objectives and for a better world." Carried back, it almost seemed, to his days in Endicott Peabody's classroom at Groton School, he rambled on as if reciting a lesson for his famous schoolmaster.

> And the Atlantic Charter stands as an objective. A great many of the previous pronouncements that go back to many centuries, they have not been attained yet, and yet the objective is still just as good as it was when it was announced several thousand years ago. And I think that the objective of the Atlantic Charter is just as sound, if you believe in that kind of objective—some people don't, some people laugh at it—just as valid as when it was announced in 1940 (1941).[29]

The president then invoked the Ten Commandments and Wilson's Fourteen Points as examples, though he hastened to add he was not comparing the Atlantic Charter with a religious document. Every once in a while, he said, someone comes forward with something else to help build the future, something like the Ten Commandments or Wilson's Fourteen Points, that are "pretty good to shoot for."

An understandably perplexed reporter asked, "Mr. President, you—did you mean to imply by that that we are as far from attaining the ends of the Atlantic Charter as the world was a thousand years ago?"

"Oh, no. Oh, no," Roosevelt protested. "The world goes a little bit by peaks and valleys, but on the whole the curve is upward; on the whole, the—over these thousands of years human life is on a great deal better scale than it was then. And we have got a long ways to go." He ended on a stern note, just as Peabody might have left his pupils: the world must work to make things better. "There are some people who don't like to work for it—some people in this room—who are—what will I say?—congenitally 'agin' that sort of thing. Well, that is part of the peaks and valleys."[30]

Roosevelt knew very well that Russia was acting in Rumania, and Churchill in Greece, according to their Moscow understanding. Such behavior might not coincide with what Roosevelt imagined for Big Four leadership in regional areas, but what was different about what they were doing and the announced intentions, say, of the French to restore their rule in Indochina? Or the Dutch in the East Indies? Rumania was not a good test case, he told Churchill on one occasion, reminding him of the prime minister's own policy. The Russians had been in control there from the beginning, and it was difficult to contest their plea of military necessity as the country lay athwart their lines of communication.[31] At press conferences on March 2 and March 9, Roosevelt had refused to be drawn into a discussion of the fate of the Baltic states and Rumania. Did developments in Rumania square with the Declaration of Liberated Europe? he was asked. "O my God!" he wailed in mock helplessness. "Ask the State Department."[32]

The harder Churchill pressed him on the Polish impasse, the more he temporized.[33] Roosevelt kept offering countersuggestions, any means to avoid confrontations. He would not tolerate a whitewash of Lublin, he said in one message, but on March 29 he cautioned the prime minister to remember that the original agreements at Yalta had been a compromise between Stalin's insistence that Lublin merely be "enlarged" and "our contention that we should start with a clean slate. . . ." "If we attempt to evade the fact that we placed, as clearly shown in the agreement, somewhat more emphasis on the Lublin Poles than on the other two groups . . . I feel we will expose ourselves to the charge that we are attempting to go back on the Crimean decision."[34]

Interspersed in these Polish "letters" to Churchill was a March 21 cable from Roosevelt suggesting a Big Three commission be sent to Greece to see how the productive power of that country might be rapidly developed "by concerted, nonpolitical action." The prime minister's responses on Poland usually took but a day or two. He did not answer the president's message about Greece for nearly two weeks, and then in very defensive tones. At a time when the Russians were excluding Western influence in Rumania, he said, "it would be rather odd to invite them unsolicited to assume some degree of responsibility in Greek affairs."[35]

Roosevelt's "odd" gestures make a long list for the historian studying his presidency. One should never make too much of such musings, but he must surely have doubted that the prime minister would like the idea about Greece. Why, then, propose it at this time? To remind Churchill that it had been *his* idea to promote spheres of influence? It is impossible to say, especially of such doings in these final weeks of FDR's life.

At bottom, as Mikolajczyk had discovered, Roosevelt believed the Poles must negotiate on their own, aided only by timely diplomatic intervention. The Polish leader despaired at Roosevelt's constantly changing mood. In one breath he would vow to see that Poland did not come out of the war "injured," in the next sigh that not much could be done. "In our dealings with Stalin we must keep our fingers crossed," Roosevelt told him, but you "must find an understanding with Russia."

> On your own, you'd have no chance to beat Russia, and let me tell you now, the British and Americans have no intention of fighting Russia.[36]

Churchill could find some solace in Roosevelt's continuing temperance, using it to excuse Western inability to budge the Soviets in discussions with the London Poles. In one session with the exile group he "grumbled mildly" that the Americans had agreed with the decision to create a Polish government of national unity but were now leaving it up to the British to bring it into existence.[37] The more common British complaint, often echoed in cold war studies, was that Roosevelt was "still living in the age of innocence." There is a case to be made in this regard, but a similar argument could be made about Churchill's constantly shifting "enthusiasms," or his blindness to the power of nationalism in India and the rest of the colonial world.

The State Department, which never cared for Roosevelt's faith in personal diplomacy, also found Britain's post-Yalta position on Poland too rigid. Indeed, Roosevelt's responses to the prime minister were often drafted in the department.[38] Ambassador Halifax encountered this line of opinion on several occasions when he talked with those in the department who had the "most influence" on Polish questions. Their view was that the longer the situation remained in stalemate, the longer any Polish government would be subservient to Moscow, and the less chance, therefore, for Western influences to make themselves felt. Halifax reported:

This does not mean that the State Department believes that we should now surrender unconditionally to Molotov's demands, but would feel that making of even fairly wide concessions to the Russians would not necessarily endanger our long term objective of creating a strong and genuinely independent Poland.[39]

London responded tersely that Halifax should "do your best to convert them to our way of thinking." Even if a Polish government ultimately stood up to Russia, this would hardly excuse acquiescing in an arrangement that could not be defended in Parliament as fulfilling the Yalta decisions.

The Foreign Office now also complained that Harriman's list of eligible Poles was in no way representative. Since these were names Roosevelt had sent to Stalin during the Yalta Conference more than a month earlier, it seemed strange that no complaint had been made before. The Foreign Office list, taken in part from Mikolajczyk's suggestions, included members of the Polish underground who were widely known to be associated with the London government. Even Clark-Kerr had his doubts here. The Russians would know only too well how that list originated, he cabled London, and it would make them all the more suspicious of everyone named by the British and Americans.[40]

At this moment the Russians further exacerbated the situation by arresting members of the Polish underground whom they had lured to Moscow with a promise of consultations on the new government. Harriman and Clark-Kerr concluded that when Beirut came to Moscow and met with Stalin, he had convinced the Russian leader that his government had no chance against any Pole with genuine nationalist credentials, hence the early switch to stalling tactics.[41]

No doubt that was the case. No doubt, also, the Polish question had become one of "legitimacy." The Russians needed to sweep away opponents to "their" Poles while the Americans and British were determined not to deny "noncommunists" legitimacy anywhere. The arrest of the Polish underground leaders was a risky step for Stalin, raising the possibility of a complete break over Poland. "I must make it quite plain to you," Roosevelt protested, "that any such solution which would result in a thinly disguised continuation of the present Warsaw regime would be unacceptable and would cause the people of the United States to regard the Yalta agreement as having failed."

Harriman read out this portion of the president's message to the next meeting of the Big Three commission. Obviously the Yalta decision meant that some members of the Warsaw government would be excluded from the new government, Molotov responded, and also some new members included from the outside. But it did not mean that the Warsaw government was simply one of three equal groups.[42]

But, insisted Harriman, Mikolajczyk must be included. Why must that be? asked Molotov. It appeared they could not get to work without the agreement of that gentleman. "Molotov could never accept this, which was not based on any Crimea decision." Harriman backed off a bit. It was only for consultations, he said, to which the Russian replied that the list might be expanded later, after the initial consultations. He could not understand—no one in the Soviet Union could understand—why they were being presented with this ultimatum. Mikolajczyk was a stimulus to "terroristic" acts in Poland, Molotov added. Every time he came to Moscow, the acts began again. Clark-Kerr objected. His Majesty's Government did not believe he had anything to do with them. "Facts were facts," said Molotov. "Mr. Mikolajczyk was not so innocent." And so the impasse persisted.[43]

The Soviets saw darker motives in the threatened breakdown of the Polish discussions. They had evidence that the West was seeking at the last minute a negotiated peace with the Germans. Secret talks with German generals commanding Nazi forces in Italy had in fact begun, engineered by Allen Dulles, the head of American intelligence, in Berne. Confusion over how much to tell the Russians of these talks, and a badly handled refusal of Molotov's demand that Russian generals also be present, led both sides to "the edge of estrangement." Dulles himself later wrote that the "secret surrender" negotiations were aimed at preventing Soviet troops or procommunist partisans from reaching Trieste "and possibly west of there before we arrived."[44]

Soviet indignation soared to levels approximating the recriminations of August 1939, before the Nazi-Soviet pact. Much of this may have been feigned injury to cover actions in Poland. Stalin announced portentously that Molotov would not attend the San Francisco Conference on the organization of the United Nations, whatever the world might think about the breakdown of Big Three unity.[45] To Roosevelt's denials that the negotiations were aimed at making a separate peace, Stalin snapped that his intelligence sources were better than the president's, and that he knew things that perhaps even the White House did not. The negotiations, Stalin insisted, were to permit a virtual cease-fire on the western front and softer peace terms for Germany while the war raged on in the east.

> And so what we have at the moment is that the Germans on the Western Front have in fact ceased the war against Britain and America. At the same time they continue the war against Russia, the Ally of Britain and the U.S.A.
>
> Clearly this situation cannot help preserve and promote trust between our countries.[46]

These messages between Stalin and Roosevelt about the Berne negotiations crisscrossed those having to do with the impasse over Poland. Why, Stalin challenged, did the Germans surrender important towns in the heart of Germany while they fought desperately for obscure places in Czechoslovakia, "which they need just as much as a dead man needs a poultice"?[47] Thus did Stalin use the Berne negotiations not only to deflect criticism from the Polish situation but to urge his generals to get to Berlin before Western forces arrived. From the end of March onward, Stalin used every report, every rumor, public and secret, of Anglo-American military plans to prod his generals to be first not only in Berlin but first as well in Vienna and Prague.[48]

Summoned to Stalin's Kremlin office, Marshal Zhukov was told that western front had collapsed. The "Hitlerites" no longer wished to stop the advance of "Allied troops" but were all the time strengthening their forces in the east. Leafing through papers on his desk, he produced a letter from a "foreign well-wisher" detailing German peace overtures. "What do you make of it?" he asked Zhukov. "I think," he said without waiting for an answer, that "Roosevelt won't violate the Yalta accords, but as to Churchill, he wouldn't flinch at anything." Lighting his pipe, Stalin remarked, "I think its going to be quite a fight. . . ."[49]

Stalin's studied gestures aimed to give the impression that he had sized up his wartime associates and knew how to counteract their presumed machinations. The picture of Roosevelt as an honest man, in danger of being duped by Churchill, justified a pretense to the Americans that Stalin's military plans did not include a race to Berlin.[50]

Harriman cabled Washington, meanwhile, that it appeared "we are at a breaking point" over Poland. If there was no satisfactory response from Stalin, he suggested that he be called home for consultations. Stalin's cable to Roosevelt on April 7, 1945, restated the Soviet position as it had been since the early days of the debate. The West wished to abolish the Warsaw government, he said. "Things have gone so far that Mr. Harriman declared . . . that it might be that not a single member of the Provisional Government would be included in the Polish Government of National Unity."[51]

Two cables to Churchill, April 10 and 11, ended Roosevelt's efforts to find a way out of the cul-de-sac. Typically, they left his successors with an uncertain idea of what he might ultimately have done. In the first he advised they must consider the implications of Stalin's reply and most carefully decide upon the next step. In the second, his last message, he suggested to the prime minister that they "minimize the general

Soviet problem as much as possible. . . ." In one form or another these difficulties seemed to arise every day, but most of them straightened out. "We must be firm, however, and our course thus far is correct."[52]

Churchill told the war cabinet that FDR's death, April 12, meant that he must take the lead in the dispute, always being sure to keep in step, of course, with Washington.[53] Churchill's influence on Harry Truman probably was not as great as that of others who felt they must take the lead with Roosevelt dead, especially Ambassador Averell Harriman. The negotiations in the Polish commission were a catalyst to Harriman, an experience that led him to send a series of cables to Washington in early April that described a rapidly disintegrating atmosphere in Moscow. Each day he and his staff were subject to insults, he said. It was becoming unbearable.

Returning to Washington, the ambassador was the principal speaker at Truman's first "seminar" on Soviet-American relations. American generosity had been misinterpreted by elements around Stalin, Harriman began. They believed they could do anything they wished, disregard American views, and not have any trouble with the United States. He could have cited Stalin's decision to sign a formal alliance with the Warsaw government on April 21 as further proof. Yet he still believed the Kremlin did not intend to force a break: Russia needed massive American aid for reconstruction. Truman interrupted at this point to say he was not afraid of the Russians, and he agreed they needed us more than we needed them.

Encouraged, Harriman plowed on. "In effect, what we were faced with was a 'barbarian invasion of Europe.'" Soviet control over any foreign country meant not only its foreign relations but an extension of the whole system of secret police, and so forth. And yet he was not pessimistic. A way could be found to get on with the Kremlin, but it would require new thinking. Then Harriman turned to Poland. The real issue was simple. Mikolajczyk would rally 80 to 90 percent of the people to him. Stalin had discovered that an honest execution of the Crimean decision would mean the end of the Soviet-backed regime in Warsaw, and so he balked.

Turning to Truman, he asked the president how important he considered the Polish question. Was it important enough to go ahead with the San Francisco Conference without Russia? Unless the Russians agreed to a Polish solution along the lines of the Crimean agreements, Truman replied, any treaty calling for American adherence to the world organization would fail. But the truth of the matter was, he admitted, there would not be much of a world organization without Russia.[54]

Harriman seemed to draw back somewhat when he met three days later with Truman's senior advisers. The gathering took place just before the president confronted Molotov, who had been sent at Harriman's special request, after Roosevelt's death, to attend the San Francisco Conference. After Secretary of State Stettinius outlined the Polish stalemate, Truman stated his position. Thus far agreements with the Soviet Union had been a one-way street. "That could not continue; it was now or never." He was going ahead with plans for San Francisco, "and if the Russians did not wish to join us they could go to hell." This said, he asked those present to state their views.

Secretary of War Stimson was taken aback. He had not expected anything like this over the Polish difficulties. Wasn't it important to find out what the Russians were driving at in Poland? Without a full understanding of how important the question was, we might be heading into very dangerous water. Twenty-five years earlier virtually all of Poland had been Russian. Navy Secretary James Forrestal, to whom Harriman had earlier confided his fears that the "outward thrust of Communism was not dead" and warned of an ideological war ahead, declared that Poland could not be treated as an isolated incident. There was too much evidence of a Russian desire to dominate adjacent countries.[55]

Harriman tried to rephrase the problem so as to meet Stimson's questions. The real issue, he said, was whether "we were to be a party to a program of Soviet domination of Poland." Obviously we were faced with a real break, he said, but if handled properly it might be avoided. The ambassador's new twist seemed to nudge the president away from now-or-never talk. Truman said he had no intention of presenting an ultimatum but merely wanted to make clear the American position.

Admiral Leahy, who had been at Roosevelt's side throughout the Yalta Conference, remarked at this point that he had left there feeling the Soviets had no intention of permitting a free government. He would have been surprised had the Russians behaved any differently. Yalta was susceptible of two interpretations. "It was a serious matter to break with the Russians but . . . we should tell them that we stood for a free and independent Poland."[56]

Truman thanked the group for their opinions and prepared for his meeting with Molotov. Had he been president for more than eleven days he might not have felt quite so pressured to act, not quite so positive about what he must say. But he had not chosen the circumstances. Suddenly everyone was talking about how ill Roosevelt had been at the end—even Harry Hopkins, who was no hard-liner. Hardly anything of FDR's recent telegrams, Hopkins confided to Halifax, had been his own.[57]

Roosevelt had postponed decisions about economic aid to Russia, about postwar treatment of Germany, about the French return to Indochina. The list was endless. And now Truman faced the consequence—and the likelihood that his fate was to be known as the man who lost the peace.

Truman opened his remarks to Molotov by recalling that in a recent cable about Poland, President Roosevelt had warned Stalin that no policy could succeed in America without public support. He would add that this applied to economic collaboration as well as political. Congress must approve all economic measures in the foreign field, and he could not expect to get that approval without public support. He hoped that Marshal Stalin would consider this aspect of the Polish question.

Molotov countered that the only basis for collaboration was equality within the Big Three. It had succeeded during the war because in no case had one or two of the Allies tried to impose their will on another. All we were asking, replied Truman impatiently, was that the Soviets carry out the Crimean decision on Poland. To a further Molotov demur, the president delivered a sharp rebuke: "An agreement had been reached on Poland and it only remained for Marshal Stalin to carry it out in accordance with his word."[58]

We cannot be sure that Roosevelt believed such a confrontation was the only way to insure a decent postwar settlement. Historians seize upon one or another of the messages from the White House in his final days as "proof" of a favored argument. As these were written by various aides, the argument goes on and probably will go on.[59] Even when arguments over the interpretation and implementation of the Yalta protocol on Poland had so divided Big Three negotiators that he feared the United Nations organizing conference might never take place, Roosevelt reverted to the most uncertain period in American history, the years under the Articles of Confederation, for his analogy with the state of international affairs in the last months of the war. He had given some thought to what he might say publicly in this regard, and an aide prepared this paragraph for his use:

> It was a time when men in a Confederation, which had been sufficiently strong to hold them together in war, were arguing in disorder about a greater union which—in unity and security— could hold for them a full measuring of their victory. They came in no calm conversation to our Constitution. It was born in invective, pamphleteering, and plain politics. . . .[60]

Roosevelt was working on a draft of this speech on April 12, 1945, when he died of a massive cerebral hemorrhage.

In the aftermath of his stormy interview with Truman, Molotov did not return home but went on to San Francisco, where the tripartite discussions continued. Churchill, meanwhile, had finally secured a statement from Mikolajczyk affirming his support for the Curzon line and all the Yalta decisions. Molotov then announced with a flourish that "progress" had been made toward a Big Three agreement. Mikolajczyk had been "a stumbling block in Moscow. This had now been settled." Eden and Stettinius did not feel that extending an invitation to Mikolajczyk represented real progress, however, until the lists for consultation were complete. It was difficult to go ahead, Eden commented, until Mikolajczyk knew whom he was to meet with in Moscow. Molotov remarked gloomily that Mikolajczyk "was always inclined to delay matters."[61]

The Russian invitation to Mikolajczyk nevertheless opened the way for the talks to continue. Truman decided to send Hopkins to Moscow where lists were brought forward and preliminary agreements reached. Hopkins knew what Roosevelt had had in mind, the special emissary told Stalin, and what Truman had in mind as well. There would be no attempt to suggest anyone for the Polish consultations who opposed the Crimea decisions. Furthermore, Roosevelt, and now Truman, had always anticipated that the members of the present Warsaw regime would constitute the majority in the new Polish provisional government.[62]

Truman received Hopkins's daily reports with growing enthusiasm, a feeling not shared by Churchill. The president had sent him Joseph Davies. And what the former ambassador to the Soviet Union had to say was shocking. Truman was considering a personal meeting with Stalin, which Churchill would be invited to join only in progress. The implication was that the disputes over Eastern and Southeastern Europe were largely Anglo-Russian affairs, to which the United States was an unwilling participant. Responding to this apparently abrupt change in American policy, the prime minister said Washington had been "as fully concerned and committed as ourselves" to the problems of the Russian threat to those areas.[63]

As fully concerned, yes, but both Roosevelt and the State Department had always believed that Churchill wished to entice them into support for his policies. One trouble with spheres of influence, the department had said in its briefing papers for the Yalta Conference, was its instability. Churchill's shifting enthusiasms were no sure guide for American policy. Hopkins had objected to a blanket approval of TOLSTOY largely for that reason, not because either he or Roosevelt wished to become involved in the internal politics of the Balkans.

In response to Truman's reports of Hopkins's success, Churchill returned a subdued note of acquiescence:

> While it is prudent and right to act in this way at this moment I am sure you will agree with me that these proposals are no advance on Yalta. They are an advance upon the deadlock but we ought by now, according to Yalta and its spirit, to have had a representative Polish Government formed.[64]

Mikolajczyk had grave doubts about accepting the invitation to Moscow. Churchill sympathized but insisted Poland needed him regardless of the outcome of the consultations. "I'm more pessimistic than you are," the prime minister told him. "I'm pessimistic about the future of all of Europe, as well as Poland. Poland will be farther away from us than ever before because the Russians will come to the Elbe and perhaps to the Rhine and establish themselves between our two countries."[65]

On July 5, 1945, the United States recognized the Polish provisional government. Mikolajczyk went to Moscow, and Churchill met with Truman and Stalin at Potsdam at the end of July. Churchill would be replaced during the conference by Clement Attlee, head of the new Labor government. Truman's secretary of state, James F. Byrnes, noted that the British and Russians traded charges at Potsdam over Yugoslavia and Greece with little purpose the Americans could see except to condemn each other. When, finally, Foreign Secretary Ernest Bevin suggested that they give it up for the time being, "Stalin quickly replied, 'Yes, welcome.'" It was a good demonstration, Byrnes quipped sarcastically, "of the seriousness with which some of the charges and countercharges were made."[66]

Truman believed that Anglo-Russian wrangling detracted from American proposals, for example, for establishing international control over all European waterways to encourage trade between industrial areas and areas producing raw materials. The president refused all Russian arguments that he grant diplomatic recognition to the Russian-installed governments in

Eastern Europe. And when he returned home he reported to the nation that Rumania, Bulgaria, and Hungary were not to be "spheres of influence of any one power."

Western leaders did not fear a Russian military invasion but rather the chaos and disorder that Stalin might exploit to subvert world economic recovery. In the summer and fall of 1945 therefore, American leaders made frequent speeches like one Byrnes delivered linking employment and economic prosperity at home to foreign policy. "A durable peace cannot be built," he claimed, "on an economic foundation of exclusive blocs . . . and economic warfare."[67]

But Potsdam decisions on German reparations set a pattern for independent action that would be a powerful spur to "blocism." In the face of contemporary understanding of the immediate postwar situation, there is some evidence to suggest that in the summer and fall of 1945 Stalin was the least inclined of the Big Three to insist upon the partition of Europe. "Public opinion" did not constrain him as it did Churchill and Roosevelt and their successors, but the situation at war's end both at home and abroad placed him in an ambiguous relationship to the Communist party and foreign communist leaders. The war, despite the invocation of patriotic themes from Russia's ancient past, had been hailed as a triumph of a superior social system, Marxism. Stalin could not have sustained his role as heir to Marx and Lenin had he abandoned the rhetoric of revolution. Nor did he wish to, for he was perfectly willing to manipulate communists abroad to gain leverage for his policies in Europe and elsewhere. Yet his problem was not unlike that facing Western leaders—neither he nor they could square their pretensions about international cooperation with a policy of "control." In the longer term, on the other hand, control harmonized with pretensions as the cold war created the world of the Berlin Crisis and the Korean War.

Stalin's hints that there was still room to maneuver went largely unnoticed as Western leaders "disregarded his statements altogether, and put him in the group of forces of disorder which they wanted to contain. . . ."[68] Put this way, both Stalin's greater desire for continued Big Three cooperation and his inability to get round the forces that had made for partition since the time of the Munich crisis, as well as Western desires to simplify their problems by lumping him in "the group of forces of disorder," become more understandable.

In mid-September 1945, while the Big Three foreign ministers were failing to resolve their differences over Poland, a group of American legislators talked with Stalin about Russia's reconstruction needs and the possibility of credits from the United States. To each question the Soviet leader's answer suggested a desire for collaboration. He was vague about Russian participation in certain international organizations, but he called attention to a recent Soviet assent to the erection of an American automobile plant in Rumania. "[The Russians] did not object to participation of other countries in trade with those nations." When the congressmen finished their interview, Stalin pulled the American chargé, George Kennan, aside: "Tell your fellows not to worry about those eastern European countries. Our troops are going to get out of there and things will be all right."[69]

The troops did not leave, of course, for nearly half a century. But the supposed threat they posed of a Russian sweep westward never materialized. In early 1946 former Prime Minister Winston Churchill spoke of an Iron Curtain dividing East and West. In the East the Soviet "bloc" was gradually "communized" over a two-year period. Ideological zeal triumphed within the context of ever tighter control from Moscow. Far from what Harriman had expected in 1945, the communist thrust in Europe was inward, away from Western Europe and back toward Moscow.

This made it no less menacing to Western policymakers. Founders of the North Atlantic Treaty Organization might not have dreaded a Soviet military attack, but they did fear a weak sense of purpose on their side of the curtain. As one policymaker, John J. McCloy, the American high commissioner in Germany, put it:

There was a deeper and more underlying motive than the fear of a direct invasion. . . . [It arose from] the contrast between Soviet strength and purpose on the one hand and Western European weakness and lack of concentrated direction on the other which prompted the formation of the Western security system.[70]

Once NATO was in place, American policymakers from Dean Acheson to Dean Rusk, from John Foster Dulles to James Baker, worried about the consequences of a Soviet collapse. In 1972, for example, a State Department official openly deplored the failure of the Soviets to achieve an "organic" unity with the satellite nations. Helmut Sonnenfeldt's remarks stirred a minor controversy, but they illustrated the basis for the Kissinger-Nixon faith in détente as a conservative alternative to the cold war.

It is difficult to imagine how the United States could have managed economic recovery without the Soviet sphere of influence in Eastern Europe. What incentive would Congress have had to support Truman's major initiatives without the cold war? After both the German and Russian armies had trampled over Eastern Europe and stripped it bare, not simply of material resources but of experienced managerial capacity, would not the economic "drain" in that region have overwhelmed the Marshall Plan? Without an "enemy" to focus on, how could the bedeviling European rivalries of the interwar years have been overcome? Very soon after World War I Britain and France fell to quarreling over practically every aspect of European political and economic security, while Germany went from villain to victim in scarcely any time at all. Spheres of influence provided—at heavy cost, to be sure—temporary security for political developments in the West, and even in the East.

Most of the advantages from Soviet actions in Eastern Europe thus accrued to the West, and if they were not essential to the success of American postwar policy they were very nearly so. Stalin's slowness (or deliberate pace) in forcing one-party rule on the "peoples' democracies" in Eastern Europe, viewed from this perspective, could have been disastrous to the West. Communist "revolutions" from the top were far safer than the chaos of "separate roads to socialism," the initial Soviet postwar policy. By early 1948 the Kremlin had no patience left for the Titoist heresy in Yugoslavia, the Greek comrades and their civil war, or an anomaly in Czechoslovakia.[71]

For some Americans and Britons it became an article of faith in the cold war that Roosevelt's shallow grasp of Stalin's motives, and his amateurish handling of foreign policy, surrendered Eastern Europe to the Soviets. Churchill led the assault in the final volume of his memoirs, not attacking Roosevelt directly but setting forth the theme: "How the Great Democracies Triumphed, and so Were able to Resume the Follies Which Had so Nearly Cost Them Their Life." But just as the first volume opened with a description of Chamberlain's folly in not accepting Roosevelt's proposed intervention in Europe as an alternative to appeasement, Churchill's final theme proved to be a "useful past" for Western policymakers. They could blame wartime mistakes for a state of affairs they had no intention of changing by force, and indeed preferred to the slightest threat of disorder and chaos.

Constructive relations with Russia would not be possible, Secretary of State Dean Acheson stressed in secret congressional hearings on NATO, until there was a much more settled situation in the West. The Soviet Union had been "drawn into the troubled situation in the West, and that made quiet relations within the rest of the world impossible."[72] When he wanted to be, when he was not employing the Holy Pretense, Acheson could be a candid witness. "I was always a conservative," he said on another occasion. "I sought to meet the Soviet menace and help create some order out of the chaos of the world. I was seeking stability and never had much use for revolution."[73] He could not be totally candid and say, "I was seeking stability and never had much use for revolution or desire for the collapse of the Soviet empire."

"What does 'the cold war' mean?" Molotov in old age would ask those around him. "They certainly hardened against us, but we had to consolidate our conquests. We made our own socialist

Germany out of our part of Germany. As for Czechoslovakia, Poland, Hungary, Yugoslavia—they were already on the move. We had to put every place in order, to know where to stop. I believe that in this consideration Stalin kept strictly within the limits."[74]

Churchill agreed. "Stalin never broke his word to me," the former prime minister told an American reporter in 1956.

> We agreed on the Balkans. I said he could have Rumania and Bulgaria; he said we could have Greece (of course, only in our sphere, you know). He signed a slip of paper. And he never broke his word. We saved Greece that way. When we went in in 1944 Stalin didn't interfere. You Americans didn't help, you know.[75]

Roosevelt would have publicly denied collaborating with Molotov and Churchill to divide Europe. But in a moment of private candor he might have pointed to a paradox: the peace process required a temporarily divided Europe in order to provide a time of healing for the nearly fatal wounds Hitler had inflicted on the Continent. Once it proved impossible to launch a second front in timely fashion, FDR's diplomatic options were severely curtailed. On the other hand he knew he could not stand behind Churchill's efforts to bargain over boundaries but must somehow regain the initiative—even if that meant going beyond what the prime minister recommended after Yalta.

When Averell Harriman went to see Stalin to discuss the meaning of Roosevelt's death, Foreign Minister Molotov kept muttering, "Time, time, time."[76] In the end, that was what spheres of influence was about.

Notes

ABBREVIATIONS USED IN THE NOTES

AK. Papers of Arthur Krock, Seeley G. Mudd Library, Princeton University, Princeton, New Jersey.

CAB. Various Cabinet Records and Minutes, Public Record Office, London, England.

CB. Papers of Charles Bohlen, National Archives of the United States, Washington, D.C.

FDRL. Papers of Franklin Delano Roosevelt, Franklin D. Roosevelt Library, Hyde Park, New York.

FO 371. General Records of the Foreign Office, Public Record Office, London, England.

FO 800. Nevile Henderson Papers, Public Record Office, London, England.

FO 800/309. Papers of Viscount Halifax, Public Record Office, London, England.

FO 954. Avon Papers, Public Record Office, London, England.

FRUS. Department of State, *Foreign Relations of the United States* (Washington, D.C., various dates).

HJM. Diary of Henry Morgenthau, Jr., Franklin D. Roosevelt Library, Hyde Park, New York.

HLH. Papers of Harry L. Hopkins, Franklin D. Roosevelt Library, Hyde Park, New York.

HLS. Papers of Henry L. Stimson, Sterling Library, Yale University, New Haven, Connecticut.

JED. Papers of Joseph E. Davies, Library of Congress, Washington, D.C.

JPM. Diary and Papers of J. Pierrepont Moffat, Houghton Library, Harvard University, Cambridge, Massachusetts.

NASD. State Department Files in the National Archives, Washington, D.C.

NC. Personal Papers of Neville Chamberlain, Birmingham University Library, Birmingham, England.

NHD. Papers of Norman H. Davis, Library of Congress, Washington, D.C.

OC. Papers of Oscar Cox, Franklin D. Roosevelt Library, Hyde Park, New York.

PREM 1. Records of the Prime Minister's Office, Neville Chamberlain, Public Record Office, London, England.

PREM 3 & 4. Records of the Prime Minister's Office, Winston S. Churchill, Public Record Office, London, England.

RCBM. Papers of Robert Cecil, Additional Manuscripts 51144, British Museum, London, England.

SIR. Samuel I. Rosenman Papers, Franklin D. Roosevelt Library, Hyde Park, New York.

Stalin Correspondence. Ministry of Foreign Affairs of the USSR, *Correspondence Between the Chairman of the Council of Ministers of the U.S.S.R. and the Presidents of the U.S.A. and the Prime Ministers of Great Britain During the Great Patriotic War of 1941–1945* (2 vols., Moscow, 1957).

T 188. Treasury Records, Public Record Office, London, England.

WAH. Papers of W. Averell Harriman, Library of Congress, Washington, D.C.

WR. Papers of Walter Runciman, University of Newcastle, Newcastle, England.

1. Roosevelt's Proposal

1. Neville Chamberlain to Hilda Chamberlain, March 13, 1938, NC 18/1/1041.
2. Winston Churchill, *The Second World War*, I, *The Gathering Storm* (Boston, 1948), 254–255.
3. *Ibid.*
4. *FRUS*, 1938, I, 115–117.
5. Lindsay to Foreign Office, January 12, 1938, PREM 1/259.
6. Welles to Roosevelt, January 10, 1938, *FRUS*, 1938, I, 115–117. For an elaboration on the proposal, see C. A. MacDonald, *The United States, Britain and Appeasement, 1936–1939* (New York, 1981), pp. 63–75.
7. Cadogan to Chamberlain, January 12, 1938, FO 371/21526 (A 2127/64/45).
8. See Ritchie Ovendale, *Appeasement and the English Speaking World* (Cardiff, Walls, 1975), pp. 97–98.
9. Chamberlain's original draft, dated January 13, 1938, PREM 1/259. The revised response is in Chamberlain to FDR, via Lindsay, January 13, 1938, FO 371/21526 (A 2127/64/45).
10. Minutes, January 24, 1938, CAB 23/92 CAB 1 (38).
11. Eden to Chamberlain, January 17, 1938, FO 954/29A, pp. 55–58.
12. *Ibid.*, pp. 257–258.
13. August 8, 1937, NC 18/1/1015.
14. G. C. Peden, *British Rearmament and the Treasury, 1932–1939* (Edinburgh, 1979), pp. 80–81.
15. NC 18/1/1026.
16. Minutes of Cabinet Meeting, December 22, 1937, CAB 23/90, Cab 49 (37).
17. Ian Colvin, *The Chamberlain Cabinet* (London, 1971), p. 38.
18. See, for example, Conclusions of the Cabinet Committee on Foreign Policy, April 6, 1937, FO 371/20735 (C 2619/G/).
19. Frederick Leith-Ross, *Money Talks* (London, 1968), p. 235.
20. London *Times* clipping of February 6, 1937, in FO 371/19925.
21. Lloyd C. Gardner, *Safe for Democracy: The Anglo-American Response to Revolution, 1913–1923* (New York, 1984), pp. 14–18.
22. *Ibid.*, p. 345.
23. "'Memorandum on Visit to Berlin, May 1937," enclosed in Sir Nevile Henderson to Sir Robert Vansittart, May 10, 1937, FO 371/20735 (C 3621/270/18).
24. *Ibid.*
25. Minute, May 27, 1937, on *ibid.*
26. Chamberlain to Ida Chamberlain, December 12, 1937, NC 18/1/1031.

27. Lothian to Henderson, September 13, 1937, FO 800/268.
28. Minutes of Cabinet Committee on Foreign Policy, March 18, 1937, F.P. (36), CAB 27/622.
29. Ovendale, *Appeasement*, pp. 95–96.
30. Record of Conversations with Hitler, November 19, 1937, and Halifax to Chamberlain, November 8, 1937, both in PREM 1/330.
31. Memorandum of Conversation with Hitler, November 19, 1937, *ibid*.
32. Cabinet Conclusions, Cab 43 (37), November 24, 1937, CAB 23/90; see also Lord Avon, *The Eden Memoirs: Facing the Dictators* (London, 1962), p. 516.
33. Minutes of Cabinet Conclusions, December 1, 1937, Cab 44 (37), CAB 23/90.
34. Ovendale, *Appeasement*, pp. 95–96; Keith Feiling, *Neville Chamberlain* (London, 1946), pp. 332–333.
35. July 4, 1937, NC 18/1/1010.
36. Feiling, *Chamberlain*, pp. 332–333.
37. Lindsay to Foreign Office, January 12, 1938, PREM 1/259.
38. *Ibid*.
39. William L. Langer and S. Everett Gleason, *The Challenge to Isolation* (New York, 1952), pp. 22–23, for the earlier evolution of the Roosevelt/Welles proposal.
40. "Memorandum of Conversation with Governor Roosevelt," Albany, August 31, 1932. Copy enclosed in Arthur J. Cummings to Walter Runciman, September 9, 1932, WR.
41. MacDonald, *The United States, Britain and Appeasement*, pp. 63, 72.
42. See Hans-Jurgen Schroeder, "Great Britain, the United States and Germany, 1937–1939," in Wolfgang J. Mommsen and Lothar Kettenacker, eds., *The Fascist Challenge and the Policy of Appeasement* (London, 1983), pp. 390–399.
43. Chamberlain to Ida Chamberlain, August 21, 1932, NC 18/1/795.
44. Norman Davis to Chamberlain, June 10, 1937, PREM 1/261.
45. Chamberlain to Hilda Chamberlain, August 29, 1937, NC 18/1/1018.
46. Chamberlain to Roosevelt, September 28, 1937, FDRL/PSF.
47. Lindsay to Foreign Office, January 12, 1938, PREM 1/259.
48. Chamberlain to Lindsay, January 13, 1938, FO 371/21526, A 2127/64/65.
49. Lindsay to Foreign Office, January 18, 1938, PREM 1/259.
50. MacDonald, *The United States, Britain and Appeasement*, p. 72. See also Keith Middlemas, *Diplomacy of Illusion: The British Government and Germany 1937–1939* (London, 1972), pp. 151–156.
51. Minutes of Cabinet Conclusions, February 19, 1938, Cab 6(38), CAB 23/92. See also Chamberlain's lengthy diary entry of February 19, 1938, NC 2/24a.
52. William C. Bullitt to Secretary of State, February 21, 1938, *FRUS*, 1938, I, 24–27.
53. *Ibid*; and Bullitt to Secretary of State, February 21, 1938, NASD 740.00/299. Bullitt had also informed Roosevelt directly at the end of January that "the real policy of Neville Chamberlain" was to achieve peace by allowing German domination over Central Europe. Bullitt to FDR, January 20, 1938, FDRL, PSF/5.
54. Messersmith to Hull, February 18, 1938, *FRUS*, 1938, I, 17–24.
55. *Ibid*.
56. MacDonald, *The United States, Britain and Appeasement*, p. 73.
57. See Robert Dallek, *Franklin D. Roosevelt and American Foreign Policy, 1932–1945* (New York, 1979), for the most recent overview.

58. Bullitt to Hull, February 21, 1938, *FRUS*, 1938, I, 24–27.
59. See Lloyd C. Gardner, *Economic Aspects of New Deal Diplomacy* (Madison, Wisc., 1964), chaps. 2 and 8.
60. *Ibid.*, pp. 106–107.
61. Diary entry, March 28, 1938, HLS.
62. John Morton Blum, *From the Morgenthau Diaries: Years of Crisis, 1928–1938* (Boston, 1959), pp. 392–393.
63. For the background of the Quarantine Speech, see Samuel I. Rosenman, *Working with Roosevelt* (New York, 1952), pp. 164–172.
64. Bernd-Jurgen Wendt, "'Economic Appeasement'—A Crisis Strategy," in Mommsen and Kettenacker, eds., *Fascist Challenge*, pp. 157–172.
65. *New York Times*, April 1, 1938.
66. Lamont to Robert Cecil, May 31,1938, RCBM.
67. December 12, 1937, NC 18/1/1031.
68. Bullitt to Hull, January 17, 1938, NHD, Box 4.
69. Blum, *From the Morgenthau Diaries*, pp. 458, 524.

2. MUNICH AND THE NAZI-SOVIET PACT

1. Quoted in Christopher Thorne, *The Approach of War, 1938–39* (New York, 1967), p. 136.
2. Maurice Baumont, *The Origins of the Second World War*, trans. by Simone de Couvreur Ferguson (New Haven, 1978), p. 233.
3. John Wiley to the Secretary of State, March 16 and 19, 1938, *FRUS*, 1938, I, 449–450, 457–460.
4. Joseph Kennedy to Secretary of State, March 15, 1938, *ibid.*, pp. 447–448.
5. Minutes of Cabinet Conclusions, March 2, 1938, Cab 10(38), CAB 23/92.
6. Cabinet Conclusions, March 9, 1938, Cab 11(38), CAB 23/92.
7. *Ibid.*
8. Middlemas, *Diplomacy of Illusion*, pp. 186–187; Minutes of Foreign Policy Committee, March 18, 1938, FP (36), 26th Meeting, CAB/27/623.
9. March 20, 1938, NC 18/1/1042.
10. Jonathan Haslam, *The Soviet Union and the Struggle for Collective Security in Europe, 1933–39* (New York, 1984), pp. 168–169; Larry William Fuchser, *Neville Chamberlain and Appeasement: A Study in the Politics of History* (New York, 1982), p. 118.
11. See Thomas R. Maddux, *Years of Estrangement: American Relations with the Soviet Union, 1933–1941* (Tallahassee, Fla., 1980), chap. 3.
12. Lloyd C. Gardner, *Architects of Illusion: Men and Ideas in American Foreign Policy, 1941–1949* (Chicago, 1970), chap. 1.
13. William Appleman Williams, *American-Russian Relations, 1781–1947* (New York, 1952), p. 241.
14. Maddux, *Years of Estrangement*, p. 51.
15. Baumont, *Origins*, pp. 249–250.
16. *Ibid.*, p. 249.
17. Kennedy to Secretary of State, May 14, 1938, *FRUS*, 1938, I, 498–500.
18. Davies to Secretary of State, March 14, 1938, *ibid.*, pp. 445–446.
19. Alan Kirk to Secretary of State, July 9, 1938, *FRUS: The Soviet Union, 1933–1939*, pp. 587–589.
20. Memorandum of Conversation, March 14, 1938, *FRUS*, 1938, I, 485–486. Washington actually sent mixed signals to Moscow all through the critical

year of 1938, notwithstanding Welles's clear-cut rejection of an international conference. Ambassador Davies had been charged by Roosevelt with delivering a special message to the Soviets suggesting informal exchanges of naval information in view of the Japanese menace to both their interests in the Far East. See Davies to Secretary of State, June 9, 1938, *FRUS: The Soviet Union, 1933–1939*, pp. 567–568, and Davies to Secretary of State, January 17, 1939, JED. Roosevelt did not pursue the matter when Stalin responded favorably to the idea, however, nor did he interfere to facilitate renewed negotiations over the prerevolution debt when they became stymied, or to overrule objections to Russian attempts to purchase an American-built battleship. See Maddux, *Years of Estrangement*, chap. 7.

21. See, for example, his comments in the spring of 1938 to Lord Astor. Thomas Jones, *A Diary with Letters, 1931–1950* (London, 1954), p. 390.

22. Bullitt to Secretary of State, May 9, 1938, *FRUS*, 1938, I, 493–494. See also Fuchser, *Chamberlain and Appeasement*, p. 127.

23. Fuchser, *Chamberlain and Appeasement*, p. 128.

24. Bullitt to Roosevelt, May 22, 1938, *FRUS*, 1938, I, 509–511.

25. Memorandum by Vansittart, August 29, 1938, FO 371, N4317/97/38. See also Ivan Maisky, *Who Helped Hitler?* (London, 1964), pp. 78–82.

26. Minutes of Cabinet Conclusions, September 14, 1938, Cab 38(38), CAB 23/95; Colvin, *Chamberlain Cabinet*, p. 153.

27. Ian Colvin, *Vansittart in Office* (London, 1965), p. 251.

28. Ivone Kirkpatrick, *The Inner Circle* (London, 1959), p. 135.

29. Neville Chamberlain to Ida Chamberlain, September 19, 1938, NC 18/1/1069.

30. Minutes of Cabinet Conclusions, September 17, 1938, Cab 39(38), CAB 23/95; Chamberlain to Ida Chamberlain, September 19, 1938, NC 18/1/1069.

31. Minutes of Cabinet Conclusions, September 25, 1938, Cab 43(38), CAB 23/95.

32. Quoted in Fuchser, *Chamberlain and Appeasement*, p. 151.

33. Bullitt to Secretary of State, *FRUS*, 1938, I, 686–689.

34. Fuchser, *Chamberlain and Appeasement*, p. 156.

35. Middlemas, *Diplomacy of Illusion*, p. 394.

36. See Klaus-Jurgen Muller, "The German Military Opposition Before the Second World War," in Mommsen and Kettenacker, *Fascist Challenge*, pp. 61–75.

37. Fuchser, *Chamberlain and Appeasement*, pp. 161–162.

38. "Notes of Conv. with Hitler in his flat at Munich," September 1938, NC 8/26/3.

39. Fuchser, *Chamberlain and Appeasement*, p. 162.

40. King to Chamberlain, J. A. Lyons to Chamberlain, J. B. M. Herzog to Chamberlain, all September 30, 1938, NC 7/2/4,5,7.

41. Hull to Kennedy, September 28, 1938, *FRUS*, 1938, I, 688.

42. Roosevelt to Hitler, September 27, 1938, *ibid.*, pp. 684–685.

43. Haslam, *The Soviet Union and the Struggle for Collective Security*, p. 179.

44. *Ibid.*, p. 181.

45. *Ibid.*, pp. 189–191.

46. Bullitt to Secretary of State, October 3, 1938, *FRUS*, 1938, I, 83–84.

47. Diary entry, October 22, 1938, in John Harvey, ed., *The Diplomatic Diaries of Oliver Harvey* (London, 1970), p. 215.

48. Kennedy to Secretary of State, October 12, 1938, *FRUS*, 1938, I, 85–86.

49. Memorandum, October 14, 1938, FO 371/21659, C14471/42/18; and

see David Dilks, ed., *The Diaries of Sir Alexander Cadogan, 1938–1945* (London, 1971), pp. 118–119.
50. Middlemas, *Diplomacy of Illusion*, p. 434.
51. Minutes of Cabinet Conclusions, November 22, 1938, Cab 56(38), CAB 23/96.
52. Minutes of Cabinet Conclusions, November 30, 1938, Cab 57(38), CAB 23/96.
53. Memorandum of a Half-hour Talk with von Schacht, December 15, 1938, T 188/227.
54. *Ibid.*
55. Neville Chamberlain to Ida Chamberlain, January 28, 1939, NC 18/1/1083.
56. Minute, January 3, 1939, FO 371/23677 (N57/57/38).
57. Minute, January 17, 1939, *ibid.*
58. Minute by Lascelles, January 5, 1939, *ibid.* And see other minutes on the Caccia memorandum by Collier, Strang, and Oliphant, who favored doing something, and Ashton-Gwatkin, who, disillusioned by von Schacht, had not, however, converted.
59. Vansittart Minute, January 20, 1939; Halifax Minute, January 21, 1939, *ibid.*
60. MacDonald, *The United States, Britain and Appeasement*, pp. 126–129.
61. Memorandum by R. A. Butler, February 3, 1939, FO 371/23677 (N669/57/38).
62. Kennedy to Secretary of State, February 17, 1939, *FRUS*, I, 1939, 14–16; Chamberlain to Henderson, February 19, 1939, PREM 1/330.
63. Hull to Kennedy, March 7, 1939, *FRUS*, 1939, I, 28–29.
64. Record of Conversation, March 9, 1939, FO 371/23677 (N1342/57/38).
65. Kirk to Secretary of State, March 11, 1939, *FRUS: The Soviet Union, 1933–1939*, pp. 739–741.
66. Haslam, *The Soviet Union and the Struggle for Collective Security*, pp. 204–205, has the best analysis of the speech and Stalin's deliberate ambiguities.
67. MacDonald, *The United States, Britain and Appeasement*, p. 140.
68. Minutes of Cabinet Conclusions, March 18, 1939, Cab 12(39), CAB 23/98; MacDonald, *The United States, Britain and Appeasement*, pp. 140–142.
69. Maisky, *Who Helped Hitler?*, pp. 102–103.
70. Chamberlain to Ida Chamberlain, March 19, 1939, NC 18/1/1090; Feiling, *Chamberlain*, pp. 402–403.
71. Chamberlain to Ida Chamberlain, March 26, 1939, NC 18/1/1091.
72. Chamberlain to Hilda Chamberlain, April 2, 1939, NC 18/1/1092.
73. *Ibid.* And See MacDonald, *The United States, Britain and Appeasement*, pp. 146–147, and Martin Gilbert, *Britain and Germany Between the Wars* (London, 1964), p. 143.
74. Maisky, *Who Helped Hitler?*, pp. 107–111. These were not Maisky's or Litvinov's views only. Former Prime Minister David Lloyd George decried Chamberlain's handling of the situation as sheer folly. "Without Russia nothing can be done. . . . So first of all there should have been an agreement with Moscow. But what does Chamberlain do? Without coming to any agreement with the Soviet Union, and in fact behind its back, he distributes 'guarantees' right and left to countries in Eastern Europe. What crying folly! What a disgrace for British diplomacy!" *Ibid.*, p. 111. The British chiefs of staff also believed that Russian commitment beforehand was essential if assistance to Poland were to be made effective. Haslam, *The Soviet Union and the Struggle for Collective Security*, p. 209.

75. Chamberlain to Ida Chamberlain, April 9, 1939, NC 18/1/1093; Minutes of Foreign Policy Committee, April 19, 1939, FP 36 (43), CAB 27/624.
76. Colvin, *Vansittart in Office*, p. 321.
77. Henderson to Halifax, May 11, 1939, NH, FO/800 270–7.
78. Minutes of Foreign Policy Committee, May 16, 1939, FP 36 (47), CAB 27/625.
79. Haslam, *The Soviet Union and the Struggle for Collective Security*, pp. 216–217.
80. Chamberlain to Ida Chamberlain, May 21, 1939, and to Hilda Chamberlain, May 29, 1939, NC 18/1/1100, 1101.
81. Chamberlain to Hilda Chamberlain, May 28, 1939, NC 18/1/1101.
82. Colvin, *Chamberlain Cabinet*, p. 229.
83. Bullitt to Secretary of State, June 5, 1939, *FR*, 1939, I, 266–269.
84. Halifax to Bernard Pares, July 19, 1939, FO 800/309, I.
85. Memorandum, July 20, 1939, PREM 1/330.
86. Kennedy to Secretary of State, July 5, 1939, *FRUS*, 1939, I, 282–283.
87. Haslam, *The Soviet Union and the Struggle for Collective Security*, p. 226.
88. Quoted by Dmitri A. Vologonov, in Keith Eubank, ed., *World War II: Roots and Causes* (2nd ed., Lexington, Mass., 1992).
89. A convenient place to locate the text is *ibid.*, pp. 254–256; the Molotov exchanges may be found in *140 Conversations with Molotov*, published in Moscow and forthcoming under a different title in an English-language edition.
90. Kirkpatrick, *The Inner Circle*, pp. 142–143.
91. Roy Medvedev, *Let History Judge: The Origins and Consequences of Stalinism*, ed. and trans. by George Shriver (rev. ed., New York, 1989), pp. 728–729.
92. *Ibid.*, p. 729.
93. Claud Cockburn, *The Devil's Decade* (London, 1973), p. 220.

3. DARKEST HOURS

1. William C. Bullitt to Roosevelt, September 13, 1939, FDRL, PSF: France.
2. August 27, 1939, NC 18/1/1115.
3. A good summary of this argument is Paul W. Schroeder's "Munich and the British Tradition," *The Historical Journal*, 19:1 (March 1976), 223–243. Schroeder makes the point that Britain had always viewed Central and Eastern Europe differently from the Lowlands and Western Europe. And in the nineteenth century it had sided with those who wished to maintain the Vienna system, adopted after Napoleon, intact. "The arguments the British used to justify this were precisely those of Munich, that the old order was outworn and untenable, that general peace was the overriding consideration, and that changes now would lead to greater peace and stability in the long run."
4. Sir Nevile Henderson, *Failure of a Mission* (London, 1940), p. 294.
5. Diary entry, September 1, 1939, JPM.
6. Joseph Alsop and Robert Kinter, *American White Paper: The Story of American Diplomacy and the Second World War* (New York, 1940), pp. 16, 74.
7. John J. McCloy, Speech Draft, August 1941, HLS.
8. See MacDonald, *The United States, Britain and Appeasement*, pp. 165–166; paraphrase of Ambassador Laurence Steinhardt cable from Moscow, August 21, 1939 HJM, vol. 206.
9. "Notes on a Visit to Washington," September 24, 1941, JPM.

10. Kennedy to Roosevelt, September 10, 1939, FDRL, PSF: Great Britain.
11. Warren F. Kimball, *The Juggler: Franklin Roosevelt as Wartime Statesman* (Princeton, N.J., 1991), p. 61. See, in general, chap. 3, "Lend-Lease and the Open Door: The Temptation of British Opulence, 1937–1942," pp. 43–62.
12. "Note for a Statement by the Prime Minister on the Lend-Lease Bill," undated [March 1941], PREM 4 17/2.
13. *Ibid.*
14. Minute, March 11, 1940, FO 371/24846 (N2779/40/38). And see Gabriel Gorodetsky, *Stafford Cripps' Mission to Moscow, 1940–42* (Cambridge, England, 1984), pp. 20–34.
15. Extract from War Cabinet Conclusions, November 16, 1939, in FO 371/23683 (N6384/92/G).
16. *Ibid.*
17. Minute by Collier, November 20, 1939, and Halifax to Churchill, November 25, 1939, FO 371/23683 (N6384/92/G).
18. Minute, October 31, 1939, FO 371/22946 (C17105/13699/62).
19. "Draft Reply to French Memorandum on War Aims," October 30, 1939, FO 371/22496 (C17104/13669/62).
20. "Draft Statement," December 1, 1940, FO 371/28899 (W587/426/49). Emphasis added.
21. Minute by Alec Cadogan, January 30, 1941, FO 371/28899 (W6189/426/49).
22. Steinhardt to Secretary of State, September 17, 1939, *FRUS: The Soviet Union, 1933–1939*, pp. 782–783.
23. "Conversation," September 27, 1939, FO 371/23682 (N4803/1459/38).
24. Steinhardt to Secretary of State, *FRUS: The Soviet Union, 1933–1939*, p. 790.
25. Steinhardt to Secretary of State, November 1, 1939, *ibid.*, pp. 786–790.
26. Seeds to Foreign Office, October 1, 1939, FO 371/23689 (N4916/518/38); Anthony Read and David Fisher, *The Deadly Embrace: Hitler, Stalin, and the Nazi-Soviet Pact, 1939–1941* (New York, 1988), p. 365.
27. Memoranda by Butler, October 17 and November 13, 1939, FO 371/23682 and 23678 (N5493/92/38 and N6477/57/38).
28. Halifax to Seeds, October 16, 1939, FO 371/23682 (N5342/92/38).
29. Minute, October 14, 1939, FO 371/23678 (N5297/57/38).
30. For a good short summary, see Read and Fisher, *The Deadly Embrace*, pp. 402–415.
31. Bullitt to Roosevelt, December 19, 1939, FDRL, PSF: France.
32. Read and Fisher, *The Deadly Embrace*, p. 408.
33. Halifax to Moscow, February 8, 1940, FO 371/24843 (N1390/30/38).
34. *Ibid.*
35. Halifax to Lothian, March 13, 1940, FO 371/24406 (C3999/G); for the origins of the Welles mission, see Dallek, *Franklin D. Roosevelt and American Foreign Policy*, pp. 416–420.
36. Halifax to Lord Lothian, March 13, 1940, FO 371/24406 (C3999/G).
37. *Ibid.*
38. Quoted in Lloyd C. Gardner, *A Covenant with Power: America and World Order from Wilson to Reagan* (New York, 1984), pp. 45–46.
39. Diary entry, June 14, 1940, Ben Pimlott, ed., *The Second World War Diary of Hugh Dalton, 1940–45* (London, 1986), pp. 39–40.
40. Gorodetsky, *Stafford Cripps' Mission to Moscow*, pp. 20–24.
41. "Note of Minister of Economic Warfare's Conversation with Soviet Ambassador on 25th May, 1940," FO 371/24840 (N5661/5/38).

42. Minute by L. Ridsdale, June 18, 1940, FO 371/24844 (N5853/G).
43. Wiley to Secretary of State, June 19, 1940, *FRUS*, 1940, I, 377.
44. Gunther to Secretary of State, June 27 and 29, 1940, *ibid.*, pp. 479–480, 485.
45. Gunther to Secretary of State, July 2, 1940, *ibid.*, pp. 488–489.
46. See "Summary of Events Since the Arrival of Sir Stafford Cripps in Moscow," February 21, 1941, FO 371/29464.
47. "Account of Interview with M. Stalin on July 1, 1940, *ibid.* It is of some interest that this memorandum of the interview was not included in Cripps's contemporary report to London. In particular, Stalin's comment that it was the USSR that had wanted to change the equilibrium, and that Germany "also" wanted a change, did not appear. Instead, Cripps's telegram said that it had been the "common desire" of the two. Nor did he include Stalin's comment that to restore equilibrium would be "very difficult." Slight as these changes were, they softened Stalin's response. See Cripps to London, July 2, 1940, FO 371/24844 (N5937/G).
48. Public Statement, July 23, 1940, *FRUS*, 1940, I, 402–403.
49. Memorandum by the Assistant Chief of the Division of European Affairs, July 15, 1940, *ibid.*, pp. 389–392.
50. Maddux, *Years of Estrangement*, p. 132.
51. Memorandum by the Secretary of State for Foreign Affairs, July 26, 1940, FO 371/24761/, W.P. (40) 287.
52. Cripps to Halifax, August 4, 1940, FO 371/24761 (N6241/G).
53. Halifax to Cripps, August 13, 1940, FO 371/28487 (N6005/40/38).
54. Cripps to Halifax, August 8, 1940, FO 371/28487 (N6105/40/38).
55. Cripps to Halifax, August 8, 10 p.m., *ibid.*
56. Gorodetsky, *Stafford Cripps' Mission to Moscow*, p. 68.
57. Halifax to Leith-Ross, September 5, 1940, FO 371/24841 (N6372/3/38).
58. "Summary of Events Since the Arrival of Sir Stafford Cripps in Moscow," February 25, 1941, FO 371/29464.
59. Steinhardt to Secretary of State, October 23, October 28, November 10, November 14, 1940, *FRUS*, 1940, I, 619–620, 623–624, 573–574, 580–581.
60. Steinhardt to Secretary of State, November 19, 1940, *ibid.*, pp. 584–586.
61. Read and Fisher, *The Deadly Embrace*, pp. 510–533. The Molotov quotation is from p. 533.
62. *Ibid.*, p. 539.
63. Memorandum, November 27, 1940, FO 371/24848.
64. Eden to Cripps, January 19, 1941, FO 954/24 (SU/41/1).
65. "Record of an Interview . . . ," February 1, 1941, FO 371/29464 (N829/G).
66. Eden to Cripps, February 8, 1941, FO 371/29463 (N411/3/38).
67. See, for example, Churchill to Halifax, March 1, 1941, FO 954/29a.
68. For a discussion of the various intelligence sources and warnings, see Robin Edmunds, *The Big Three: Churchill, Roosevelt, and Stalin in Peace and War* (New York, 1991), pp. 232–242.
69. John Erickson, *The Road to Stalingrad* (New York, 1975), p. 89.
70. Diary entry, March 17, 1941, in Beatrice Bishop Berle and Travis Beal Jacobs, eds., *Navigating the Rapids, 1918–1971: From the Papers of Adolf A. Berle* (New York, 1973), p. 365.
71. Vic Schneierson, trans., *Marshal of the Soviet Union G. Zhukov: Reminiscences and Reflections* (2 vols., Moscow, 1985), I, 268.
72. Eden to Cripps, April 16, 1941, FO 371/29465 (N1658/3/38).
73. Eden to Cripps, April 17, 1941, FO 371/29464 (N1386/G).
74. Gorodetsky, *Stafford Cripps' Mission to Moscow*, pp. 128-129; Cripps to

Eden, April 24, 1941, and Eden to Cripps, April 27, 1941, FO 371/29465 (N1778/3/38).

75. The fullest account, using Russian records, is John Costello, *Ten Days to Destiny* (New York, 1991), especially pp. 413–460. A more extreme version of the Hess conspiracy holds that he was, in fact, part of a plan to make peace with Germany.

76. Gorodetsky, *Stafford Cripps' Mission to Moscow*, pp. 132-134; and see Sir Llewellyn Woodward, *British Foreign Policy in the Second World War* (5 vols., London, 1971), I, 614–615.

77. Eden to Cripps, June 2, 1941, FO 371/29465 (N2570/3/38). Interestingly, the official history of British foreign policy during the war leaves the impression that Maisky took the lead in suggesting mutual concessions when in fact Eden had first asked to know what Russia would do in exchange for recognition. Woodward, *British Foreign Policy*, pp. 616–617.

78. Eden to Moscow, June 14, 1941, FO 954/24/B (SU41/17).

79. Waldo Heinrichs, *Threshold of War: Franklin D. Roosevelt and American Entry into World War II* (New York, 1988), pp. 95–96.

80. Erickson, *The Road to Stalingrad*, p. 106.

81. Zhukov, *Reminiscences*, I, 282.

82. Read and Fisher, *The Deadly Embrace*, p. 642.

83. Steven Merritt Miner, *Between Churchill and Stalin: The Soviet Union, Great Britain, and the Origins of the Grand Alliance* (Chapel Hill, 1988), p. 144.

4. THE ATLANTIC CHARTER

1. This quotation was included in a truncated version of the interview that Eden gave to American Ambassador James G. Winant. Winant to Hull, January 19, 1942, *FRUS*, 1942, III, 494–503.

2. Anthony Eden, *The Reckoning* (Boston, 1965), p. 312.

3. Winant's role was recorded shortly after the war in a memorandum by Lord Beaverbrook, who was among those present that day. It is reproduced, with a tantalizing ellipsis, in A. J. P. Taylor, *Beaverbrook* (London, 1972), p. 475.

4. John Colville, *The Fringes of Power: 10 Downing Street Diaries, 1939–1955* (New York, 1985), pp. 406–407.

5. Martin Gilbert, *Finest Hour: Winston S. Churchill, 1939–1941* (London, 1983), p. 1120.

6. *FRUS*, 1941, I, 766–767.

7. Stimson to FDR, June 23, 1941, FDRL, PSF.

8. See William C. Bullitt to Roosevelt, July 1, 1941, FDRL, PPF 1124; and Berle and Jacobs, *Navigating the Rapids*, pp. 372–373.

9. *FRUS*, 1941, I, 342. The pact with Russia is not mentioned in this message, nor is Russia mentioned at all. Instead, Roosevelt's references are to rumored promises to Yugoslavia. But there can be no doubt that the primary concern was Anglo-Soviet diplomacy. FDR's message was drafted by him immediately after he received a memorandum from Assistant Secretary of State Adolf Berle discussing British efforts to act as a go-between in negotiations between the Soviets and the Polish Government in Exile in London, and the possibility that Churchill's government would accept Moscow's demand that its title to the Baltic countries be recognized. The whole file at the Roosevelt Library in Hyde Park consists of the memorandum from Berle to FDR, July 8, 1941, Roosevelt's draft, and memos between Roosevelt and his favorite adviser in the State Department, Under Secretary of State Sumner Welles. FDRL: PSF, Great Britain.

10. Gilbert, *Finest Hour*, p. 1123.
11. *Ibid.*, p. 1134.
12. Quoted in Miner, *Between Churchill and Stalin*, p. 147.
13. Eden to Halifax, July 9, 1941, PRO, FO 371/29467 (N3603/3/38).
14. Edmunds, *The Big Three*, p. 218.
15. See William Hardy McNeill, *America, Britain and Russia: Their Cooperation and Conflict, 1941–1946* (New York, 1953).
16. Eden, *The Reckoning*, p. 316.
17. "Notes on a Visit to Washington," July 10–12, 1941, JPM.
18. Gardner, *Economic Aspects of New Deal Diplomacy*, pp. 278–279.
19. Heinrichs, *Threshold of War*, pp. 149–150.
20. *FRUS*, 1941, I, 343–354.
21. Memorandum, August 9, 1941, *ibid.*, pp. 345–354.
22. In this regard see Cadogan's memorandum on the Atlantic Conference, August 20, 1941, FO 371/28904 (W10301/426/49).
23. Winston S. Churchill, *The Second World War*, III, *The Grand Alliance* (Boston, 1951), 442. Churchill admitted, however, that the president had first raised the question of a joint declaration.
24. David Reynolds, *The Creation of the Anglo-American Alliance, 1937–41: A Study in Competitive Cooperation* (Chapel Hill, 1982), pp. 276–279.
25. Memorandum, August 20, 1941, FO 371/28904 (W10301/426/49).
26. Colville, *Fringes of Power*, p. 434.
27. (WC) 84, August 19, 1941, Public Record Office, CAB 65/19.
28. Elting E. Morison, *Turmoil and Tradition: A Study of the Life and Times of Henry L. Stimson* (Boston, 1960), p. 582.
29. Churchill, *The Grand Alliance*, pp. 444–445.
30. Roosevelt's fascination with his British colleague, his anxiousness never to miss out when the prime minister held forth on any subject, is well documented in James MacGregor Burns, *Roosevelt: The Soldier of Freedom, 1940–1945* (New York, 1970), pp. 175–180.
31. Press Conference #761, August 16, 1941, FDRL: PPF-1, vol. 18, 4–5.
32. Quoted in Steven Miner, "Stalin's 'Minimum Conditions' and the Military Balance, 1941–1942," in *Soviet-U.S. Relations, 1933–1942* (Moscow, 1989), pp. 72–87.
33. Quoted in L. V. Pozdeeva, "The USSR in the Grand Alliance, Foreign Policy Aspects," forthcoming, p. 16.
34. *Ibid.*
35. Christopher Thorne, *Allies of a Kind: The United States, Britain and the War Against Japan, 1941–1945* (New York, 1978), p. 61.
36. "Soviet Declaration . . . ," September 18, 1941, FO 954/24/B (SU/41/88).
37. Notes by Averell Harriman, September 28, 1941, HLH.
38. *Ibid.*
39. *Ibid.*, and "Supplement Governing Balance of Conversation with Mr. Stalin at Meeting with Lord Beaverbrook and Mr. Harriman, Sunday, September 28, 1941," WAH, Box 160.
40. "Memorandum of Conversation . . . ," September 30, 1941, HLH.
41. Churchill, *The Grand Alliance*, pp. 457–458.
42. Gorodetsky, *Stafford Cripps' Mission to Moscow*, p. 209.
43. Maisky, *Memoirs*, pp. 201–202.
44. Roosevelt to Harriman, September 22, 1941, HLH.
45. Hopkins to Harriman, September 24, 1941, and "Arming of the Poles in Russia," October 16, 1941, HLH.
46. Eden to Cripps, October 21, 1941, FO 371/29469 (N6125/3/38).

47. Churchill to Stalin, received November 7, 1941, *Stalin Correspondence*, I, 32–33.
48. Eden to Cripps, November 4, 1941, FO 371/29470 (N6374/5279/G).
49. Stalin to Churchill, November 8, 1941, *ibid.*, pp. 33–34.
50. Gorodetsky, *Stafford Cripps' Mission to Moscow*, p. 268.
51. Minutes of Conclusions, November 11, 1941, WM 41, CAB 65/24.
52. "Record of a Conversation...," November 12, 1941, FO 954/24B (SU/41/159).
53. Eden to Cripps, November 20, 1941, *ibid.*, SU/41/169.
54. Maisky, *Memoirs*, p. 221.
55. *Ibid.*, p. 231.
56. W.P. (41) 288, November 29, 1941, and Eden's draft memo for Winant, December 4, 1941, FO 371/29472 (N6835/G).
57. Memorandum to Churchill, December 15, 1941, PREM 4 32/1.
58. Dilks, *The Diaries of Sir Alexander Cadogan*, p. 414.
59. WM (41) 120th Mtg, November 27, 1941, Confidential Annex, CAB 65/24, PRO.
60. Bullitt to Roosevelt, December 5, 1941, FDRL:PPF 1124.
61. Hull to Winant, December 5, 1941, *FRUS*, 1941, I, 194.
62. The minutes of the Kremlin conversations, December 16–20, and Eden's full report to the war cabinet, January 5, 1942, are all in FO 371/32874, N109/G.
63. Eden to Foreign Office, December 18, 1941, CAB 65/24; and Dominions Office to Dominions, December 19, 1941, PREM 3, 394/2.
64. Churchill to Eden, December 19, 1941, PREM 3, 399/7.
65. *Ibid.* (All quotations in this section are to this complete file of the Eden-Stalin conversations.)
66. This quotation was included in a truncated version of the talks that Eden gave to Ambassador Winant. It is interesting to look at the highlights Eden chose to communicate, though these did include the foreign secretary's pledge to take up the matter of Russia's frontiers with the dominions and the United States. See Winant to Hull, January 19, 1942, *FRUS*, 1942, III, 494–503.
67. Historians are prone to risk the dangers of overcausation, and certainly overspeculation. It may well be that Eden's position was the straightforward concern he felt not to leave matters where they were, knowing that a second front was not about to happen. It may also be, however, that he imagined an important war aim was to preserve Great Britain's freedom of action in European affairs, and that there were worse things than dealing with the Russians as equals. There is also the chance that he considered Stalin's overtures a serious bid to "get along" with the West. Eden's behavior as prime minister during the 1956 Suez crisis would tend to support the former speculation, while his 1943 conversations with Roosevelt over postwar Europe and the chances for cooperation with Russia offer hard evidence that he wanted to give the latter a try. See Sherwood, *Roosevelt and Hopkins*, pp. 707–721.
68. Miner, *Between Churchill and Stalin*, p. 192.
69. WM (42), 1st meeting, confidential annex, January 1, 1942, CAB 65/29, PRO.
70. Churchill to Eden, January 8, 1942, FO 371/32874 (N109/86/G). Possibly to protect Eden's political future, Churchill altered a key sentence of this message in his memoirs, thereby moderating the tone. He also did not quote Eden's comment on the unlikelihood of influencing affairs in postwar Eastern Europe. As an opposition MP with his own aspirations to return to

power, Churchill probably also did not want even this much of a Conservative "soft line" to go on record. See *The Grand Alliance*, pp. 695–696. In his memoirs the first two sentences of the cable to Eden are condensed to this one: "No one can foresee how the balance of power will lie or where the winning armies will stand at the end of the war."

71. Churchill to Lord Privy Seal, December 20, 1941, PREM 3, 399/6, PRO.

72. Churchill to War Cabinet, December 23, 1941, quoted in *The Grand Alliance*, pp. 664–665.

5. PILGRIMAGES TO WASHINGTON

1. Warren F. Kimball, *Churchill and Roosevelt: The Complete Correspondence* (3 vols., Princeton, N.J., 1984), I, 394.

2. Gilbert, *Finest Hour*, p. 1274.

3. Martin Gilbert, *Winston S. Churchill: Road to Victory, 1941–1945* (Boston, 1986), p. 16.

4. A. A. Berle, "And What Shall We Do Then?" *Fortune* 24 (October 1941), 102–104ff.

5. Berle and Jacobs, *Navigating the Rapids*, p. 394.

6. "Memorandum of a Conversation," December 22, 1941, PREM 3, 458/7.

7. Berle and Jacobs, *Navigating the Rapids*, p. 391.

8. Robert E. Sherwood, *Roosevelt and Hopkins: An Intimate History* (New York, 1948), pp. 447–453.

9. War Cabinet Conclusions, January 1, 1942, WM 42, CAB 65/29.

10. Churchill to Eden, January 7, 1942; Gilbert, *Road to Victory*, p. 17.

11. Halifax to Eden, January 12, 1942, enclosing Halifax to Churchill, January 11, 1942, FO 954/29.

12. Eden to Halifax, January 22, 1942, *ibid.*

13. "Policy Towards Russia," W.P. (42) 48, January 28, 1942, in FO 371/32875 (N563/G).

14. Winston S. Churchill, *The Second World War*, IV, *The Hinge of Fate* (Boston, 1950), 291, *et passim*.

15. *Ibid.*, p. 81.

16. Memorandum by Theodore Achilles, March 6, 1942, NASD 841.00/1572; Hoover to Berle, February 16, 1942, NASD 841.00/1547; and Winant to Hull, February 20, 1942, NASD 841.00/1548.

17. The memorandum is in the Sherwood Collection, taken from the Hopkins Papers at the Roosevelt Library.

18. Cabinet Conclusions, February 6, 1942, WM 42, CAB 65/29; Eden to Halifax, February 25, 1942, FO 954/29A.

19. Memorandum of Conversation, February 18, 1942, *FRUS*, 1942, III, 512–521.

20. *Ibid.*

21. Memorandum of Conversation, February 20, 1942, *ibid.*, pp. 521–524.

22. Memorandum, "Policy Towards Russia," February 18, 1942, PREM 3, 395/2.

23. Beaverbrook to Eden, with enclosures, March 3, 1942, FO 954/25A (SU/42/21).

24. Press Conference #807, February 24, 1942, FDRL: PPF-1, vol. 19, 3–4.

25. Aide-Mémoire, February 25, 1942, FO 954/29A.

26. Cabinet Conclusions, February 25, 1942, 42 WM, CAB 65/29.

27. Eden to Kuibyshev, February 26, 1942, FO 954/25A (SU/42/17).
28. Eden to Churchill, March 6, 1942, PREM 3, 395/12.
29. Gilbert, *Road to Victory*, pp. 67–68.
30. Kimball, *Churchill and Roosevelt*, I, 394.
31. *Ibid*.
32. Gilbert, *Road to Victory*, p. 73.
33. Halifax to Foreign Office, February 12, 1942, FO 371/32876 (N897/5/G).
34. Diary entry, December 31, 1942, *ibid*., p. 160.
35. Miner, *Between Churchill and Stalin*, p. 218.
36. Quoted in Hugh Phillips, "Mission to America: Maksim M. Litvinov in the United States, 1941–1943," *Diplomatic History* 12 (Summer 1988), 261–275.
37. Eden to Clark-Kerr, March 17, 1942, FO 954/25A (SU/42/27).
38. Eden to Clark-Kerr, March 23, 1942, *ibid*., SU/42/3.
39. Kimball, *Churchill and Roosevelt*, I, 421.
40. Halifax to Foreign Office, March 26, 1942, FO 371/32878 (N1614/38/G).
41. "Memorandum for the Chief of Staff," February 12, 1942, in HLH.
42. Stimson to FDR, March 27, 1942, FDRL, PSF.7.
43. "Memorandum of Conversation," April 1, 1942, *FRUS*, 1942, III, 538–539.
44. Kimball, *Churchill and Roosevelt*, I, 437, 441.
45. *FRUS*, 1942, III, 536–542.
46. *Ibid*., pp. 542–543.
47. Sherwood, *Roosevelt and Hopkins*, p. 528.
48. D.O. (42) 10th Meeting, in PREM 3, 333/6.
49. *Ibid*.
50. Halifax to Foreign Office, April 17, 1942, and Churchill's minute, April 18, 1942, FO 371/32907 (N2000/G).
51. Undated, Untitled Memorandum, ca. April 25, 1942, FO 371/32880 (N2182/G). An added complication was the territorial demands of the Polish Government in Exile. If a treaty was signed with Russia, it was sure to cause trouble with Sikorski's provisional government and, as both the U.S. and British governments were fully aware, spill over into the press. See, for example, Biddle to Roosevelt and Hull, April 24, 1942, SD 741.6111/7.
52. Eden to Clark-Kerr, April 13, 1942, with enclosure, FO 954/25A (SU/42/49).
53. Eden to Clark-Kerr, May 1, 1942, FO 371/32880 (N2336/86/G).
54. Eden to Clark-Kerr, May 5, 1942, FO 371/32880 (N2385/86/G).
55. Minute, May 7, 1942, FO 371/32881 (N2524/G).
56. April 24, 1942, FO 954/25A (SU/42/74).
57. Eden to Halifax, May 9, 1942, FO 954/25A.
58. Eden to Halifax, May 21, 1942, FO 954/25A (SU/42/108).
59. Strang, *At Home and Abroad*, p. 159.
60. The minutes of these sessions are in Churchill Papers, PREM 3, 333/8.
61. See *FRUS*, 1942, III, 558, for a discussion of the circumstances.
62. Cordell Hull, *The Memoirs of Cordell Hull* (2 vols., London, 1948), II, 1172.
63. Winant to Hull, May 24, 1942, *FRUS*, 1942, III, 558–563.
64. Richard C. Lukas, *The Strange Allies: The United States and Poland, 1941–1945* (Knoxville, Tenn., 1978), pp. 29–30.
65. WM (42), 68th Concl., Min 2, Confidential Annex, May 25, 1942, CAB 65/30.
66. Maisky, *Memoirs of a Soviet Ambassador*, p. 267; Molotov, "Conversations."

67. Miner, *Between Churchill and Stalin*, p. 249.
68. *The Road to Great Victory*, trans. by Lev Bobrov (Moscow, 1985), p. 76.
69. Hopkins, "Memorandum of Conversation," May 29, 1942, HLH, Sherwood Collection. For some reason the latter half of Hopkins's memorandum is not printed in *FRUS*, 1942, III, though it bears very strongly on the issues. The sentence quoted is from the unprinted section. The implication of that sentence is that Hopkins was truly depressed by Roosevelt's hunting around in the underbrush when the quarry was plainly in sight in front of him. In other parts of the unprinted section, Hopkins refers to friction between Litvinov and his superior, Molotov's desire to spend at least one night in the White House (as opposed to Litvinov's seeming wish to separate FDR and the foreign minister), and the latter's desire "that one of the girls he brought over as secretaries be permitted to come and that has been arranged." For the official minutes and the first half of Hopkins's memorandum, see *ibid.*, pp. 566–568, 571–572.
70. These paragraphs are taken, in part, from both the official (Cross) minutes and Hopkins notes, in *ibid.*, pp. 568–569, 572–574.
71. Once again this portion of the Cross minutes was not published with the records in *ibid.*, pp. 569–570, and is available in manuscript form in the Hopkins Papers, Sherwood Collection. It is hard to explain this omission, for an understanding of Roosevelt's emphasis on making a firm commitment to Molotov later in the conference would seem to stem from this fear as much as anything else.
72. FDR's comment is likewise excised from the printed minutes, and is in Hopkins Papers, Sherwood Collection.
73. Memorandum, May 30, 1942, 11 a.m., *FRUS*, 1942, III, 575–578.
74. Yet again an important paragraph is omitted in the printed version, and one must go to the manuscript in the Hopkins Papers, Sherwood Collection.
75. "Memorandum... , June 1, 1942," *ibid.*, pp. 578–583.
76. HLH, Sherwood Collection. Marshall made a last effort to qualify Molotov's proposed draft which mentioned 1942, but when Hopkins called this to FDR's attention specifically, "he, nevertheless, wished to have it included...." "Memorandum," June 3, 1942, *ibid.*
77. A reader of the major American news publications for the week following the announcement of Molotov's visit and the signing of the treaties could almost piece together the whole story from December 1941 to June 1942. Here is another example of the failure of "secret diplomacy," a point historians should always keep in mind.
78. *New York Times*, June 23, 1942, p. 12.
79. Mountbatten to Roosevelt, June 15, 1942, FDRL, Map Room File.
80. Marshall to FDR, with attachments, June 19, 1942, FDRL, PSF.
81. Stimson to Roosevelt, July 15, 1942, *ibid.*
82. Diary entries, July 15 and 23, 1942, quoted in Elting E. Morison, *Turmoil and Tradition: A Study of the Life and Times of Henry L. Stimson* (Boston, 1960), p. 587.
83. Sherwood, *Roosevelt and Hopkins*, pp. 609–610; Roosevelt to Hopkins, undated [July 23, 1942?], FDRL, PSF.
84. Stimson to FDR, July 25, 1942, *ibid.*
85. June 22, 1942, p. 34.
86. Molotov, "Conversations."

6. PONDERING THE RUSSIAN SPHINX

1. *FRUS*, 1944, IV, 951.

2. (2 vols. New York, 1948), II, 1247.
3. *Ibid.*
4. Halifax to Foreign Office, March 28, 1943, FO 371/35366, U 1430/G.
5. Hull, *Memoirs*, II, 1297.
6. *Ibid.*
7. For the full story of American financial planning with the British to make sure the ghost of Ottawa did not rise again, the standard work remains Richard N. Gardner, *Sterling-Dollar Diplomacy* (Oxford, 1956).
8. The initiative might come from another direction; it might come from London. For these fears, see Lloyd C. Gardner, "A Tale of Three Cities," paper prepared for the first Soviet-American Conference on World War II, October 1986. And for concern about Churchill's aims in 1943 and 1944, see Williams, *American-Russian Relations*, pp. 270–273.
9. At the outset of the New Deal there had been a struggle between traditional internationalist liberals and the new "intranationalists" of the Brains Trust. As World War II approached, many of the most stalwart intranationalists conceded that capitalism in one country had not insured economic recovery or political stability. See Gardner, *Economic Aspects of New Deal Diplomacy*, chap. 8.
10. Berle and Jacobs, *Navigating the Rapids*, p. 421.
11. Maddux, *Years of Estrangement*, p. 156.
12. For a discussion of Bullitt's about-face on Russian-American relations, see Beatrice Farnsworth, *William C. Bullitt and the Soviet Union* (Bloomington, Ind., 1967), especially chaps. 1–7.
13. January 19, 1934, NASD, 711.61/471.
14. Bullitt to Hull, April 26, 1936, *FRUS: The Soviet Union, 1933–1939*, pp. 291–296. Comments inside the department were congratulatory on this "remarkable despatch" which should be "highly commended." Robert Kelley, head of the East European Division, told Cordell Hull that Bullitt's conclusions on the impossibility of really friendly relations with the Soviets or "with any Communist Party or Communist individual" and the lack of any permanency in trade relations would be concurred in by most competent observers of Russia. See NASD 861.01/2120.
15. Maddux, *Years of Estrangement*, p. 134.
16. Warren F. Kimball, "'They Don't Come Out Where You Expect': America Reacts to the German-Soviet War, June–November 1941," paper presented at the first Soviet-American Conference on World War II, Moscow, October 1986.
17. Hull, *Memoirs*, II, 977. Roosevelt also outlined for Oumansky other requirements he would need to make Lend-Lease aid available, including a Russian submission of its gold assets and a detailed proposal for what barter trade could be carried on between the countries. Roosevelt's presentation was based on a memorandum prepared by Harry Hopkins, "Memorandum for the President," September 5, 1941, FDRL, PSF. See also the basic studies by George Herring, *Aid to Russia, 1941–1946* (New York, 1973), and Raymond Dawson, *The Decision to Aid Russia, 1941: Foreign Policy and Domestic Politics* (Chapel Hill, 1959).
18. Burns's memo is in Sherwood, *Roosevelt and Hopkins*, pp. 641–643. Sherwood reprints it in full because, he writes, it reflected Hopkins's own views.
19. Bullitt to Roosevelt, January 29, 1943, FDRL, PSF.
20. *Ibid.*
21. Gilbert, *Road to Victory*, pp. 177–181.
22. Edmunds, *The Big Three*, p. 301.

23. Elisabeth Barker, *British Policy in South-East Europe in the Second World War* (London, 1976), p. 134.

24. Gardner, *Architects of Illusion*, pp. 38–39.

25. Churchill's efforts, which were not supported by the war cabinet, are detailed in *The Hinge of Fate*, pp. 685–689; Roosevelt's concern about Russia is detailed in Forrest C. Pogue, *George C. Marshall: Organizer of Victory, 1943–1945* (New York, 1973), pp. 32–33.

26. Gardner, *A Covenant with Power*, p. 61.

27. John Erickson, *The Road to Berlin* (Boulder, Colo., 1983), pp. 43–44.

28. *Ibid.*

29. David Carlton, *Anthony Eden: A Biography* (London, 1981), p. 208.

30. Barker, *British Policy in South-East Europe*, p. 134.

31. *Ibid.*, p. 135.

32. Memorandum of Conversation, March 16, 1943, *FRUS*, 1943, III, 19–24.

33. Eden to Churchill, March 16, 1943, FO 371/36991 (N1748/G).

34. Minute, March 24, 1943, on *ibid.*

35. FO 371/35661 (U1528/320/70).

36. Bullitt to FDR, May 12, 1943, FDRL, PSF 1.

37. That a choice between the Balkans and Central Europe might have to be made was the burden of an untitled memorandum by Russian expert Charles Bohlen, dated June 24, 1943. CB, Box 4.

38. *FRUS*, 1943, III, 40–41.

39. "Roosevelt's World Blueprint," *Saturday Evening Post*, April 10, 1943, pp. 20–21, 109–110.

40. Kimball, *The Juggler*, p. 102.

41. For a fuller discussion, see Elizabeth Kimball MacLean, "Joseph Davies and Soviet-American Relations, 1941–1943," *Diplomatic History* 14 (Winter 1980), 73–93.

42. Churchill to Roosevelt, June 25, 1943, in Kimball, *Churchill and Roosevelt*, II, 278–279. See also Kimball, *The Juggler*, pp. 90–91.

43. Roosevelt to Churchill, June 28, 1943, *ibid.*, pp. 282–283.

44. Harriman to Roosevelt, July 5, 1943, FDRL, PSF.

45. Churchill to Eden, September 15, 1943, FO 371/35398 (U4486/402/70).

46. Stimson to Roosevelt, August 10, 1943, included in diary entry for August 10, 1943, HLS.

47. "Minutes of Meeting Held at the White House," August 10, 1943, FDRL.

48. Bullitt to FDR, August 11, 1943, FDRL, PSF, Bullitt.

49. *Ibid.*

50. Burns to Hopkins, August 10, 1943, HLH.

51. Eden to A. Cadogan, August 19, 1943, FO 954/2.

52. For a brief discussion of the dinner conversation, see Eden, *The Reckoning*, p. 468. Eden's minute of the conversation is much fuller and includes his protest along with other crucial details. Eden to Cadogan, August 21, 1943, FO 954/2.

53. Eden to Cadogan, August 21, 1943, FO 954/2.

54. *FRUS*, 1943, I, 755–756.

55. *Ibid.*, p. 739.

56. Herbert Feis, *Churchill, Roosevelt, Stalin: The War They Waged and the Peace They Sought* (Princeton, N.J., 1957), p. 238.

57. *Ibid.*, p. 239, and Harriman to Roosevelt, November 5, 1943, *FRUS*, 1943, III, 589–591.

58. Gardner, *A Covenant with Power*, p. 63.
59. Diary entry, September 3, 1943; Berle and Jacobs, *Navigating the Rapids*, p. 446.
60. *FRUS*, 1943, III, 586–589.
61. *Ibid.*, pp. 710–716.
62. Harriman to Hopkins, November 9, 1943, *ibid.*, pp. 786–778.
63. Memorandum, November 29, 1943, *ibid.*, pp. 722–723.
64. *Ibid.*
65. Lord Moran, *Winston Churchill: The Struggle for Survival, 1940–1965* (London, 1966), pp. 133–134; see also Kimball, *The Juggler*, pp. 100–101.

7. FROM TEHERAN TO TOLSTOY

1. Carlton, *Anthony Eden*, pp. 236–237.
2. "Minutes of Meeting Between the President and the Chiefs of Staff . . . , November 19, 1943, FDRL, Map Room Collection.
3. Sherwood, *Roosevelt and Hopkins*, p. 780.
4. Kimball, *The Juggler*, pp. 100–101.
5. Feis, *Churchill, Roosevelt, Stalin*, pp. 284–285.
6. After the Teheran Conference, Eden reviewed the situation for Churchill. The British were committed on the point of the Baltic states going to Russia but could not say anything publicly because of a clamor about the Atlantic Charter and "difficulties with the Americans." So while FDR was willing to make the concession to Stalin directly at Teheran, British policymakers were not aware of the change, or, if they were, did not wish to put Roosevelt on the spot in an election year (which amounted pretty much to the same thing as far as London was concerned). It was a difficult situation. The repetition of this situation was one of the reasons why Churchill sought his own meeting with Stalin and was determined not to let Roosevelt interfere. See Eden to Churchill, January 25, 1944, PREM 3 399/6.
7. Diary entry, December 18, 1943, John Morton Blum, ed., *The Price of Vision: The Diary of Henry A. Wallace, 1942–1946* (Boston, 1973), pp. 283–284.
8. "Memorandum of Meeting at the State Department with Hull and Knox," January 11, 1944, HLS.
9. *FRUS*, 1944, IV, 1032–1035.
10. Herring, *Aid to Russia*, pp. 146–160.
11. Feis, *Churchill, Roosevelt, Stalin*, p. 643.
12. Cox to Hopkins, January 15, 1944, OC.
13. *Ibid.*
14. Hull to Harriman, February 8, 1944, *FRUS*, 1944, IV, 1047–1048.
15. *FRUS*, 1944, IV, 951.
16. *Ibid.*, pp. 1052–1053.
17. Hull to Roosevelt, February 7, 1944, FDRL, PSF.
18. Herring, *Aid to Russia*, p. 157.
19. "Russia—Seven Years Later," September [?], 1944, *FRUS*, 1944, IV, 902–912.
20. Molotov, "Conversations."
21. (WM 44), 11th Concl., Min 1, January 25, 1944, CAB 65–45.
22. Hull to Roosevelt, March 20, 1944, including Russian memorandum of March 19, 1944, FDRL, PSF, Russia. The maneuvers can be followed in Sir Llewellyn Woodward, *British Foreign Policy in the Second World War*, II, chap. 33.
23. See Woodward, *British Foreign Policy*, II, 538, *et passim.*
24. Minute on FO 371/43304, N1908/G.

25. Minute, April 1, 1944, on *ibid.*, WM 44, 43 concl., min. 4, confidential annex, April 3, 1944, CAB 65–46.

26. Minute April 1, 1944, FO 371/43304 (N2128/36/G), and "Account by Dr. Bowman of his Private Talk with the P.M. on Saturday, April 15th," 1944, FO 371/40689 (U3316/180/70).

27. Letters quoted in, Carlton, *Anthony Eden*, pp. 236–237.

28. During the last weeks of the campaign, local Democratic leaders complained to White House aides that Republican candidate Thomas E. Dewey was making dangerous progress in efforts to hang the communist label on the administration. "There were charges that Roosevelt had secretly begun to sell out to Uncle Joe Stalin at Teheran and that after the war he would complete the process of delivering the American free enterprise system over to Communist control." Sherwood, *Roosevelt and Hopkins*, p. 829.

29. Eden to Churchill, May 9, 1944, FO 371/43636 (R7380/68/G).

30. One could extend these thoughts something like this: The British did not want spheres of influence in Europe simply for geopolitical reasons, but neither did they want the internal triumph of communist political forces anywhere. It would be better, then, that where communists ruled they be seen to be imposed by the Red Army. A spheres-of-influence arrangement would promote such a realization.

31. Eden to Clark-Kerr, May 18, 1944, FO 371/43636 (R7903/G).

32. *Ibid.* When Eden reported to the war cabinet he used the bluntest language yet: "The Secretary of State for Foreign Affairs told the War Cabinet that he had recently put it to the Russians that if they wished us to allow them to take the lead in Roumania, they should be prepared to reciprocate by allowing His Majesty's Government to do likewise in Greece." Extract from meeting of May 18, 1944, in *ibid.* The language used also makes nonsense of the idea that all Eden and Churchill had in mind was a temporary military arrangement. It might have been temporary but certainly not military, for the British were in no position to challenge Russian leadership in Rumania.

33. Halifax to Eden, May 31, 1944, PREM 3, 66/7,

34. Halifax to Foreign Office, June 3, 1944, FO 371/40694 (U5011).

35. Churchill to Roosevelt, June 1, 1944, Kimball, *Churchill and Roosevelt*, III, 155–156.

36. Halifax to Foreign Office, June 7, 1944, FO 371/43646 (R8988/G).

37. Churchill to Halifax, June 8, 1944, *ibid.*

38. Stettinius to Roosevelt, June 10, 1944, and Roosevelt to Churchill, June 11, 1944, both in *FRUS*, 1944, V, 117–118.

39. Minutes and draft telegram dated June 8, 1944, FO 371/43646 (R8988/9/G).

40. Minute on Roosevelt to Churchill, June 11, 1944, in *ibid.*

41. Churchill to Roosevelt, June 11, 1944, Kimball, *Churchill and Roosevelt*, III, 178–180.

42. Roosevelt to Churchill, June 12, 1944, and Churchill to Roosevelt, June 14, 1944, *ibid.*, pp. 182, 185–186.

43. Eden to Gousev, June 19, 1944, FO 371/43646 (R9472/9/G).

44. Ambassador Winant learned from Churchill firsthand that the prime minister did distinguish "between long term policy and the necessity for prompt decision in the military phase." Winant to FDR, June 13, 1944, FDRL, Map Room Papers.

45. Hull to Roosevelt, June 17, 1944, *FRUS*, 1944, V, 124–125.

46. Roosevelt to Churchill, June 22, 1944, *ibid.*, p. 125.

47. Churchill to Roosevelt, June 23, 1944, *ibid.*, pp. 126–127.

48. Barker, *British Policy in South-East Europe*, p. 141.
49. *FRUS*, 1944, V, 128–129.
50. Department of State to Soviet Embassy, July 15, 1944, *ibid.*, pp. 130–131.
51. Campbell to Foreign Office, July 27, 1944; Minutes by Churchill and Eden, August 1 and 3, 1944, all in FO 371/43676 (R11461/G).
52. Minute by D. S. Laskey, August 6, 1944, and draft of Eden to Churchill, August 8, 1944, in *ibid.*
53. W.M. (44), 103rd Concl., Min 1, Confidential Annex, August 9, 1944, PREM 3, 212/1.
54. Churchill to Eden, August 16, 1944, and Eden to Churchill, August 17, 1944, PREM 3, 212/1.
55. Churchill to Roosevelt, August 17, 1944, in Kimball, *Churchill and Roosevelt*, III, 278–279.
56. Halifax to Foreign Office, August 20, 1944, and Cairo to Foreign Office, August 21, 1944, both in PREM 3, 212/2.
57. Churchill to General Walter Bedell Smith, August 24, 1944; Churchill to Hopkins, August 24, 1944; and Halifax to Foreign Office, September 8, 1944, all in *ibid.*
58. Churchill to Roosevelt, August 25, 1944, and Roosevelt to Churchill, August 26, 1944, in Kimball, *Churchill and Roosevelt*, III, 296–297.
59. *Ibid.*, p. 297.
60. Erickson, *Road to Berlin*, p. 345.
61. Winston S. Churchill, *The Second World War*, VI, *Triumph and Tragedy* (Boston, 1953), pp. 208–209.
62. Moran, *Churchill: The Struggle for Survival*, p. 190.
63. *Ibid.*, p. 191.
64. Molotov quoted in Barker, *British Policy in South-East Europe*, p. 137. American policymakers were also well aware of Russia's concern about so-called Eastern European confederations. Charles Bohlen called State Department colleagues' attention to an article in *War and the Working Classes* denouncing all such plans as contraventions of the 1942 Anglo-Russian treaty. The inference, said the Russian expert, was that the Soviet Union intended to deal bilaterally with all the countries in Eastern Europe, thereby insuring its predominance. Bohlen to J. C. Dunn, August 26, 1943, CB, Box 4.
65. Churchill to Roosevelt, October 3, 1944, in Kimball, *Churchill and Roosevelt*, III, 342–343.
66. Sherwood, *Roosevelt and Hopkins*, pp. 832–833, remains the most important account of Washington's concern as well as the most graphic of Hopkins's intervention.
67. Kimball, *Churchill and Roosevelt*, III, 345.
68. Bohlen to Hopkins, October 3, 1944, HLH, Box 140–141A.
69. Sherwood, *Roosevelt and Hopkins*, pp. 833–834; FDR to Harriman, October 4, 1944, HLH, Box 140–141A. There are different wordings of the cable available, probably because of encoding procedures. I have used the wording in the Hopkins Papers.
70. Sherwood, *Roosevelt and Hopkins*, p. 834.
71. Churchill, *Triumph and Tragedy*, pp. 227–228.
72. Record of Meeting at the Kremlin, October 9, 1944, 7 p.m., "Records of Meetings at the Kremlin, Moscow, October 9–October 17, 1944," copy in PREM 3, 434/2.
73. Record of Meeting . . . , October 9, 1944, 10 p.m., *ibid.*, p. 5.
74. *Ibid.*, p. 7.

75. *Ibid.*, p. 8.
76. Harriman to Roosevelt, October 10, 1944, *FRUS*, 1944, IV, 1006–1007.
77. Record of Meeting at the Kremlin, October 10, 1944, *ibid.*, pp. 10–15; Eden to Orme Sargent, October 11, 1944, PREM 3, 66/7.
78. Moran, *Churchill: The Struggle for Survival*, pp. 194–195.
79. Carlton, *Anthony Eden*, p. 245. Carlton makes the very good point that the Balkans deal remained a wholly informal arrangement, and that there never was a final agreed statement on the percentages. He suggests that Eden held out more than Churchill for a larger percentage in those areas Russia wished to control because in fact he believed there was a difference, say, between 10 percent and 25 percent. He finally accepted the fact that the Russians intended to control things in Rumania, Bulgaria, and Hungary, and there was nothing to be done. Yet both Churchill's efforts, discussed in the text, and Molotov's attempt to give some meaning to the percentages cannot be entirely dismissed.
80. Churchill to Stalin, October 11, 1944, PREM 3, 66/7.
81. When he arrived in Moscow Churchill was greeted by Harriman along with the Russians. The prime minister asked the ambassador to convey to Roosevelt his disappointment that Marshall had not been sent, or that Harriman had been designated only an observer. Under those circumstances Churchill thought it better, reported Harriman, "for me not to participate in his tete-a-tete talks with Stalin. . . ." Churchill actually delighted in the situation. Harriman to Roosevelt, October 9, 1944, *FRUS*, 1944, IV, 1004–1005.
82. Churchill to Hopkins, October 11, 1944, in Foreign Office to Washington, October 13, 1944, FO 371/43647 (R16726/G).
83. Harriman to FDR, October 11, 1944, *FRUS*, IV, 1009–1010.
84. Churchill to Roosevelt, October 11, 1944, in Kimball, *Churchill and Roosevelt*, III, 353.
85. October 11, 1944, *FRUS*, 1944, IV, 1009.
86. *FRUS*, 1944, IV, 988–990.

8. Denouement: Poland and Yalta

1. Lord Halifax to Churchill, December 20, 1944, PREM 3, 355/14
2. John Balfour to Christopher Warner, October 9, 1944, FO 371/43306 (N6565/G).
3. Moran, *Churchill: The Struggle for Survival*, p. 193.
4. Sherwood, *Roosevelt and Hopkins*, pp. 796–797.
5. R. I. Campbell to David Scott, December 20, 1943, FO 371/38516 (A7/G).
6. *Ibid.* Evidence that the Poles had been shot by the Russians later demonstrated the Germans had been right, but at the time it was considered only a ploy to divide the Allies.
7. See Geir Lundestad, *The American Non-Policy Towards Eastern Europe, 1943–1947* (New York, 1975), pp. 188–189.
8. Jan Ciechanowski, *The Warsaw Rising of 1944* (London, 1974), p. 243.
9. See Alexander Werth, *Russia at War* (New York, 1964), chap. 8.
10. "Memorandum," H. Freeman Matthews to Secretary of State, October 16, 1944, *FRUS*, 1944, IV, 1016–1019.
11. Record of Meeting Held at Spirdonovaka House, October 13, 1944, PREM 3, 66/7, 20–26.
12. Eden to Foreign Office, October 16, 1944, PREM 3, 355/13.
13. Eden to Foreign Office, October 16 and 17, 1944; Churchill to Attlee, October 17, 1944, PREM 3.

14. Quoted from Mikolajczyk's account of their conversation, later confirmed by Churchill. See Lord Moran, *Churchill: The Struggle for Survival*, pp. 199–200.
15. Eden to Cadogan, October 19, 1944, PREM 3.
16. Churchill to Roosevelt, October 18, 1944, in Kimball, *Churchill and Roosevelt*, III, 358–359.
17. *Ibid.*
18. Moran, *Churchill: The Struggle for Survival*, p. 206.
19. Arthur Bliss Lane, *I Saw Poland Betrayed* (Indianapolis, 1948), p. 66.
20. Martin Herz, *Beginnings of the Cold War* (Bloomington, Ind., 1966), pp. 62–63.
21. Lundestad, *The American Non-Policy Towards Eastern Europe*, p. 191.
22. Ben Pimlott, *The Second World War Diary of Hugh Dalton, 1940–45* (London, 1986), p. 563.
23. The principal source for this intriguing episode is Samuel I. Rosenman, *Working with Roosevelt* (New York, 1952), pp. 464–476. It was charged that Roosevelt leaked a letter to Willkie to the press in order to use the idea to his immediate advantage in the presidential campaign. He may have, but that does not negate the interest both he and Willkie displayed in such a reorientation of American politics.
24. Hopkins to Winant, September 4, 1944, HLH, Box 157.
25. See Thomas M. Campbell and George Herring, eds., *The Diaries of Edward R. Stettinius, Jr., 1943–1946* (New York, 1975), pp. 156–157. The 1944 presidential campaign, therefore, saw the first manifestation of the conservative-ethnic alliance that reappeared in various forms in domestic and foreign policy for the next five decades.
26. See M. R. Wright's account of his conversation with Hopkins, in Wright to P. M. Broadmead, November 14, 1944, PREM 4, 27/7.
27. Memorandum, "The Washington Negotiations . . . ," December 12, 1944, CAB 66.
28. Colville, *The Fringes of Power*, pp. 534–535.
29. Winant to Hopkins, December 11, 1944, HLH, Sherwood Collection.
30. Cox to Hopkins, December 19, 1944, HLH, Box 338.
31. Extract of Churchill's speech in CAB 66/61, p. 12.
32. Campbell and Herring, *Stettinius Diaries*, pp. 196–202.
33. Churchill to Halifax, December 19, 1944; Halifax to Churchill, December 20, 1944, PREM 3, 355/14.
34. Wright to Phillip Broadmead, January 7, 1945, FO 371/44555.
35. Stimson to Roosevelt, September 9, 1944, HLS.
36. Lamont to Villard, December 7, 1944, Papers of Oswald Garrison Villard, Houghton Library, Harvard University, Cambridge, Mass.
37. FDR to Stalin, December 30, 1944, *FRUS*, Yalta, pp. 224–226.
38. *Ibid.*, pp. 226–227.
39. "Memorandum for the President," January 16, 1945, FDRL, PSF/State Department.
40. "The necessity of the three principal Allies arriving at a common political program for liberated countries," undated [January 1945], pp. 1–2, HLH, Box 169–171.
41. "Reconstruction of Poland and the Balkans: American Interests and Soviet Attitude," undated [January 1945], p. 1, *ibid.*
42. Stettinius broached the idea of a European High Commission to function until the new world organization was established to a very receptive Anthony Eden at a pre-Yalta meeting on February 1, 1945. He and his aides

warned the British foreign secretary that since it involved Poland they would have to be careful with the Russians, and that Roosevelt himself had serious doubts about the plan as perhaps prejudicing the long-term prospects of the world organization. "Meeting of the Foreign Ministers," February 1, 1945, *FRUS*, Yalta, pp. 498–507.

43. Diaries, January 5, 1945, OC, Box 151.

44. See Lloyd C. Gardner, "The Riddle of the Sphinx: Russia and Reconstruction," paper presented at the third Soviet-American Conference on World War II in Moscow, October 1988, pp. 20–26.

45. The exchanges between Harriman and Washington can best be followed in *FRUS*, 1945, V, 937–945.

46. John Morton Blum, *From the Morgenthau Diaries: Years of War, 1941–1945* (Boston, 1967), pp. 304–305. Someone in the Treasury Department may have leaked the secret request to James Reston of the *New York Times*, who then wrote a story that some members of the administration felt the present was not a propitious time for discussing a postwar deal of that magnitude. Embassy officials were annoyed, fearing, said George Kennan, that the Russians would be even more hesitant now to enter into frank discussions of "matters involving both our governments." Grew to American Embassy, January, 26, 1945, and Kennan to Grew, January 29, 1945, NASD, 861.51/1-2645, and 861.51/1-2945.

47. Cited in Winifred N. Hackel, "Political Currents in Liberated Europe," *Foreign Policy Reports* 21 (June 1, 1945), 66–78.

48. *Life*, January 22, 1945, p. 22.

49. See the minutes of Roosevelt's meeting with his advisers on February 4, 1945, and the brief notes made by Alger Hiss of that same meeting, in *FRUS*, Yalta, pp. 566–570.

50. Hiss notes, *ibid.*

51. "Luncheon Meeting of the Foreign Ministers," February 5, 1945, *FRUS*, Yalta, pp. 608–610. An interesting difference occurs in the minutes taken by British and American recorders of this meeting. In the British version Molotov also "informed" his colleagues that Russia expected to receive reparations in kind, while in the American minutes he "indicated" that would be the case. See FO 371/45775 (ME671/624/G77). The British minutes suggest a more decided and unilaterally determined issue.

52. Edward R. Stettinius, *Roosevelt and the Russians: The Yalta Conference* (Garden City, N.Y., 1949), p. 49.

53. Memo by Eden, "Poland's Western Frontier," January 23, 1945, CAB 66/61.

54. Eden to Churchill, February 1, 1945, *FRUS*, Yalta, pp. 508–509.

55. *Ibid.*

56. "United States Delegation Memorandum: Concrete Proposals on the Polish Question," undated [February 1, 1945], *ibid.*, pp. 510–511; for the earlier paper, with the American position outlined on a map of Europe, see *ibid.*, pp. 231–234.

57. "Tripartite Dinner Meeting," February 4, 1945, *ibid.*, pp. 589–590.

58. Gilbert, *Road to Victory*, pp. 1171–1175.

59. "Tripartite Dinner Meeting," February 4, 1945, *FRUS*, Yalta, pp. 589–590.

60. Gilbert, *Road to Victory*, p. 1184.

61. *Ibid.*

62. All the above, except for Gilbert citations, from Bohlen Minutes of the Third Plenary Session, February 6, 1945, *FRUS*, Yalta, pp. 667–671.

63. Gilbert, *Road to Victory*, p. 1185.
64. The minutes are in PREM 3/51/4.
65. *The Teheran, Yalta and Potsdam Conferences: Documents* (Moscow, 1969), p. 97.
66. *FRUS*, Yalta, pp. 727–728.
67. In the British minutes, however, Roosevelt is recorded as saying that he did not think it was necessary "to contact only *émigrés* and that people in Poland should also be found." PREM 3/51/4. But the Russian minutes affirm the American version—"he believed that it was not at all necessary to invite specifically persons from abroad to take part in the Polish Government. Suitable men could be found inside Poland herself." *Teheran, Yalta and Potsdam*, p. 105.
68. Bohlen Minutes, Fourth Plenary Meeting, February 7, 1945, *FRUS*, Yalta, pp. 709–718. H. Freeman Matthews's minutes give a somewhat different impression still of Roosevelt's response to the Molotov proposals, perhaps explaining why Stalin so readily agreed to the inclusion of democratic leaders inside Poland. "It is not necessary to take *émigrés*. There may be people who are now in Poland who are now satisfied." What did "who are now satisfied" mean? *Ibid.*, pp. 718–721.
69. Bohlen Minutes, Roosevelt-Stalin Meeting, February 8, 1945, *ibid.*, 766–771.
70. Gilbert, *Road to Victory*, p. 1191.
71. The British minutes, again, differ substantially. "The President said that, as inhabitants of another hemisphere, it was the great objective of the Americans that there should be an early election in Poland. The only problem was how the country was to be governed between now and then, and he hoped it would be possible to hold elections before the end of the present year. The problem was, therefore, limited in time." PREM 3/51/4.
72. Bohlen Minutes, Fifth Plenary Meeting, February 8, 1945, *FRUS*, Yalta, pp. 771–782.
73. Gilbert, *Road to Victory*, p. 1195.
74. "Meeting of the Foreign Ministers," February 9, 1945, *FRUS*, Yalta, pp. 802–811.
75. Bohlen and Matthews Minutes, Sixth Plenary Meeting, February 9, 1945, *ibid.*, pp. 841–855. The Russian minutes of this telling exchange have Roosevelt making an even clearer statement about where he thought trouble would arise. The elections must be absolutely pure, he said, "so pure that no one could cast any doubt on them, and that the Poles themselves—very hot-headed people—could accept the elections without any reservations." *Teheran, Yalta and Potsdam*, p. 123.
76. William D. Leahy, *I Was There* (New York, 1950), p. 314.

9. Let's Pretend It Never Happened

1. *Mr. Citizen* (New York, 1960), p. 165.
2. For the argument that Roosevelt had seen the light in regard to Russian postwar aims, see Dallek, *Franklin D. Roosevelt and American Foreign Policy*, pp. 533–535. The letter to Lamont is dated March 29, 1945, FDRL, President's Personal File, (PPF) 70.
3. Kimball, *The Juggler*, p. 7.
4. Gardner, *Architects of Illusion*, p. 76.
5. Confidential Annex, WM (45), February 19, 1945, CAB 65/51.
6. Cited in Gardner, *Architects of Illusion*, p. 56.
7. Robert Rhodes James, *Anthony Eden* (London, 1986), p. 290.

8. John Boettiger to FDR, February 13, 1945, FDRL, Map Room Papers, Box 21.

9. Jonathan Daniels to Early, February 13, 1945, *ibid.*

10. Press Conference #992, February 23, 1945. FDRL, PPF-1, vol. 25, 16.

11. Bohlen to Samuel I. Rosenman, February 18, 1945, SIR, Box 27. Four years later Bohlen had decided that the Russians had never intended to carry out the Yalta agreements and that Roosevelt had designed them as a "test" of Stalin's intentions. Quite a different view. Bohlen to Rosenman, August 23, 1949, *ibid.*, Box 18.

12. "Memorandum," Turner Catledge to Arthur Krock, February 26, 1945, AK, Box 1.

13. Gilbert, *Road to Victory*, p. 1208.

14. Kevin Jeffreys, *The Churchill Coalition and Wartime Politics, 1940-1945* (Manchester, 1991), p. 180.

15. *Ibid.*, p. 182.

16. Quoted in Kimball, *The Juggler*, p. 176.

17. WM (45), 22nd Concl., Min 1, Confidential Annex, February 19, 1945, CAB 65/51.

18. WM (45), 26th Concl., Min 5, Confidential Annex, March 6, 1945, CAB 65/51.

19. Count Edward Raczynski, *In Allied London* (London, 1962), p. 266.

20. *Ibid.*, p. 271.

21. Zhukov, *Reminiscences and Reflections*, II, 340–341.

22. "Record of Meeting...," February 23, 1945, FO 371/47582 (N2454/G); Harriman to Stettinius, February 24, 1945, *FRUS*, 1945, V, 123–124.

23. Commission on Poland, "Second Meeting," February 27, 1945, FO 371/47582 (N2458/G).

24. Note 90, *FRUS*, 1945, V, 135.

25. Clark-Kerr to Foreign Office, March 6, 1945, FO 371/47582.

26. See Orme Sargent to Eden, March 10, 1945, and Eden's comments thereon, FO 371/47582 (N2481/G).

27. From a marked-up copy showing FDR's verbal changes, FDRL, Speech File, Box 86.

28. Press Conference #984, December 19, 1944, FDRL, PPF 1, vol. 24, 7–12.

29. Press Conference #985, December 22, 1944, *ibid.*, pp. 5–7.

30. *Ibid.*

31. WM (45), 26th Concl., Min 5, Confidential Annex, March 6, 1945, CAB 65/51; Roosevelt to Churchill, March 11, 1945, PREM 3, 356/9.

32. Press Conferences #993 and #995, March 2 and 9, 1945, FDRL, PPF-1, vol. 25, 10, 9.

33. The first cable in the series that lasted until Roosevelt's death was February 28, 1945. Kimball, *Churchill and Roosevelt*, III, 547–631.

34. *Ibid.*, pp. 593–594.

35. Roosevelt to Churchill, March 21, 1945, and Churchill to Roosevelt, April 3, 1945, *ibid.*, 579–580, 606–607.

36. Stanislaw Mikolajczyk, *The Rape of Poland* (New York, 1948), p. 60.

37. Raczynski, *In Allied London*, p. 278.

38. See, for example, Charles Bohlen to Stettinius, March 15, 1945, CB, Box 4.

39. Halifax to Foreign Office, March 26, 1945, FO 371/ 47583 (N3317/6/G).

40. Foreign Office to Washington, March 28, 1945, FO 371/47584 (N3404/6/G); Minute by O. G. Sargent, March 29, 1945, FO 371/47584 (N3346/6/G); Clark-Kerr to Foreign Office, March 27, 1945, FO 371/47584 (N3346/6/G).

41. Clark-Kerr to Foreign Office, April 3, 1945, FO 371/47485 (N32587/6/G).
42. Roosevelt to Stalin, April 1, 1945, *FRUS*, 1945, V, 194–196; Sixth Meeting, Commission on Poland, April 2, 1945, FO 371/47589.
43. Sixth Meeting, Commission on Poland, April 2, 1945, FO 371/47589.
44. Erickson, *Road to Berlin*, pp. 526–527; Dulles, *The Secret Surrender* (New York, 1966), pp. 147, 161, 164–165. Dulles wrote to his brother John Foster on February 6, 1945, "I feel apprehensive as to what we will find in Europe for years to come. We are moving toward the dramatic finale which will leave a large part of Central Europe in chaos." Papers of John Foster Dulles, Seeley G. Mudd Library, Princeton University, Princeton, N.J.
45. Erickson, *Road to Berlin*, p. 527.
46. See Stalin to Roosevelt, April 3, 1945, *Stalin's Correspondence*, I, 206–207.
47. Stalin to Roosevelt, April 7, 1945, *ibid.*, pp. 208–210.
48. See Vojtech Mastny, *Russia's Road to the Cold War* (New York, 1979), chap. 7.
49. Zhukov, *Reminiscences and Reflections*, II, 346–347.
50. Erickson, *Road to Berlin*, p. 329.
51. Harriman to Stettinius, April 3, 1945; Stalin to Roosevelt, April 7, 1945, *FRUS*, 1945, V, 196–198, 201–204.
52. *Ibid.*, pp. 209, 210.
53. WM (45), 44th Concl., Min 3, April 13, 1945, CAB 65/52, PRO.
54. "Memorandum of Conversation...," April 20, 1945, *FRUS*, 1945, V, 231–234.
55. Diary entry, April 20, 1945, in Walter Millis, ed., *The Forrestal Diaries* (New York, 1951), p. 47.
56. "Memorandum...," April 23, 1945, *ibid.*, pp. 252–255.
57. Gilbert, *Road to Victory*, p. 1282.
58. Memorandum of Conversation, April 23, 1945, *FRUS*, 1945, V, 256–258.
59. For the most recent evaluation, see Kimball, *The Juggler*, pp. 178–183.
60. "Jonathan Daniels Draft for Jefferson Day Speech," and Robert Sherwood to Samuel I. Rosenman, April 16, 1949, both in SIR, Box 18.
61. Memorandum of Conversation, May 2, 1945, *ibid.*, pp. 272–276.
62. Memorandum of Conversation, May 30, 1945, *ibid.*, pp. 301–306.
63. Churchill, *Triumph and Tragedy*, pp. 576–578.
64. Churchill to Truman, June 4, 1945, *FRUS*, 1945, V, 320–321.
65. Mikolajczyk, *The Rape of Poland*, p. 117.
66. Gardner, *Architects of Illusion*, p. 76.
67. Walter LaFeber, *America, Russia and the Cold War* (6th ed., New York, 1990), pp. 25–26.
68. William O. McCagg, Jr., *Stalin Embattled, 1943–1948* (Detroit, 1978), p. 312.
69. Kennan to Secretary of State, September 15, 1945, *FRUS*, 1945, V, 881–884.
70. John J. McCloy, *The Atlantic Alliance: Its Origins and Future* (New York, 1969), pp. 22–26.
71. McCagg, *Stalin Embattled*, pp. 298–300.
72. U.S. Senate, Committee on Foreign Relations, *Hearings: The Vandenberg Resolution and the North Atlantic Treaty*, 80th Cong., 2nd. Sess. (Historical Series) (Washington, D.C., 1973), p. 86.
73. Quote in *Time*, October 25, 1971, p. 19.
74. Molotov, "Conversations."
75. C. L. Sulzberger, *The Last of the Giants* (New York, 1970), p. 304.
76. Memorandum of Conversation, April 13, 1945, *FRUS*, 1945, V, 826–829.

Bibliography of Published Sources

1. DIARIES AND MEMOIRS

Avon, Lord. *The Eden Memoirs: Facing the Dictators.* London, 1962.
Berle, Beatrice Bishop, and Travis Beal Jacobs, eds. *Navigating the Rapids, 1918–1971: From the Papers of Adolf A. Berle.* New York, 1973.
Blum, John Morton, ed. *The Price of Vision: The Diary of Henry A. Wallace, 1942–1946.* Boston, 1973.
———. *From the Morgenthau Diaries, Years of War, 1941–1945.* Boston, 1967.
Campbell, Thomas M., and George C. Herring, eds. *The Diaries of Edward R. Stettinius, Jr., 1943–1946.* New York, 1975.
Churchill, Winston S. *The Second World War,* 6 vols. Boston, 1950–1953.
Colville, John. *The Fringes of Power: 10 Downing Street Diaries, 1939-1955.* New York, 1985.
Dilks, David, ed. *The Diaries of Sir Alexander Cadogan, 1938–1945.* London, 1971.
Eden, Anthony. *The Reckoning.* Boston, 1965.
Harvey, John, ed. *The Diplomatic Diaries of Oliver Harvey.* London, 1970.
Henderson, Sir Nevile. *Failure of a Mission.* London, 1940.
Hull, Cordell. *The Memoirs of Cordell Hull,* 2 vols. London, 1948.
Jones, Thomas. *A Diary with Letters, 1931–1950.* London, 1954.
Kimball, Warren F., ed. *Churchill and Roosevelt: The Complete Correspondence,* 3 vols. Princeton, 1984.
Kirkpatrick, Ivone. *The Inner Circle.* London, 1959.
Lane, Arthur Bliss. *I Saw Poland Betrayed.* Indianapolis, 1948.
Leahy, William D. *I Was There.* New York, 1950.
Leith-Ross, Frederick. *Money Talks.* London, 1968.
Maisky, Ivan. *Memoirs of a Soviet Ambassador,* trans. by Andrew Rothstein. New York, 1967.
———. *Who Helped Hitler?,* trans. by Andrew Rothstein. London, 1964.
Mikolajczyk, Stanislaw. *The Rape of Poland.* New York, 1948.
Millis, Walter, ed. *The Forrestal Diaries.* New York, 1951.
Moran, Lord. *Winston Churchill: The Struggle for Survival, 1940–1965.* London, 1966.
Pimlott, Ben, ed. *The Second World War Diary of Hugh Dalton, 1940–45.* London, 1986.
Rosenman, Samuel I. *Working with Roosevelt.* New York, 1952.
Schneierson, Vic, trans. *Marshal of the Soviet Union G. Zhukov: Remininiscences and Reflections,* 2 vols. Moscow, 1985.
Stettinius, Edward R. *Roosevelt and the Russians: The Yalta Conference,* ed. by Walter Johnson. Garden City, N.Y., 1949.
Truman, Harry S. *Mr. Citizen.* New York, 1960.

2. SECONDARY WORKS

Alsop, Joseph, and Robert Kinter. *American White Paper: The Story of American Diplomacy and the Second World War.* New York, 1940.

Barker, Elisabeth. *British Policy in South-East Europe in the Second World War.* London, 1976.

Baumont, Maurice. *The Origins of the Second World War*, trans. by Simone de Couvreur Ferguson. New Haven, 1978.

Burns, James MacGregor. *Roosevelt: The Soldier of Freedom, 1940–1945.* New York, 1970.

Carlton, David. *Anthony Eden: A Biography.* London, 1981.

Ciechanowski, Jan. *The Warsaw Rising of 1944.* London, 1974.

Cockburn, Claud. *The Devil's Decade.* London, 1973.

Colvin, Ian G. *The Chamberlain Cabinet.* London, 1971.

———. *Vansittart in Office.* London, 1965.

Costello, John. *Ten Days to Destiny.* New York, 1991.

Dallek, Robert. *Franklin D. Roosevelt and American Foreign Policy, 1932–1945.* New York, 1979.

Dawson, Raymond. *The Decision to Aid Russia, 1941: Foreign Policy and Domestic Politics.* Chapel Hill, 1959.

Edmunds, Robin. *The Big Three: Churchill, Roosevelt, and Stalin in Peace and War.* New York, 1991.

Erickson, John. *The Road to Berlin.* Boulder, Colo., 1983.

———. *The Road to Leningrad.* New York, 1975.

Eubank, Keith, ed. *World War II: Roots and Causes*, 2nd ed. Lexington, Mass., 1992.

Farnsworth, Beatrice. *William C. Bullitt and the Soviet Union.* Bloomington, Ind., 1967.

Feiling, Keith. *Neville Chamberlain.* London, 1946.

Feis, Herbert. *Churchill, Roosevelt, Stalin: The War They Waged and the Peace They Sought.* Princeton, N.J., 1957.

Fuchser, Larry William. *Neville Chamberlain and Appeasement: A Study in the Politics of History.* New York, 1982.

Gardner, Lloyd C. *Architects of Illusion: Men and Ideas in American Foreign Policy, 1941–1949.* Chicago, 1970.

———. *A Covenant with Power: America and World Order from Wilson to Reagan.* New York, 1984.

———. *Economic Aspects of New Deal Diplomacy.* Madison, Wisc., 1964.

———. *Safe for Democracy: The Anglo-American Response to Revolution, 1913–1923.* New York, 1984.

Gilbert, Martin. *Britain and Germany Between the Wars.* London, 1964.

———. *Finest Hour: Winston S. Churchill, 1939–1941.* London, 1983.

———. *Winston S. Churchill: Road to Victory, 1941–1945.* Boston, 1986.

Gorodetsky, Gabriel. *Stafford Cripps' Mission to Moscow, 1940–42.* Cambridge, England, 1984.

Haslam, Jonathan. *The Soviet Union and the Struggle for Collective Security in Europe, 1933–39.* New York, 1984.

Heinrichs, Waldo. *Threshold of War: Franklin D. Roosevelt and American Entry into World War II.* New York, 1988.

Herring, George C. *Aid to Russia, 1941–1946: Strategy, Diplomacy, and the Origins of the Cold War.* New York, 1973.

Herz, Martin. *Beginnings of the Cold War.* Bloomington, Ind., 1966.

James, Robert Rhodes. *Anthony Eden.* London, 1986.

Jeffreys, Kevin. *The Churchill Coalition and Wartime Politics, 1940–1945.* Manchester, England, 1991.

Kimball, Warren F. *The Juggler: Franklin Roosevelt as Wartime Statesman.* Princeton, N.J., 1991.

Kimball-MacLean, Elizabeth. "Joseph Davies and Soviet-American Relations, 1941–1943," *Diplomatic History* 14 (Winter 1980), 73–93.

LaFeber, Walter. *America, Russia and the Cold War*, 6th ed. New York, 1990.

Langer, William L., and S. Everett Gleason. *The Challenge to Isolation*. New York, 1952.

Lukas, Richard C. *The Strange Allies: The United States and Poland, 1941–1945*. Knoxville, Tenn, 1978.

Lundestad, Geir. *The American Non-Policy Towards Eastern Europe, 1943–1947*. New York, 1975.

MacDonald, C. A. *The United States, Britain and Appeasement, 1936–1939*. New York, 1981.

Maddux, Thomas R. *Years of Estrangement: American Relations with the Soviet Union, 1933–1941*. Tallahassee, Fla., 1980.

Mastny, Vojtech. *Russia's Road to the Cold War*. New York, 1979.

McCagg, William O., Jr. *Stalin Embattled, 1943–1948*. Detroit, 1978.

McCloy, John J. *The Atlantic Alliance: Its Origins and Future*. New York, 1969.

McNeill, William Hardy. *America, Britain and Russia: Their Cooperation and Conflict, 1941–1946*. New York, 1970.

Medvedev, Roy. *Let History Judge: The Origins and Consequences of Stalinism*, ed. and trans. by George Shriver, rev. ed. New York, 1989.

Middlemas, Keith. *Diplomacy of Illusion: The British Government and Germany, 1937–1939*. London, 1972.

Miner, Steven Merritt. *Between Churchill and Stalin: The Soviet Union, Great Britain, and the Origins of the Grand Alliance*. Chapel Hill, 1988.

———. "Stalin's 'Minimum Conditions' and the Military Balance, 1941–1942," in *Soviet-U.S. Relations, 1933–1942*. Moscow, 1989.

Mommsen, Wolfgang J., and Lothar Kettenacker, eds. *The Fascist Challenge and the Policy of Appeasement*. London, 1983.

Morison, Elting E. *Turmoil and Tradition: A Study of the Life and Times of Henry L. Stimson*. Boston, 1960.

Ovendale, Ritchie. *Appeasement and the English Speaking World*. Cardiff, Wales, 1975.

Peden, G. C. *British Rearmament and the Treasury, 1932–1939*. Edinburgh, 1979.

Pogue, Forrest C. *George C. Marshall: Organizer of Victory, 1943–1945*. New York, 1973.

Raczynski, Count Edward. *In Allied London*. London, 1962.

Read, Anthony, and David Fisher. *The Deadly Embrace: Hitler, Stalin, and the Nazi-Soviet Pact, 1939–1941*. New York, 1988.

Reynolds, David. *The Creation of the Anglo-American Alliance, 1937–41: A Study in Competitive Cooperation*. Chapel Hill, 1982.

Schroeder, Paul W. "Munich and the British Tradition," *Historical Journal* 19 (March 1976), 223–243.

Sherwood, Robert E. *Roosevelt and Hopkins: An Intimate History*. New York, 1948.

Taylor, A. J. P. *Beaverbrook*. London, 1972.

Thorne, Christopher. *Allies of a Kind: The United States, Britain and the War Against Japan, 1941–1945*. New York, 1978.

———. *The Approach of War, 1938–39*. New York, 1967.

Werth, Alexander. *Russia at War*. New York, 1964.

Williams, William Appleman. *American-Russian Relations, 1781–1947*. New York, 1952.

Woodward, Sir Llewellyn. *British Foreign Policy in the Second World War*, 5 vol. London, 1971.

Index

Abyssinia, 14, 19, 20
Acheson, Dean, 74–75, 180;
  Soviet Union, fear of
  collapse of, 263–264
Adriatic operation. *See*
  Balkan strategy.
Africa: proposals to
  repartition before World
  War II, 9–26 *et passim*, 28
Albania, 228; invasion by
  Italy, 54
Anschluss, 27, 29, 37
Anti-Comintern (1936), 8
Appeasement: Britain in
  regard to Germany, x,
  3–26 *et passim*; Churchill
  compared with
  Chamberlain, 131–132;
  and colonialism, 96; and
  economic blocs, 96; and
  spheres of influence, 166
Argentina, 187
Articles of Confederation,
  258
Ashton-Gwatkin, Frank, 46
Atlantic Charter, xii, 91–116;
  application to all
  countries, 102–103;
  Argentia,
  Newfoundland, meeting,
  97–102; Churchill's writing
  of first draft, 98; eight
  common principles, 99;
  exclusions to, 164–165;
  expansion of, 119; and
  questions of Russian
  frontiers, 117–147 *et passim*;
  Roosevelt's retreat from,
  241, 247–248; signing of
  by Soviet Union, 103;
  Stalin's response to, 91,
  104–105, 114, 125
Attlee, Clement, 102, 116,
  125, 192, 212, 260

Australia, 126
Austria: German invasion
  of, 27–29; pre–World War
  II, 20, 21
Axis Tripartite, 81, 82;
  invitation to Soviets to
  join, 82–83

Badoglio, Marshal Pietro,
  183
Baker, James, 263
Balance of Impotence, 155
Baldwin, Stanley, 8
Balkan agreement, 201–206
Balkan confederation, 134,
  157, 159
Balkan states, xi, 41, 163,
  184; cooperation with
  refugee groups, 67;
  Greece/Rumania bargain,
  184–206 *et passim*; Stalin's
  attitude toward, 77, 148,
  174–206 *et passim*; TOLSTOY
  Conference, discussion of,
  198–206 *et passim*
Balkan strategy, 174–175
Baltic-Americans, 175
Baltic states, 57, 58, 66;
  gold assets in Britain, 84;
  and military agreement
  between Soviets and
  Britain, 139; and new
  equilibrium, 78, 80;
  postwar military bases,
  debate over, 123; postwar
  status, debate over,
  117–147 *et passim*, 159–160,
  175; Soviet appropriation
  of, 70–90 *et passim*; Stalin's
  postwar plans for, 113,
  117–147 *et passim*, 159–160,
  Beaverbrook, Max, 91–92,
  103–104, 107; resignation,
  124–125; as Russophile,

122–123
Beck, Colonel Jozef, 32
Beirut, Boleslaw, 245
Berle, Adolf, 63, 86, 117,
  118, 119, 122; diary entry
  on postwar Europe, 153
Berne negotiations, 252–253
Bessarabia, Rumania, 58,
  76, 81, 125
Bevin, Ernest, 260
Big Four, 142; leadership in
  regional areas, 248–249;
  and question of
  disarmament, 150
Big Three, 72, 167, 168;
  Declaration on Liberated
  Europe, 226; harmony of,
  149, 162; at Yalta
  Conference, ix–xiv *et
  passim*, 207–237 *et passim*
Bilateralism versus
  multilateralism, 96–97
Birmingham speech
  (Chamberlain), 51–52
Black Sea, 200
Boettiger, John, 241
Bohlen, Charles, 197, 229,
  242
Bolshevism. *See*
  Communism.
Bonnet, Georges, 43, 45
Bowman, Isaiah, 184
Brest-Litovsk, 47, 100
*Brest-Litovsk: The Forgotten
  Peace* (Wheeler-Bennett),
  47
Britain (*see also* Chamberlain,
  Neville; Churchill,
  Winston; *specific conferences;
  specific treaties*): air power
  of, 44; arms race of, 9,
  24, 39, 85; Balkan
  countries, trade with, 41;
  Czechoslovakia, attitude

295

A NOTE ON THE AUTHOR

Lloyd C. Gardner is the Charles and Mary Beard Professor of History at Rutgers University. Born in Delaware, Ohio, he studied at Ohio Wesleyan University and at the University of Wisconsin, Madison, where he received a Ph.D. in history. He has been a Woodrow Wilson Fellow, a Guggenheim Fellow, and a Fulbright Exchange Professor, and in addition to a great many articles has written and edited more than a dozen books dealing with American diplomatic history, the most recent being *A Covenant with Power: America and World Order from Wilson to Reagan* and *Approaching Vietnam: From World War II to Dienbienphu*.

ELEPHANT PAPERBACKS

ELEPHANT PAPERBACKS

Literature and Letters

Stephen Vincent Benét, *John Brown's Body*, EL10
Isaiah Berlin, *The Hedgehog and the Fox*, EL21
Anthony Burgess, *Shakespeare*, EL27
Philip Callow, *Son and Lover: The Young D. H. Lawrence*, EL14
James Gould Cozzens, *Castaway*, EL6
James Gould Cozzens, *Men and Brethren*, EL3
Clarence Darrow, *Verdicts Out of Court*, EL2
Floyd Dell, *Intellectual Vagabondage*, EL13
Theodore Dreiser, *Best Short Stories*, EL1
Joseph Epstein, *Ambition*, EL7
André Gide, *Madeleine*, EL8
John Gross, *The Rise and Fall of the Man of Letters*, EL18
Irving Howe, *William Faulkner*, EL15
Aldous Huxley, *After Many a Summer Dies the Swan*, EL20
Aldous Huxley, *Ape and Essence*, EL19
Aldous Huxley, *Collected Short Stories*, EL17
Sinclair Lewis, *Selected Short Stories*, EL9
William L. O'Neill, ed., *Echoes of Revolt: The Masses,
    1911–1917*, EL5
Ramón J. Sender, *Seven Red Sundays*, EL11
Wilfrid Sheed, *Office Politics*, EL4
Tess Slesinger, *On Being Told That Her Second Husband Has
    Taken His First Lover, and Other Stories*, EL12
B. Traven, *The Bridge in the Jungle*, EL28
B. Traven, *The Carreta*, EL25
B. Traven, *Government*, EL23
B. Traven, *March to the Montería*, EL26
B. Traven, *The Night Visitor and Other Stories*, EL24
B. Traven, *The Rebellion of the Hanged*, EL29
Rex Warner, *The Aerodrome*, EL22
Thomas Wolfe, *The Hills Beyond*, EL16

Theatre and Drama

Robert Brustein, *Reimagining American Theatre*, EL410
Robert Brustein, *The Theatre of Revolt*, EL407
Irina and Igor Levin, *Working on the Play and the Role*, EL411
Plays for Performance:
    Aristophanes, *Lysistrata*, EL405
    Pierre Augustin de Beaumarchais, *The Marriage of Figaro*,
        EL418
    Anton Chekhov, *The Seagull*, EL407
    Fyodor Dostoevsky, *Crime and Punishment*, EL416
    Euripides, *The Bacchae*, EL419
    Georges Feydeau, *Paradise Hotel*, EL403
    Henrik Ibsen, *Ghosts*, EL401
    Henrik Ibsen, *Hedda Gabler*, EL413
    Henrik Ibsen, *The Master Builder*, EL417
    Henrik Ibsen, *When We Dead Awaken*, EL408
    Heinrich von Kleist, *The Prince of Homburg*, EL402
    Christopher Marlowe, *Doctor Faustus*, EL404
    The Mysteries: Creation, EL412
    The Mysteries: The Passion, EL414
    Sophocles, *Electra*, EL415
    August Strindberg, *The Father*, EL406